For Reference

Not to be taken from this room

Preventing Violence in America

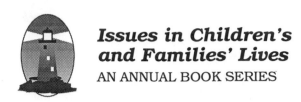

Issues in Children's and Families' Lives

AN ANNUAL BOOK SERIES

Senior Series Editor

Thomas P. Gullotta, *Child and Family Agency, Connecticut*

Editors

Gerald R. Adams, *University of Guelph, Ontario, Canada*

Bruce A. Ryan, *University of Guelph, Ontario, Canada*

Robert L. Hampton, *University of Maryland, College Park*

Roger P. Weissberg, *University of Illinois at Chicago, Illinois*

Drawing upon the resources of Child and Family Agency of Southeastern Connecticut, one of this nation's leading family service agencies, Issues in Children's and Families' Lives is designed to focus attention on the pressing social problems facing children and their families today. Each volume in this series will analyze, integrate, and critique the clinical and research literature on children and their families as it relates to a particular theme. Believing that integrated multidisciplinary approaches offer greater opportunities for program success, volume contributors will reflect the research and clinical knowledge base of the many different disciplines that are committed to enhancing the physical, social, and emotional health of children and their families. Intended for graduate and professional audiences, chapters will be written by scholars and practitioners who will encourage the reader to apply their practice skills and intellect to reducing the suffering of children and their families in the society in which those families live and work.

Volume 1:   Family Violence: Prevention and Treatment
LEAD EDITOR: Robert L. Hampton
CONSULTANTS: Vincent Senatore, *Child and Family Agency, Connecticut*; Ann Quinn, *Connecticut Department of Children, Youth, and Family Services, Connecticut*

Volume 2:   The Family-School Connection
EDITORS: Bruce A. Ryan and Gerald R. Adams

Volume 3:   Adolescent Dysfunctional Behavior
EDITORS: Gary M. Blau and Thomas P. Gullotta

Volume 4:   Preventing Violence in America
EDITORS: Robert L. Hampton, Pamela Jenkins, and Thomas P. Gullotta

Volume 5:   Primary Prevention Practices
AUTHOR: Martin Bloom

VPreventing Violence in America

Editors
Robert L. Hampton
Pamela Jenkins
Thomas P. Gullotta

Vol. 4 *Issues in Children's and Families' Lives*

SAGE Publications
International Educational and Professional Publisher
Thousand Oaks   London   New Delhi

For information address:

SAGE Publications, Inc.
2455 Teller Road
Thousand Oaks, California 91320
E-mail: order@sagepub.com

SAGE Publications Ltd.
6 Bonhill Street
London EC2A 4PU
United Kingdom

SAGE Publications India Pvt. Ltd.
M-32 Market
Greater Kailash I
New Delhi 110 048 India

Printed in the United States of America

Library of Congress Cataloging-in-Publication Data

Main entry under title:

Preventing violence in America / editors Robert L. Hampton, Pamela Jenkins, Thomas P. Gullotta.
    p.   cm.—(Issues in children's and familes' lives; v. 4)
    Includes bibliographical references and index.
    ISBN 0-7619-0040-3 (cloth: alk. paper).—ISBN 0-7619-0041-1
(pbk.: alk. paper)
    1. Violence—United States—Prevention. 2. Family violence—
United States—Prevention. I. Hampton, Robert L. II. Jenkins, Pamela.
III. Gullotta, Thomas 1948- . IV. Series.
HN90.V5P74 1996
303.6—dc20   95-34981

This book is printed on acid-free paper.

96 97 98 99 10 9 8 7 6 5 4 3 2 1

Sage Production Editor: Tricia K. Bennett
Sage Typesetter: Andrea D. Swanson

Dedication

This book is dedicated to Alva B. Gimbel, who spent much of her life and many resources on behalf of those who were less advantaged than she. Her generosity knew no boundaries of country, color, or class. She was an inspiration to all who came to know her.

The Gimbel Learning Community
on the Prevention of Violence in America

In addition to the chosen Gimbel Child and Family Scholars, a small select group of practitioners, policymakers, and scholars were invited to the retreats that were held in 1994 and 1995. These individuals, some of whom contributed to this volume, significantly enriched the discussions that were held. The Alva and Bernard Gimbel Foundation and Child and Family Agency of Southeastern Connecticut would like to acknowledge the important role of the following individuals:

Susan Addiss
Lynn Andrews
Kathleen Beland*
Martin Bloom
Patricia Crittenden*
Steven Danish
Stephen Gardner
Donna Garske*
Chris Gullotta
Thomas Gullotta
Robert Hampton
Pamela Jenkins*
Garry Lapidus*
Linda Lausell*
Aleta Meyer*
Eli Newberger
Susan Patrick
Brian Ragsdale
Rose Alma Senatore
Vincent Senatore
Margot Stern Strom*
Earl Stuck, Jr.
Jeffrey Trawick-Smith
Billie Weiss*
Betty Yung*

* Denotes Gimbel Scholar

Contents

Preface

Not a day passes in which some courtships do not sour violently, some spouses do not strike their mates, some adults do not harm their offspring, some elderly do not feel the wrath of their progeny, some children do not kill other children, some legal authorities do not overzealously fulfill their responsibilities, and some citizens do not violently abuse the rights of others unknown to them. Not a day passes in which violence does not occur.

With each new day, voices over the airwaves warn of clans of youth, born not of blood but of circumstance, gathering on street corners. They organize in long-forgotten shells of neighborhoods and in ignored public institutions such as schools. With each new day, photographers capture mothers cradling motionless loved ones in their arms. With each new day, news programs telecast—live and on scene—twisted forms of past lives bathed in clotted pools of darkness, draped in sheets, and arranged in neatly ordered rows. With each new day, images flash across screens of family members and friends clutching one another at funerals. With each new day, people die in vain.

This fourth volume in the **Issues in Children's and Families' Lives** book series represents a year-long effort by a talented group of scholars and practitioners to address the problem of violence in the United States. It is the result of a unique experiment being conducted by the Bernard and Alva Gimbel Foundation of New York, which seeks to identify promising mid-career scholars and practitioners working on issues of critical social importance to American society. Clearly, no issue is more pressing than the problem of violence.

This volume comprises 13 chapters that are organized into three unlabeled sections. The first section is intended to provide the reader with an understanding of the subject matter. Thus, in Chapter 1, Thomas P. Gullotta, Pamela Jenkins, and Robert L. Hampton introduce the reader to selected writings of two of Western literature's greatest social commentators, Charles Dickens and Samuel Clemens. Revisiting these authors' observations on the human condition may temper nostalgic views of the past and sensitize readers to the material that follows. Chapter 2, by Jenkins, Hampton, and Gullotta, provides a selected theoretical overview of explanations for violence within families. Jenkins continues this selected theoretical overview in Chapter 3 by linking violence within families to community violence.

The next section, which consists of five chapters, explores subjects deserving of special consideration in the attempt to understand population aspects of violence and possible preventive factors. Accordingly, Robert L. Hampton and Betty R. Yung, in Chapter 4, examine the disproportionate presence of violence within minority populations and discuss preventive interventions. Martin Bloom explores the concept of psychological resilience in Chapter 5, followed by Aleta L. Meyer and Linda Lausell's examination in Chapter 6 of the influence spirituality may have as a possible protective factor. In Chapter 7, Steven J. Danish and Thomas R. Donohue review the dark side of television programming and discuss opportunities for improving television's prosocial programming. This part of the book concludes with Chapter 8 by Stephen E. Gardner and Hank Resnik in which they examine gang formation and discuss efforts by the Federal Center for Substance Abuse Prevention, through its High-Risk Youth Demonstration Grant Program, to promote positive youth development.

The final five chapters provide illustrations of different efforts under way to reduce the incidence of violent behavior in American society. In Chapter 9, Garry Lapidus and Mary Braddock review the calls of public health authorities for training models for health care professionals and describe a model educational project that is under way in Connecticut. In Chapter 10, Billie P. Weiss shares the efforts of the Los Angeles, California, community to form a collaborative multiagency response to violent behavior. In Chapter 11, Kathleen R. Beland discusses the social competence literature and her experiences in developing and implementing the Second Step curriculum for use in school systems. In Chapter 12, Lynn Andrews and Jeffrey Trawick-Smith, drawing on the social competence and resilience literature, describe their efforts to develop a community program to reduce aggressive behaviors among preschool youth. Finally, challenging many of the programmatic concepts of this volume, Donna Garske uses a thought-provoking feminist perspective in Chapter 13 to explore behavior within society.

It is our hope that readers will find the work of the Gimbel Child and Family Scholars and associates to be a starting point for their own efforts to reduce violent behavior in the United States. We hope that community leaders, practitioners, and graduate students in such applied disciplines as social work, public health, psychology, nursing, and child and adolescent development will use this volume to build local and state programs aimed at promoting a society in which peace can prosper.

—Robert L. Hampton
—Pamela Jenkins
—Thomas P. Gullotta

Acknowledgments

Many people were involved in the development of this project. The authors were the principal players in transforming initial ideas into final drafts. They are both scholars and practitioners and share a common commitment to reducing violence. This book would not have been possible without them.

I want to thank Thomas P. Gullotta, CEO of the Child and Family Agency of Southeastern Connecticut, for first developing the concept for the Gimbel Scholars Program and the board of directors of the agency for supporting his efforts to make this learning community a reality. I would also like to thank the many individuals who assisted with the research and other related tasks that go into completing an edited volume: Marianne Eismann, Diane Gaboury, Tawanna Gaines, Heather Gendler, Judy Lovelace, Sarah Rogers, Sandra Toussaint, and Wendy Traub. Finally, I want to thank my colleagues in the Departments of Family Studies and Sociology and in Academic Affairs at the University of Maryland for their support.

—Robert L. Hampton

CHAPTER 1

Of Dickens, Twain, and Violence

THOMAS P. GULLOTTA
PAMELA JENKINS
ROBERT L. HAMPTON

[Nancy] was lying, half dressed. . . . "Get up!" said [Sikes]. "It is you, Bill!" said [Nancy], with an expression of pleasure at his return. "It is. . . . Get up . . . " "Bill," said [Nancy] in the low voice of alarm, "why do you look like that at me!" [Sikes] sat regarding her, for a few seconds, with dilated nostrils and heaving breast; and then, grasping her by the head and throat, dragged her into the middle of the room, and looking once towards the door, placed his heavy hand upon her mouth. "Bill, Bill!" . . . gasped [Nancy]. . . . [Sikes] freed one arm, and grasped his pistol. The certainty of immediate detection if he fired flashed across his mind even in the midst of his fury; and he beat it twice, with all the force he could summon, upon [Nancy's] up-turned face. . . . She staggered and fell, nearly blinded with the blood that rained down from a deep gash in her forehead. [Nancy struggled to raise herself, whereupon Sikes], shutting out the sight [of her] with his hand, seized a heavy club and struck her down. (Dickens, 1837/ 1894e, pp. 383-384)

Violence such as Sikes's against Nancy (in what many would consider their common-law marriage) in *Oliver Twist* (Dickens, 1837/1894e) is not a rare occurrence in Western literature. For centuries, writers have recorded the violent times in which they lived, at times expressing their outrage over these conditions and at others simply reflecting the societal norms that governed the periods in which they wrote. For this reason, it is hard to understand

1

why, until a little more than two decades ago, family violence was not mentioned in the professional literature (Gelles, 1980). It is hard to understand how, until street violence spilled from urban streets and into schools, young people harming other young people could have been ignored. It is hard to understand how, until the publication of Kempe, Silverman, Steele, Droegemuller, and Silver's 1962 work on the battered child syndrome, child abuse could have gone unnoticed. In this chapter, we examine several selected passages from the works of certain prominent authors and discuss their handling of violent themes.

It is our intention to reawaken the reader to the reality that violence has been and remains an integral part of Western culture in general, and American culture in particular. What with daily media announcements of serial killings, planned executions of family members, and gang-related retaliations for real or imagined affronts, it would seem unnecessary for us to remind readers of the presence of violence. However, our concern is not with the present, but with the past. Furthermore, our concern is not with history, but with literature. Not that literature is reality—it is not, just as the film *Boys Town* is not reality. But the images in fiction have become—have always been—powerful representations of the past, of family life, of societal values, of what life should really be like.

In the fictionalized world, rivers are wide and lazy, offering refuge and avenues of escape to those who seek them. When evil presents itself, no messy mitigating factors interfere with the swift application of justice. Such clear literary images enable reporters, politicians, and common citizens to be transported to mythical places in the imagined past, when, if all was not good with the world, at least decided action could be taken to make it so.

But did such a time and place ever really exist? In a society where the printed word has become digitized, abridged, animated, scripted, and taped, it has become all too easy to lose the original intent of some authors' language. Like the October leaf separated from its branch, literary passages cut free from their stories are left to drift into oblivion. Meanings change and so, literally cleansed, Scrooge, Tom Sawyer, and others become available to market the commodities of the new day, whether they be automobiles, paint, or fast food. Our intention here is to ask the reader to pause and reflect on the circumstances surrounding us, to reconnect with the authors of the works we will discuss and with those authors' stories, and, in doing so, to approach the remainder of this volume with heightened awareness and sensitivity.

Western literature is rich with examples of violence between family members, from the Bible to children's stories such as Cinderella, Hansel and Gretel, and Snow White. Cruelty is a recurring theme in Shakespeare's plays—the cruelty of offspring toward an elderly parent (*King Lear*), the cruelty of one spouse toward the other (*Othello*), the cruelty of youth toward youth (*Romeo and Juliet*), and the cruelty of adult toward youth (*Titus Andronicus*).

When we consider the position of children and women in Western societies in premodern times—that is, prior to 1620—we should not be surprised at the violence that was often visited upon them (see Edward Shorter's *The Making of the Modern Family*, 1977, for a seminal discussion of this issue). Children were considered the property of their parents, and society rarely intervened in parent-child relationships, even when children were being abused. Similar attitudes existed concerning men's rights over women; for example, consider the ancient practice of wife selling. In *The Life and Death of the Mayor of Casterbridge,* Thomas Hardy (1886/1966) incorporates an episode of wife selling as a crucial element in the novel's plot:

> "For my part I don't see why men who have got wives and don't want 'em, shouldn't get rid of 'em as these gypsy fellows do their old horses. . . . Why shouldn't they put 'em up and sell 'em by auction to men who are in need of such articles? Hey? Why begad, I'd sell mine this minute if anybody would buy her!"
>
> She turned to her husband and murmured, "Michael, you have talked this nonsense in public places before. A joke is a joke, but you may make it once too often, mind!"
>
> "I know I've said it before; I meant it. All I want is a buyer."
>
> [An offer of 5 guineas is made.] "Now," said the woman, breaking the silence, so that her low dry voice sounded quite loud, "before you go further, Michael, listen to me. If you touch that money, I and this girl go with the man. Mind it is a joke no longer."
>
> "A joke? Of course it is not a joke!" shouted her husband, his resentment rising at her suggestion. "I take the money: the sailor takes you. That's plain enough. It has been done elsewhere—and why not here?"
>
> . . . "Mike," she said, "I've lived with thee a couple of years, and had nothing but temper! Now I'm no more to 'ee, I'll try my luck elsewhere. 'Twill be better for me and Elizabeth-Jane, both. So good-bye!"

Seizing the sailor's arm with her right hand, and mounting the little
girl on her left, she went out of the tent sobbing bitterly. (pp. 8-11)

Premodern values, however, cannot explain the prevalence of
family violence in literature of modern family times. To illustrate
that prevalence, we have chosen two modern Western authors
regarded as social commentators on their time—Charles Dickens
and Samuel Clemens (Mark Twain). Curiously enough, both lived
during a period many family historians have described as the time
of the "cult of domesticity" (Shorter, 1977). This was supposedly a
time in Western societies when apple pie, motherhood, and children
were valued. Although these were valued in comparison with prior
times, as television's Captain Kangaroo, Bob Keeshan (1983), once
observed, "In reality we can't eat very much apple pie, we divorce
mother, and we usually ignore children." Both Dickens and Clemens
illustrated this point throughout their long careers. Their novels
abound with episodes of abuse and cruelty toward children and
families and the neglect of dependent women and children.

For example, consider the plight of Pip, living with his sister, the
wife of the village blacksmith, in *Great Expectations:* "My sister,
Mrs. Joe Gargery was more than twenty years older than I, and had
established a great reputation with herself and the neighbors because she had brought me up 'by hand' " (Dickens, 1861/1894c,
p. 6). "By hand" often translated into the liberal application of a
waxed piece of cane called a "tickler" to Pip's body:

"Mrs. Joe has been out a dozen times, looking for you, Pip. And she's
out now, making it a baker's dozen."

"Is she?"

"Yes Pip," said Joe; "and what's worse, she's got tickler with her. . . .
She sat down," said Joe, "and she got up, and she made a grab at tickler,
and she Ram-paged out. That's what she did . . . she Ram-paged out,
Pip."

"Has she been gone long, Joe?"

"Well . . . she's been on the Ram-page, this last spell, about five
minutes, Pip. She's a coming! Get behind the door old chap, and have
the jack-towel betwixt you."

I took the advice. My sister, Mrs. Joe, throwing the door wide open,
and finding an obstruction behind it, immediately divined the cause,
and applied tickler to its further investigation. She concluded by

throwing me—I often served her as a connubial missile—at Joe, who glad to get hold of me on any terms, passed me on into the chimney and quietly fenced me up there [protecting me] with his great leg. (Dickens, 1861/1894c, p. 7)

Great Expectations is not Dickens's only comment on a caretaker's inhumanity to a child. In *Oliver Twist* (1837/1894e), Bumble, the parish beadle, cruelly mistreats the young waif Oliver. Smike is no better treated by the infamous Wachford Squeers, headmaster of Dotheboys Hall, in *Nicholas Nickleby* (1839/1894d). Furthermore, the poor and working-class are not alone in their mistreatment of others, as Florence's treatment by her father in *Dombey and Son* (1848/1894b) and David Copperfield's (1849/1894a) treatment by his stepfather Murdstone, ably assisted by his sister, Miss Murdstone, and a tyrannical headmaster named Creakle, amply demonstrate.

In fact, we believe parental neglect helps to explain why Ebenezer Scrooge, in *A Christmas Carol* (1843/1967), became a cruel, mean-spirited man:

"The school is not quite deserted," said the ghost. "A solitary child, neglected by his friends, is left there still."

Scrooge said he knew it. And he sobbed. . . .

[The boy, Scrooge, in his loneliness glanced at a door when] it opened; and a little girl, much younger than the boy, came darting in, and putting her arms about his neck, and often kissing him, addressed him as her "Dear, dear brother."

"I have come to bring you home, dear brother!" said the child, clapping her tiny hands, and bending down to laugh. "To bring you home, home, home!"

"Home, little Fan?" returned the boy.

"Yes!" said the child, brimful of glee. "Home for good and all. Home, for ever and ever. Father is so much kinder than he used to be, that home's like heaven! He spoke so gently to me one dear night when I was going to bed, that I was not afraid to ask him once more if you might come home; and he said yes, you should; and sent me in a coach to bring you." (pp. 48, 51-52)

By Dickens's time, the value of women and children had improved from an earlier age when Romans operating under the

principle of *patria potestas* permitted the male head of the household to sell, disfigure, or kill his wife and children at will (Bybee,
1979; Dobash & Dobash, 1979). But not enough progress had been
made to prevent passage of laws like the one passed in Mississippi
in 1824 that gave husbands immunity from prosecution for physically assaulting their wives (Davidson, 1977; Star, 1980). Nor was
the 17th-century concept of *parens patriae* yet strong enough to
protect a child from mistreatment (Brown, 1979-1980). Children
were still chattel (Bross, 1979) who, like one young child named
Mary Ellen, might be saved from mistreatment not because they
were human beings but because they were animals. It was with this
argument that the Society for the Prevention of Cruelty to Animals
interceded on Mary Ellen's behalf to save her from starvation and
physical abuse. The organization argued that, as a member of the
animal kingdom, she was protected by laws prohibiting cruelty to
animals (Bybee, 1979).

About this same time, Samuel Clemens was working on *The
Adventures of Tom Sawyer* (1876/1993). Tom Sawyer was no Hora-
tio Alger figure. Hard work and honesty were character traits
Clemens omitted when creating this young rascal. As his story's
narrator observes, "He was not the Model Boy of the village. He
knew the model boy well enough—and loathed him" (Clemens,
1876/1993, p. 13). Still, Tom was a well-meaning fellow with a
vivid imagination and enthusiasm born of youth that was communicated to all who have ever read his story. His adventures—running
away with Huck and Joe Harper, his graveyard antics with dead
cats, and his encounters with Injun Joe—were all well chronicled.
Or were they? Certainly, Clemens wrote of these and other occur-
rences. But over the years, as Tom's adventures were adapted and
readapted, certain story elements were omitted. The images etched
in film, comic, and cartoon that linger in many people's memories
are of sleepy summer days on the banks of the Mississippi and
whitewashed picket fences, but these form an incomplete story.

For example, consider Aunt Polly, Tom's caretaker. A generous
woman, a religious woman, a kind and compassionate woman
trying her level best to raise a difficult youth who could have easily
found himself today before a judge for delinquent offenses—are
these the images that emerge? To these images permit us to add
further complexity to her character. Reflective of the time, Dickens's tickler becomes Clemens's switch:

"Forty times I've said if you didn't let that jam alone I'd skin you. Hand me that switch."

The switch hovered in the air—the peril was desperate.

"My! Look behind you, aunt!"

The old lady whirled. . . . The lad fled. . . . His Aunt Polly stood surprised a moment, and then broke into a gentle laugh. . . .

"I ain't doing my duty by that boy, and that's the Lord's truth, goodness knows. Spare the rod and spile the child, as the Good Book says. I'm a-laying up sin and suffering for us both, I know. He's full of the Old Scratch, but laws-a-me! he's my own dead sister's boy, poor thing, and I ain't got the heart to lash him, somehow." (Clemens, 1876/1993, p. 10)

When Sid, Tom's half brother, broke a sugar bowl, Aunt Polly assumed Tom to be the culprit:

And the next instant he was sprawling on the floor! The potent palm was lifted to strike again, when Tom cried out:

"Hold on, now, what're you belting *me* for? Sid broke it!"

Aunt Polly paused, perplexed, and Tom looked for healing pity. But when she got her tongue again she only said:

"Umf! Well, you didn't get a lick amiss, I reckon. You been into some other audacious mischief when I wasn't around, like enough."

Then her conscience reproached her, and she yearned to say something kind and loving; but she judged that this would be construed into a confession that she had been wrong, and discipline forbade that. (Clemens, 1876/1993, pp. 27-28)

Make no mistake—Aunt Polly is not Mrs. Joe Gargery. She is a kind soul. Still, both women subscribe to an understanding that encourages the liberal application of tickler or switch to instill rule and discipline in young lads and lasses—a belief that carries beyond the home and into the classroom, as Tom Sawyer soon discovers when he not only arrives late but admits to talking with Huckleberry Finn:

"Thomas Sawyer, this is the most astounding confession I have ever listened to; no mere ferule will answer for this offence. Take off your jacket."

The master's arm performed until it was tired, and the stock of switches notably diminished. (Clemens, 1876/1993, pp. 56-57)

This is only the first of several lashings applied to Tom for reasons ranging from classroom inattention, to an ink-soiled spelling book (not his fault), to taking blame for Becky Thatcher's indiscretion in damaging schoolmaster Dobbins's anatomy book. These events pale, however, in comparison with the principal plot involving Tom's and Huck's encounters with Injun Joe. From the grave-looting scene, when Dr. Robinson is knifed, to the attempted maiming of the Widow Douglas, to Injun Joe's ultimate demise from starvation, Tom Sawyer's world is anything but lazy and carefree.

Omitted from grade-school plays, films, and animated features based on the book are such scenes as the attempted mutilation of the Widow Douglas, which present a more sobering view of life in St. Petersburg. In this scene, Huck Finn, who has followed Injun Joe and an accomplice to the Widow Douglas's, learns that her deceased husband, a justice of the peace, had had Injun Joe horsewhipped. Joe plans to avenge this indignity.

> "He had me *horsewhipped*!—horsewhipped in front of the jail, like a nigger!—with all the town looking on! HORSEWHIPPED!—do you understand? He took advantage of me and died. But I'll take it out of *her*!"
>
> "Oh, don't kill her! Don't do that!" [Joe's accomplice says].
>
> "Kill! Who said anything about killing. . . . When you want to get revenge on a woman you don't kill her—bosh! you go for her looks. You slit her nostrils—you notch her ears like a sow!"
>
> "By God, that's—"
>
> "Keep your opinion to yourself! It will be safest for you. I'll tie her to the bed. If she bleeds to death, is that my fault? I'll not cry if she does." (Clemens, 1876/1993, pp. 201-202)

Huck's actions save the widow from Injun Joe's malicious intent. Becky and Tom ultimately emerge from the darkness of the caves that seal Injun Joe's fate. With newfound wealth of $6,000 apiece and heroic actions on both their parts, as the novel ends the boys are giving up thoughts of piracy for robbery. Romantic? Unquestionably! Joyous? Undoubtedly! Adventurous? Assuredly! *The Adventures of Tom Sawyer* is all these things and more. Clemens provides the reader with a view of a world in which cruelty coexists with kindness—a world not unlike our own.

In *The Adventures of Huckleberry Finn*, Clemens (1884/1962) continues the exploits of Tom and Huck in a society in which child and adult are the property of others and where violence exists for reasons long ago forgotten. The principal character, Huckleberry, has a plainer style than Tom Sawyer. Oh, he lies and cheats, when necessary, but more than anything else he is driven by the need to escape. He has no mother, and his father is a mean drunkard. Abandoned for most of his life, he has lived by his wits in the village and on the river. It appears too that for most of that life he has been shunned by proper society. The schoolmaster reacts violently to the mention of Tom Sawyer's meeting with Huck. Parents dread their children's coming into contact with his corrupting behavior—that is, until Huck finds redemption at the conclusion of Tom Sawyer's book.

The second story is again set in St. Petersburg. Huck, who has been taken in by the Widow Douglas and is ever so slowly growing accustomed to sleeping under a roof, with bedsheets, clean clothing, and schoolbook learning, is reunited with pap, his alcoholic father. The reader soon learns that Huck cannot escape his father's drunken rages through civilized avenues. Like the Negro slave, Jim, he is considered property.

> The judge and the widow went to the law to get the court to take me away from him and to let one of them be my guardian; but it was a new judge that had just come, and he didn't know the old man; so he said courts mustn't interfere and separate families if they could help it; he said he druther not take a child away from its father. . . . That pleased the old man till he couldn't rest. He said he'd cowhide me till I was black and blue if I didn't raise some money for him. I borrowed three dollars . . . and pap took it and got drunk and went a-blowing . . . till most midnight; then they jailed him. . . . But he said *he* was satisfied; said he was the boss of his son, and he'd make it warm for *him*. (Clemens, 1884/1962, p. 42)

Unable to secure Huck's wealth and frustrated by the widow's continued interference, pap decides he will "show who was Huck Finn's boss" (p. 45). And so the boy is abducted by his father and taken across the river to Illinois. The story's narrator relates that it took Huck 2 months to lose his taste for the widow's clean living and to rediscover the pleasures of smoking, cussing, and laying about. But no amount of time could bring Huck to appreciate pap's beatings: "Pap got too handy with his hick'ry, and I couldn't stand it. I was all over welts" (p. 47).

Huck's circumstances reach desperate proportions when pap, having consumed enough whiskey "for two drunks and one delirium tremens," lights after Huck:

> "[Pap] jumped up on his feet . . . and went for me. He chased me . . . with a clasp-knife, calling me the Angel of Death and saying he would kill me. . . . I begged, and told him I was Huck, but he laughed . . . and kept on chasing me up. . . . Pretty soon he was all tired out . . . and said he would rest a minute and then kill me. He put his knife under him, and said he would sleep and get strong, and then he would see who was who. So he dozed off, pretty soon. By-and-by I got the old split-bottom chair and clumb up, as easy as I could, not to make any noise, and got down the gun. I slipped the ramrod down it to make sure it was loaded, and then I laid it across the turnip barrel, pointing towards pap, and set down behind it to wait for him to stir. And how slow and still the time did drag along. (Clemens, 1884/1962 p. 52)

To survive, Huck must engage in deception and flee. His travels bring him into contact with much that is evil (or is it confused?) in this world—both then and now. For example, consider the Granger-fords and the Shepherdsons. A feud, as Huck learns, has thinned their ancestral ranks for years. Buck Grangerford—with Huck in tow—has attempted to kill Harney Shepherdson as he was riding:

> "Did you want to kill him, Buck?"
> "Him? He never did nothing to me."
> "Well, then, what did you want to kill him for?"
> "Why nothing—only it's on account of the feud."
> "What's a feud? . . ."
> "Well," says Buck, "a feud is this way. A man has a quarrel with another man, and kills him; then that other man's brother kills *him*; then the other brothers, on both sides, goes for one another; then the *cousins* chip in—and by-and-by everybody's killed off, and there ain't no more feud. But it's kind of slow, and takes a long time."
> "Has this one been going on long, Buck?"
> "Well I should *reckon*! It started thirty year ago, or som'ers along there. There was trouble 'bout something and then a lawsuit to settle

it; and the suit went agin one of the men, and so he up and shot the
man that won the suit—"

"What was the trouble about, Buck?—land?"

"I reckon maybe—I don't know."

"Well, who done the shooting?—was it a Grangerford or a Shepherdson?"

"Laws, how do *I* know? it was so long ago."

"Don't anybody know?"

"Oh, yes, pa knows, I reckon, and some of the other old folks; but
they don't know, now, what the row was about in the first place."
(Clemens, 1884/1962 pp. 146-147)

It is not our intent to relate the rest of Huck's story here, but a
rich story it is—filled with more violence, more cruelty, and still
more deceptions. Indeed, it might be observed that Huck's deceptions and those practiced on Pip are a true commentary on human
nature. That is, we soften those elements that bring us displeasure
such that over time we reinvent the story; we revise history, or we
readjust our understandings to fit what we wish to believe at the
time—our time.

But this is not a chapter of desperation. Rather, we hope it is an
expression of inspiration for our readers. First, reconnect with the
literature. Rediscover the conditions and the social climates that
actually existed in the times past that are so fondly regarded as
better than today. In so doing, we suspect, readers will find that the
past offered few idyllic marriages and wide, lazy rivers of escape.
It did not provide simple, caring extended families for all children
left parentless. It held secrets in graveyards.

Know that the feuds of Clemens's time are today called gang
warfare and ethnic cleansing. Know that corporal punishment is
still permitted in many American schools. Know that individuals
still act to maim others they perceive as having mistreated them.
Know that there are still plenty of prisons; "union workhouses"
have been replaced by homeless shelters; and orphanages—whether
in the form experienced by Oliver Twist or that envisioned by the
speaker of the House—exist as residential treatment centers. Know
that the "poor law" of Dickens's time may become the welfare
reform of today. Most of all, however, know that you and the others
who read this volume who hope to diminish the incidence of
violence in this society are the Aunt Pollys, the Judge Thatchers,

and the Abel Magwitchs of our time—imperfect and flawed like those fictional characters, but sincere in wanting a better tomorrow for our children and in being willing to work toward it.

References

Bross, D. C. (1979). Analysis of the protected status of maltreated children and youth. *Journal of Social Issues, 35,* 72-81.

Brown, J. A. (1979-1980). Combatting the roots of family violence. *Journal of Social Welfare, 6,* 17-24.

Bybee, R. W. (1979). Violence toward youth: A new perspective. *Journal of Social Issues, 35,* 1-14.

Clemens, S. (1962). *The adventures of Huckleberry Finn.* San Francisco: Chandler. (Original work published 1884)

Clemens, S. (1993). *The adventures of Tom Sawyer.* New York: Oxford University Press. (Original work published 1876)

Davidson, T. (1977). Wifebeating: A recurring phenomenon throughout history. In M. Roy (Ed.), *Battered women.* New York: Van Nostrand Reinhold.

Dickens, C. (1894a). *David Copperfield.* Cambridge, MA: Houghton Mifflin. (Original work published 1849)

Dickens, C. (1894b). *Dombey and son.* Cambridge, MA: Houghton Mifflin. (Original work published 1848)

Dickens, C. (1894c). *Great expectations.* Cambridge, MA: Houghton Mifflin. (Original work published 1861)

Dickens, C. (1894d). *Nicholas Nickleby.* Cambridge, MA: Houghton Mifflin. (Original work published 1839)

Dickens, C. (1894e). *Oliver Twist.* Cambridge, MA: Houghton Mifflin. (Original work published 1837)

Dickens, C. (1967). *A Christmas carol.* Cambridge, MA: Houghton Mifflin. (Original work published 1843)

Dobash, R. E., & Dobash, R. P. (1979). *Violence against wives: A case against the patriarchy.* New York: Free Press.

Gelles, R. J. (1980). Violence in the family: A review of research in the seventies. *Journal of Marriage and the Family, 42,* 873-885.

Hardy, T. (1966). *The life and death of the mayor of Casterbridge.* New York: St. Martin's. (Original work published 1886)

Keeshan, B. (1983, January 30). [Untitled comments]. *Hartford Courant,* p. A2.

Kempe, C. H., Silverman, F. H., Steele, B. F., Droegemuller, W., & Silver, H. K. (1962). The battered child syndrome. *Journal of the American Medical Association, 181,* 17-24.

Shorter, E. (1977). *The making of the modern family.* New York: Basic Books.

Star, B. (1980). Patterns in family violence. *Social Casework, 61,* 339-346.

CHAPTER 2

Understanding the Social Context of Violent Behavior in Families: Selected Perspectives

PAMELA JENKINS

ROBERT L. HAMPTON

THOMAS P. GULLOTTA

The media today are filled with stories of violence—husbands killing wives, wives killing husbands, parents killing children, children killing parents. Violence has become the hot topic—alleged perpetrators and victims of domestic violence are now household names (e.g., O. J. Simpson, Lyle and Erik Menendez, Susan Smith). In our view, the media and much of society treat such instances of violent behavior as uncommon events that affect only people who can somehow be set apart from the rest of society. However, violent acts do not occur in isolation, separate from social and historical contexts.

Violence in families can occur between any members—parent and parent, child and child, grandparent and grandchild, parent and child. Often, the role of the victim of violence in an intimate setting has been explained by his or her dependence; for example, that children are dependent on their parents, that elderly persons are dependent on their adult children, or that citizens are dependent on government (in the case of police brutality). Although dependency plays a part in the dynamics of violence and other forms of maltreatment, it cannot explain all of its aspects. Currently in the

13

United States, researchers have contended that "with the exception of the police and the military, the family is perhaps the most violent social group, and the home is the most violent social setting in our society" (Gelles & Straus, 1979, p. 15). From pushing and shoving to the death of a parent, child, or spouse, inflicting physical harm is a common practice in intimate settings.

This particular historical moment has witnessed enormous academic debate over the causes and understanding of violence, in turn resulting in controversies over what constitutes effective policy and prevention efforts (Gelles, 1993; Gelles & Straus, 1988). All would agree that violence is a serious social problem, yet little consensus exists about the etiology, the incidence, and the perpetrators of this behavior. Differing perspectives and policies answer these questions in a variety of ways. Any student of violent behavior can become confused by the myriad explanations that have been offered for why violence occurs, how often it occurs, and who commits violent acts.

This volume reflects some of the most recent issues and debates concerning our understanding of violence. Violence in the home and violence in the streets are serious problems in the late 20th century—we attempt in this book to add to the current understanding of violence and to the development of strategies to prevent it. This chapter highlights the debate about why violence occurs from several theoretical perspectives.

A Social-Historical Context

Throughout the history of the Western world, violence toward wives and children has been seen as the right of the head of the household. In those rare instances when punishment was imposed for such violence, the sanctions were mild. For example, in the United States, the Puritans saw violence as a moral issue and against the laws of God and the state. As reflected in the Puritans' own records of occurrence and prohibition, premarital sex and adultery received far more punitive attention than did violence in the home (Pleck, 1987). The public record on violence in families is silent for the latter half of the 18th century and for many years of the 19th century. This period encompassed the height of the "cult of domesticity," when such behaviors were thought to be unimaginable.

Although the maltreatment of wives and children was never the central issue, the prevention of abuse became a part of several reform movements, including the women's rights and temperance movements. For example, in the late 1800s, protective legislation was enacted to restrict child labor and women's labor (Matthaei, 1982); this same period was one of the first times in history when rape and incest were discussed publicly. Especially in the United States, many of the reform movements' concerns were for wives who were at the mercy of their drunken and abusive husbands and unable to divorce them. The demand for reform to prevent the abuse of women and children did not last long, and many of the relatively liberal divorce laws that the movements had led to were later repealed. The public discourse during this reform period focused on the higher morality of women compared with men and linked the cause of most social evils to alcohol. Through the great social reform movements of the 19th century, violence was first viewed as caused by alcohol abuse and later, with the arrival of immigrants, as a reflection of the lack of morality of lower-class families (Gordon, 1988; Pleck, 1987).

During the late 19th and early 20th centuries, maltreatment of children was framed as child cruelty. In 1874 in New York, the case of a young girl named Mary Ellen led to the founding of children's anticruelty societies (e.g., the Society for the Prevention of Cruelty to Children) based on the model of societies set up to prevent cruelty to animals (Pleck, 1987). In this case, a young girl's plight stirred the imagination of some of the wealthiest families and individuals in New York. Nearly 40 years later, there were almost 500 anticruelty societies in the United States. Most of the early reform movements aimed at saving children involved private agencies and targeted a population that was thought not to have the proper skills for raising children because of poverty and immigrant status (Pleck, 1987).

At the end of the 19th century, serious scientific examination of maltreatment in families began with the growth of professions interested in the study of families. Researchers believed that it should be possible to formulate a social scientific understanding of the motivations and attributions of perpetrators and victims of domestic violence. Emphasis on the "social self" replaced earlier reform movements that focused on morals and ethics. For example, the psychologist G. Stanley Hall, in his lectures presented at meetings of the National Congress of Mothers, "promised a glorious union of science and motherhood" (Ehrenreich & English, 1978, p. 199). Experts became increasingly interested in the lives of children and families (Ehrenreich & English, 1978; Gordon, 1988; Pleck, 1987).

In addition, the maltreatment of wives and children was perceived through class and racial filters and was explained as resulting from environmental stress, lack of education, and/or lack of mental stability (Gordon, 1988). These filters allowed the society to identify particular victims and perpetrators in several ways. First, portraying the perpetrator as "the other"—that is, as a stranger, someone unlike oneself—focused society's attention on lower-class families, and the occurrence of violence in the home could be distanced from the middle-class "norm." Second, focusing on the victim's pathology helped to defend the social institution of the family. "Blaming the victim" describes a pattern of discourse and thought in which the attributes or characteristics of the victim are seen to contribute to his or her victimization. For example, a child's unwillingness to obey a parent may be said to have caused the parent to have to harm the child physically. Theories based in the victim's culpability were especially useful in cases of child sexual abuse, where young children were perceived as seductive (Olafson, Corwin, & Summit, 1993). Another example of victim blaming would be the perception of a wife who complained or who could not keep house adequately as an appropriate target for spouse abuse.

Both blaming the victim and making the perpetrator "the other" enabled society to contain family violence to a select part of the population that was overwhelmingly lower-class and believed to be pathological. If society could distinguish the problems of some as not part of the "normal family experience," it could more easily dismiss the problem. In individual and psychological terms, these families and individuals were dysfunctional.

The elderly population was not perceived as a problem until the end of the 19th century, when the status of older people had clearly deteriorated. Aschenbaum and Kusnerz (1978) attribute this decline to the growth of science, which lessened the value of the knowledge of elders, and the medical practice of approaching old age as a disease state. These two factors, plus the increasing dominance of an industrial society that valued strength and stamina over experience, contributed to the development of a youth culture that denigrated older Americans. Aging became a social problem, one so serious that the government had to assume greater responsibility for elders' well-being, which it did in 1935 with the passage of the Social Security Act.

Society could dismiss the suggestion that many family members were victims of cruelty and neglect—individual children, spouses, or elderly parents might be abused, but families were not abusive. In this way, the belief in the family as a healthy institution was preserved. This benevolent view of the family continued until the early 1960s, when reports began to appear about "battered child syndrome" (Kempe, Silverman, Steele, Droegemuller, & Silver, 1962); the 1970s discovered battered women (Schechter, 1982), and in the late 1970s, elder abuse emerged (Conner, 1992).

Our search of the historical literature suggests that until the latter part of the 20th century, society and its helping professions ignored the presence of cruelty in families. Because violence in the family was acceptable or hidden, the explanations for it were embedded in the social arrangements of the period.

Currently, we are aware that violence occurs in all kinds of families, regardless of class, race, ethnicity, or social status. Yet why violence occurs in families is still debated. Recent work is still very much concerned with issues concerning perpetrators, the situations in which violence takes place, and incident rates.

Selected Theoretical Perspectives in Family Violence

The study of domestic violence has resulted in findings that display many inconsistencies, caused in part by the complexity of subject matter and the varying perspectives of the researchers involved, whose disciplines range from psychiatry, psychology, social work, and human development to education and sociology. Researchers within these different disciplines subscribe to a multitude of theoretical constructs that extend from biological and individually focused theories to broader sociological perspectives. Each of the perspectives to be examined here offers a unique but incomplete understanding of violent behavior.

Using the medical model, a group of physicians led by Kempe can be credited with focusing the public's attention on the issues of child maltreatment (Kempe et al., 1962). It was this initial attention that challenged long-held and cherished beliefs about the family and that would later open the door to discussions of spouse abuse (Schechter, 1982) and elder abuse (Conner, 1992). The medical model that Kempe and his associates used was a biological paradigm that examines individuals against a standard for the presence of specific, identifiable symptoms that have been linked to dysfunctional or ill states of health. Illnesses are explained in this model by (a) the expanding presence of a noxious foreign bacterial or viral organism, (b) trauma to the host, and (c) genetic deficiencies or imperfections. For example, physicians have long been aware that the bacteria responsible for syphilis, *Treponema pallidum,* is also responsible for the organic brain syndrome that often accompanies this disease in its tertiary stage. This organic disease can result in unpredictable violent outbursts. Similarly, the retrovirus responsible for AIDS often causes an AIDS-related dementia in many of those afflicted with the disease. Unfortunately, these two syndromes, which can be clearly traced to a foreign infectious presence within the body, are the exception and not the rule. It does not appear that most forms of violent behavior have such clear biological markers.

To illustrate the second factor, it has been suggested that trauma early in life correlates with later violent behavior. Studies have shown positive correlations between lead levels, premature birth, and pre- and postnatal nutritional deprivation and aggressive behavior. However, correlation does not establish causation. The life experiences of such unfortunate young children are complicated by a multitude of interacting environmental variables, such as poverty and the stresses accompanying it, that have equal if not greater predictive value (Reiss & Roth, 1993).

The third medical explanation focuses on genetic deficiencies or imperfections. Research in this area is often collected by studying identical twins living with or apart from their biological families. Using the life histories of identical twins, who share the same 23 pairs of chromosomes, researchers assume that similar patterns of behavior are genetic in origin. Findings from twin studies point to the possibility that intelligence has strong biological origins. There is also agreement that the genes individuals inherit at conception provide strong explanations for height, eye color, and weight. There is significantly less agreement that genes explain individuals' personalities or behaviors (Plomin, 1990a, 1990b).

A growing body of research is discovering relationships between the body's biochemical activity and behavior. For example, the relationship between violent behavior and the use of alcohol and other psychoactive drugs has been documented (Reiss & Roth, 1993).

Although the medical model has made vitally important contributions to the improved physical health of society, its focus on the host limits the explanatory power of this paradigm. Sociobiology seeks to explain cultural patterns as the product, in part, of biological causes (Macionis, 1994). For example, Wilson (1975) links biological and genetic conditions to the perception and learning of social behaviors, which are then linked to existing environmental structures. To sociobiologists, biology, environment, and learning are interdependent factors. Some sociobiologists state that through the evolutionary process, human beings have acquired tendencies, such as aggression, selfishness, and territoriality, that determine much of our current behavior. In recent years, sociobiology has gained new prominence. Daly and Wilson (1988) link violence in intimate relationships to the need for the reproductive success potential of children and subsequent parental investment. Smuts (1992) and Burgess and Draper (1989) link male aggression against females to genetic influences.

The growing sophistication of the biological and sociobiological models has led to renewed interest in the link between individuals' genetic and physical makeup and violent behavior. Whether physiological predispositions to violence can be separated from the cultural context is an area for future research and speculation.

Psychological Perspectives

Rather than being concerned with biological influences, researchers who approach the problem of violence from psychological perspectives focus on individual internal thought processes and emotional states that influence behavior. For example, early explanations for woman abuse were based on a belief in women's masochism (Snell, Rosenwald, & Robey, 1964). Other psychological approaches examined the traits and personality characteristics of the abuser and, to some extent, the victim (Tower, 1989).

These studies suggest that the individual has symptoms of an illness, such as an inability to cope or an inability to manage frustration. It is from this perspective that the traits of the abusive parent are often derived. Neglectful mothers are often diagnosed as apathetic/futile, impulse ridden, mentally retarded, suffering from reactive depression, or suffering from psychosis (Polansky, Chalmers, Buttenwieser, & Williams, 1981). With the sexual abuse of children, fathers (as perpetrators) are portrayed as having deep-seated feelings of helplessness and a sense of vulnerability and dependency (Meiselman, 1978). This view looks toward individuals, both victims and perpetrators, who have some deficit in their characters or personalities.

More recent psychological theories have attempted to connect certain psychological characteristics with aggression and violent behavior that may predict child and spouse abuse. Current psychological analysis has also described a continuum of aggression for perpetrators of violence toward intimates (O'Leary, 1993).

Explanations from a psychological perspective state that abuse follows a particular symptomatic pattern. With this knowledge it is assumed that vulnerable individuals can be identified before dysfunctional behavior occurs, and preventive interventions can be initiated with the hope of reducing the incidence of dysfunctional behavior.

Social psychological explanations expand on individual factors to incorporate the environment as well. For example, the social psychological literature clearly identifies babies who are perceived as different as targets for parental abuse. Such children may be premature infants, twins, retarded children, or sickly or unwanted babies. Another example of this approach is the characterization of sexually abused girls with traits that describe their behavior as in some way contributing to the abuse, such as "She is in awe of adults"; "She has been taught to submit to authority"; "She loves and trusts her father"; "She is desperately seeking attention" (deYoung, 1982; Mayer, 1983). An additional explanation provided by this model is that a family develops a specific dysfunctional set of behaviors; members may sometimes be totally enmeshed with each other, but at other times are distanced from each other.

Using a social psychological focus, Lenore Walker's (1979, 1984, 1989) studies of battered women in clinical settings represent some of the first such research into domestic violence. Walker's work sought to answer the question: Why do women stay in abusive relationships? She answered this question by developing a theory based on the three-stage cycle of violence model. The initial stage of the cycle, "tension building," is described as a gradual escalation of tension manifested by discrete acts that cause increased friction. The second stage, the battering incident, occurs when the woman's efforts at amelioration deteriorate and, according to Walker (1984), "she precipitates the inevitable explosion so as to control where and when it occurs, allowing her to take better precautions to minimize her injuries and pain" (p. 96). At this stage, battering usually occurs. The third stage, the honeymoon phase, follows the violence, when the batterer is contrite. The woman wants to believe that he is truly repentant and deserves her forgiveness. From this point, the tension begins to build again, and the cycle repeats.

The cyclical nature of the violence and the battered woman's passiveness in response, together called "battered woman syndrome," is an attempt to explain the violence that battered women experience and the psychological effects of such violence on victims. It characterizes the battered woman as suffering from a reactive condition produced by the violence in which she lives and the history of her individual upbringing. Walker's explanations challenge the notion that women stay in violent intimate settings because of some form of masochism. Instead of asking how women provoke the violence against them, Walker describes battered women as trapped by the violence and held hostage by their own perceptions. In Walker's perspective, the woman who is abused by her intimate partner cannot help herself because she cannot act.

The social psychological model is richer in complexity than the psychological model, but it still does not capture many of the aspects of violent behavior.

Social Learning Theories

Both psychology and sociology embrace social learning theories to explain behavior. Learning theories view the individual human's development as the cumulative effects of a multitude of learning experiences that are integrated to form a personality. Social learning theories take into consideration how adults were treated as children and the bearing that has on their subsequent treatment of their own children and of their parents. Researchers who take this perspective believe that people who witness or experience maltreatment within their families as children are more likely than those who have not had such experiences to mistreat family members later.

The witnessing or experiencing of maltreatment can lead to later violent behavior in two manners. The first involves the concept of reinforcement. Reinforcement is any event that occurs after a behavior and affects the chances that the behavior will occur again. In positive reinforcement, a desirable stimulus follows a given behavior, increasing the chances that the behavior will recur. In negative reinforcement, an unwanted stimulus is removed following a given behavior, also increasing the chances that the behavior will recur. In punishment, an undesirable stimulus (e.g., pain) is presented after a behavior, or a desirable stimulus is removed, decreasing the chances that the behavior will recur. The second way in which individuals exposed to violence learn to repeat the violence later in their own lives is through modeling. In modeling, people imitate the behavior of others whom they admire or respect.

Social learning theories suggest how individuals learn aggressive behaviors. Often, this is conceptualized as understanding aggressive behavior as a response to frustration or as a way to achieve desired goals. Aggression as a learned response to frustration is used to explain family violence. It also is used to show how children learn in intimate settings that aggression is an acceptable form of behavior.

One example of the extension of social learning theory to explain some aspect of violent behavior can be found in the work of Mildred Pagelow (1981), whose research concerns how institutional responses influence the how and the when of women's decisions to leave or remain in abusive situations. Pagelow's research represents one of the first attempts to identify the social context of woman abuse from a sociological perspective. It examines institutional responses to battering, the resources of battered women (both external and internal), and the belief systems of battered women. *Institutional responses,* in this context, refers to the ways in which social institutions, such as police departments, respond to battered women who are seeking help. Pagelow defines *external resources* as objective assets, such as the ability to drive a car and the possession of money and job skills; she defines *internal resources* subjectively as self-esteem and self-confidence. The final factor is the degree to which a woman believes in traditional gender role arrangements. Pagelow hypothesizes that the more resources a woman has, the more she does not believe in traditional ideology about gender roles, and the more the institutions respond to her helpfully, the more likely she is to leave a violent domestic situation.

Conversely, the fewer resources she has, the more she believes in traditional gender roles, and the more institutions do not respond to her, the more likely she is to stay. In other words, the answer to the question of why any particular woman stays in an abusive situation is more complicated than simply that she is masochistic, trapped, or helpless.

General critics of social learning models express the belief that humans show far more complexity than these mechanistic models account for. Social learning theories often present an oversocialized view of human behavior.

Sociological Perspectives

Sociologists have contributed enormously to our understanding of domestic violence. Initially, sociological studies concentrated on measuring the incidence of family abuse. We might think that just collecting data on the incidence of violence in the home would not be controversial, but the research techniques used have caused a storm of debate. For example, Straus and Gelles (1990) used a survey instrument with national samples to document the rate of violence of families in the United States. They used a variety of theoretical perspectives, but linked violence to larger structural factors, such as violence in the society at large, generational transmission of violent norms, sexism, unemployment, and poverty.

The accumulated work of Gelles and Straus and their colleagues has shown how prevalent family violence is in our society (e.g., Gelles & Straus, 1988; Straus & Gelles, 1990). Their studies, which represent some of the most important work in this area, portray women as active participants in domestic violence. Their theoretical and causal analyses show violence as pandemic and an everyday part of the American way of life; their methods reveal that anyone can be violent in the home. This gender-neutral view has been challenged by scholars who contend that intimate violence must be understood primarily as male violence (Dobash & Dobash, 1979, 1992; Kurz, 1989).

General Systems Theory

Sociological theories expand the factors that may influence violent behavior. Systems theorists use several terms when speaking of families. One of these is *boundaries*. Boundaries define a system by establishing what elements belong to it. If a family is described as having open boundaries, this suggests that its members have a great deal of interaction with the outside world, through friends, clubs, organizations, and church activities. A family with closed boundaries keeps to itself, with a minimal amount of outside interaction— members have few if any friends and little if any involvement in civic or community affairs. A family is a system, made of units, that has established more or less open or closed boundaries with other systems. Systems theorists suggest that an incoming stimulus, or input, is mediated within the family and that a response, or output, is returned. Using the general systems perspective, the family's use of violence can be understood through an examination of the ways in which a system (family) adjusts to violent behaviors. In other words, the use of violence becomes part of the general set of inputs that are mediated within a family in a particular manner.

Social Exchange Theory

Another sociological theory that helps to explain family violence is social exchange theory, which states that individuals trade, as in a marketplace, emotions for other emotions. The business of exchange is transacted among family members and also between family members and others in society. Gelles (1983) states that wife and child abuse can be explained within a system of costs and rewards. Violence is used when the positive rewards for it are higher than the costs of refraining from violence.

Both general systems theory and social exchange theory explain a wide range of violent behaviors. The following discussion, however, suggests a structural explanation of specific perpetrators and victims.

Sociological Perspectives on Woman Abuse

Another segment of research in this area may be referred to as perspectives on woman abuse (Dobash & Dobash, 1979, 1992; Kurz, 1989). Researchers who take this perspective are concerned with the violence of men toward women and identify women as the primary victims in violent intimate relationships. They ask questions concerning how battered women think, what they do, and how institutions have responded to their requests for help.

Dobash and Dobash (1979, 1992) have presented the most critical challenge to individual and other structural perspectives on violence. These authors connect violence to the larger social and cultural relations of patriarchy. They show that violence in families reflects cultural arrangements that place men in a position of dominance both in public and in the home. More important, these cultural arrangements place men in the position to maintain this dominance. By asking why men hit their wives, and not why the women do not leave, Dobash and Dobash are able to show how wives predictably become the outlet for men's violence.

In their published work, Dobash and Dobash (1979, 1992) characterize battered women as active and courageous. They have found that these women might be depressed and anxious, but they are also determined and brave. These women strive continuously to find solutions to the violence. Over time, battered women change toward their relationships and toward the violence perpetrated on them. After the first episode of violence, battered women are typically shocked and seek to understand the violence. Instead of being trapped and helpless, Dobash and Dobash (1992) note, these women are "engaging in an active process we refer to as 'staying, leaving and returning' " (p. 231). This is a dynamic process in which the women are evaluating and learning how to solve the problem. They state that "for most women, active pursuit of assistance is a continual aspect of their lives, ebbing and flowing with their experiences at the hands of violent men and of the institutions from which they seek assistance" (p. 232).

According to Dobash and Dobash (1979), women stay in violent relationships not because of their own psychological characteristics or traits, but because of the myriad barriers they face as they attempt to leave. These barriers include cultural supports for remaining in the home, economic barriers to their ability to support themselves and their children, and lack of protection by the criminal justice system. Similarly, their attempts to leave are unsuccessful in a context of increasing violence and coercion, not from any perceived inability to "see the door."

Issues in Furthering an
Understanding of Violence

All of the perspectives described above add to our understanding of violence, and each in some way attempts to address the questions of why violence occurs and who commits violent acts. Without theory, there is no understanding. Each of these theories, however, must contend with violence in the context of the late 20th century and possibly the early 21st century. Any perspective on violence finds it difficult to separate an explanation for behaviors from the issue of identifying a perpetrator and victim and the circumstance of the violent event. In the following discussion, we speculate on future areas of research, including issues that range from the identification of victims and perpetrators to types of situations that increase the risk for violence or harm.

We began this chapter with a brief historical reference because context is important, not only to our understanding of violence, but also to our understanding of societal responses to violence. The problems outlined below are mostly structural; they include family neglect and poverty, being a witness to violence, and other custodial situations (for elderly and children) in which violence can occur. Many of these problems, which have generally been ignored by earlier theories, are related to systems of structural inequities that are implicit and explicit elements of American society. Integrated theoretical perspectives may be needed if we are to design effective prevention measures to address such problems. The following examples do not represent all the issues of the future, but they do represent areas for which any student of violence must begin to consider theoretical and policy directions.

Poverty and Neglect

There is a growing recognition that children are as victimized as adults, and this victimization leads to a multitude of serious long-term problems (Finkelhor & Dziuba-Leatherman, 1994). For example, violence toward children is not limited by a definition of physical harm, but by their life circumstances. Poverty accounts for much of the abuse and neglect of children (Nelson, Saunders, & Landsman, 1993), and child poverty is a major social problem in the United States today. The poverty rate in the United States for all children is nearly 20%; the poverty rate for children in single-parent households is nearly 55% (Smeeding, 1992).

Although the poverty rate represents families' income, it does not reflect how the lives of children are affected by this deprivation. Being poor in this country means not eating well, not having adequate clothing, living in substandard housing conditions, and having fewer educational opportunities than the nonpoor. Many poor children die from neglect; those who survive are often permanently damaged. Even though neglect is a much more prevalent problem than violence and contributes to violence, it does not garner the same amount of theoretical or substantive speculation ,that violent acts do.

Discussion of the neglect of elderly family members often distinguishes between active and passive neglect. Intentional or active neglect involves deliberate failure to provide for the elderly family member, whereas unintentional or passive neglect involves failure to provide care because of lack of knowledge or infirmity (Pillemer & Wolf, 1986, 1989). Neglect of the elderly is complicated further by the need to identify the perpetrator and to locate the elderly victim. Perpetrators of elder neglect can be spouses, adult children, nursing home staff members, or elders themselves. The neglect can occur in the elder's home or in an institutional setting and can consist of lack of food, inadequate shelter, inadequate health care, and other forms of unfulfilled need.

Another indicator of neglect among the elderly is poverty. As we noted earlier, poverty among the elderly, once the most severely affected of all age groups, has been ameliorated by social security and other benefits. Still, poverty among groups who have historically received the fewest benefits persists into old age. For example, the poverty rate for African Americans is estimated at 33.9%, whereas the rate of poverty for white Americans is 10.1% (Greenstein & Shapiro, 1988). Self-neglect in terms of poverty is the consequence of structural inequities and may be manifested by an inadequate diet, substandard housing, and little medical care (Griffin & Williams, 1992).

Witnessing Violence

Another structural phenomenon that affects children is the amount of violence some children witness. Violence in some neighborhoods has reached, in public health terms, epidemic proportions. The rate of homicide, for example, of African American males aged 15 to 24 is 85 per 100,000; comparable homicide rates exist only in some Third World countries (Reiss & Roth, 1993). Children living in many urban neighborhoods are exposed to very dangerous conditions. Parents must teach their children how to avoid the violence in their everyday surroundings and what to do when violence occurs. People in the United States who are not exposed to this danger on a daily basis often find it hard to imagine what it is like to live in what amounts to a war zone. In their study of children in one Chicago neighborhood, Bell and Jenkins (1994) estimated that one third of all school-age children in the neighborhood had witnessed a homicide and two thirds of all school-age children had witnessed a serious assault. As with poverty, witnessing violence exposes children to extremely traumatic events and reflects a form of cultural and societal neglect. Witnessing violence, either in the home or in the streets, is a factor that will continue to be important for any future research on violence in the United States.

Custodial Settings

Neglect and abuse of the elderly and children also occurs in custodial settings. More than 1.5 million Americans now reside in nursing homes (Pillemer & Moore, 1990). Sengstock, McFarland, and Hwalek (1990) note that elderly persons are at risk in nursing home settings for two reasons: First, the elderly are dependent and physically, and sometimes mentally, disabled; second, the personnel responsible for their care have low status and receive little training. Another difficulty is that *adequate care* has been defined differently within different state and federal standards for nursing home and other custodial care facilities. The regulation of care and the expansion of the definition of *adequate care* remain recurring and chronic problems (Pillemer & Moore, 1990). Custodial care by the state and by private caregivers also may contain elements of abuse and neglect that are seen as separate from family violence, although they are based on surrogate family relationships. Issues of abuse in custodial institutions are critical for children as well as the elderly.

Each historical era has defined the problem of violence in different ways. Our present era has shown concern and has generated an enormous amount of research about the dynamics of violence. Yet serious disagreements persist about how to explain violence. Such controversies and debates can make for exciting reading, but the prevention and intervention efforts based on these differing opinions can have serious consequences for the victims of violence, its perpetrators, and society in general.

References

Aschenbaum, W. A., & Kusnerz, P. (1978). *Images of old age in America: 1790 to present*. Ann Arbor: University of Michigan-Wayne State University, Institute of Gerontology.

Bell, C., & Jenkins, E. (1994). Community violence and children in Chicago's Southside. *Psychiatry, 56*, 46-54.

Burgess, R. L., & Draper, P. (1989). The explanation of family violence: The role of biological, behavioral, and cultural selection. In L. Ohlin & M. Tonry (Eds.), *Family violence: Crime and justice—a review of research* (Vol. 11, pp. 59-116). Chicago: University of Chicago Press.

Conner, K. A. (1992). *Aging America: Issues facing an aging society*. Englewood Cliffs, NJ: Prentice Hall.

Daly, M., & Wilson, M. (1988). *Homicide*. New York: Aldine de Gruyter.

deYoung, M. (1982). *The sexual victimization of children*. Jefferson, NC: McFarland.

Dobash, R. E., & Dobash, R. P. (1979). *Violence against wives: A case against the patriarchy*. New York: Free Press.

Dobash, R. E., & Dobash, R. P. (1992). *Women, violence and social change*. London: Routledge.

Ehrenreich, B., & English, D. (1978). *For her own good*. London: Pluto.

Finkelhor, D., & Dziuba-Leatherman, J. (1994). Victimization of children. *American Psychologist, 49*, 173-183.

Gelles, R. J. (1983). An exchange/social control theory. In D. Finkelhor, R. J. Gelles, G. T. Hotaling, & M. A. Straus (Eds.), *The dark side of families: Current family violence research* (pp. 151-165). Beverly Hills, CA: Sage.

Gelles, R. J. (1993). Family violence. In R. L. Hampton, T. P. Gullotta, G. R. Adams, E. H. Potter III, & R. P. Weissberg (Eds.), *Family violence: Prevention and treatment* (pp. 1-24). Newbury Park, CA: Sage.

Gelles, R. J., & Straus, M. A. (1979). Violence in the American family. *Journal of Social Issues, 35*(2), 15-39.

Gelles, R. J., & Straus, M. A. (1988). *Intimate violence: The causes and consequences of abuse in the American family*. New York: Simon & Schuster.

Gordon, L. (1988). *Heroes of their own lives: The politics and history of family violence, Boston 1880-1960*. New York: Penguin.

Greenstein, R., & Shapiro, I. (1988). *Holes in the safety net: Poverty programs and policies in the states*. Washington, DC: Center on Budget and Policy Priorities.

Griffin, L. W., & Williams, O. J. (1992). Abuse among African-American elderly. *Journal of Family Violence, 7*, 19-35.

Kempe, C. H., Silverman, F. H., Steele, B. F., Droegemuller, W., & Silver, H. K. (1962). The battered child syndrome. *Journal of the American Medical Association, 181,* 17-24.

Kurz, D. (1989). Social science perspectives on wife abuse: Current debates and future directions. *Gender & Society, 3,* 489-505.

Macionis, J. J. (1994). *Society: The basics* (2nd ed.). Englewood Cliffs, NJ: Prentice Hall.

Matthaei, J. A. (1982). *An economic history of women in America.* New York: Schocken.

Mayer, A. (1983). *Incest: A treatment manual for therapy with victims, spouses and offenders.* Holmes Beach, FL: Learning Publications.

Meiselman, K. (1978). *Incest.* San Francisco: Jossey-Bass.

Nelson, K. E., Saunders, E. J., & Landsman, M. J. (1993). Chronic child neglect in perspective. *Social Work, 38,* 661-671.

Olafson, E., Corwin, D. L., & Summit, R. C. (1993). Modern history of child sexual abuse awareness: Cycles of discovery and suppression. *Child Abuse and Neglect, 17,* 7-24.

O'Leary, K. D. (1993). Through a psychological lens: Personality traits, personality disorders, and levels of violence. In R. J. Gelles & D. R. Loseke (Eds.), *Current controversies in family violence* (pp. 7-30). Newbury Park, CA: Sage.

Pagelow, M. (1981). *Women battering: Victims and their experience.* Beverly Hills, CA: Sage.

Pillemer, K., & Moore, D. W. (1990). Highlights from a study of abuse of patients in nursing homes. *Journal of Elder Abuse & Neglect, 2*(1/2), 5-29.

Pillemer, K., & Wolf, R. (1986). *Elder abuse: Conflict in the family.* Dover, MA: Auburn House.

Pillemer, K., & Wolf, R. (1989). *Helping elderly victims: The reality of elder abuse.* New York: Columbia.

Pleck, E. (1987). *Domestic tyranny.* Oxford: Oxford University Press.

Plomin, R. (1990a). *Nature and nurture.* Pacific Grove, CA: Brooks/Cole.

Plomin, R. (1990b). The role of inheritance in behavior. *Science, 248,* 183-188.

Polansky, N., Chalmers, M. A., Buttenwieser, E., & Williams, D. (1981). *Damaged parents: An anatomy of child neglect.* Chicago: University of Chicago Press.

Reiss, A. J., Jr., & Roth, J. A. (Eds.). (1993). *Understanding and preventing violence.* Washington, DC: National Academy Press.

Schechter, S. (1982). *Women and male violence: The visions and struggles of the battered women's movement.* Boston: South End.

Sengstock, M. C., McFarland, M. R., & Hwalek, M. (1990). Identification of elder abuse in institutional settings: Required changes in existing protocols. *Journal of Elder Abuse & Neglect, 2*(1/2), 31-50.

Smeeding, T. (1992, January/February). Why the U.S. anti-poverty system doesn't work very well. *Challenge,* pp. 30-35.

Smuts, B. (1992). Male aggression against women: An evolutionary perspective. *Human Nature, 3*(1), 1-44.

Snell, J., Rosenwald, R., & Robey, A. (1964). The wifebeater's wife: A study of family interaction. *Archives of General Psychiatry, 11,* 107-112.

Straus, M. A., & Gelles, R. J. (Eds.). (1990). *Physical violence in American families: Risk factors and adaptations to violence in 8,145 families.* New Brunswick, NJ: Transaction Books.

Tower, C. C. (1989). *Understanding child abuse and neglect.* Boston: Allyn & Bacon.

Walker, L. E. A. (1979). *The battered woman.* New York: Harper & Row.

Walker, L. E. A. (1984). *The battered woman syndrome.* New York: Springer.

Walker, L. E. A. (1989). *Terrifying love: Why battered women kill and how society responds.* New York: HarperCollins.

Wilson, E. O. (1975). *Sociobiology: The new synthesis.* Cambridge, MA: Harvard University Press.

CHAPTER 3

Threads That Link Community and Family Violence: Issues for Prevention

PAMELA JENKINS

Violence exists in many forms in our culture—some of which we condone, some of which we fear, and some of which we ignore. During the 1992 Los Angeles rebellion, Rodney King asked, "Why can't we just get along?"[1] He did not differentiate between stranger violence and nonstranger violence or between street violence and domestic violence. He spoke simply about the necessity for citizens to live in a civil society. Public violence such as occurred during the L.A. rebellion diverts society's attention from the more common type of violence that occurs—violence between individuals who know each other. However, society tends to treat the various kinds of violence the same. For example, a common response to the violence in Los Angeles was to make the rioters and strangers "the other"—that is, those who assault or kill are different from the rest of us.

At first glance, domestic violence and street violence appear to be very different expressions of harm. Using the victim-offender relationship for definitional purposes, we can separate violence into three categories. *Domestic violence* can be defined as harm that occurs between members of the family (or people who share intimacy in some fashion), including spouse abuse, child abuse, child neglect, child sexual abuse, elder abuse, parent abuse, and sibling abuse.[2] Other types of violence can be labeled either *acquaintance violence* (occurring between people who know each other) or *stranger violence*. In this chapter, I classify violence that occurs in neighborhoods that is not domestic violence as *community violence,* which includes acquaintance and stranger violence occurring in a given community.

In public and academic discourses, domestic violence is regarded as separate and distinct from community violence (Fagan & Wexler, 1987). However, when violence in the streets and violence in the home are placed in their social and historical context, these distinctions are diminished. This chapter addresses these forms of violence and attempts to identify a few critical issues for understanding the social context of both types. This discussion does not assume that these types of violence reflect the same set of behaviors; rather, the assumption is that there are similarities in the dynamics of domestic violence and community violence that might be useful to examine.

Social Science and Violence

Criminology has long recognized that much of the violence that takes place in our culture occurs between people who know each other (Rojek & Williams, 1993). Few studies, however, have linked domestic and community violence, even though both types of violence may have some of the same attributes: physical harm that consists of assaults and homicides, and psychological harm that includes threats, intimidation, and terror. As the following review suggests, there is little crossover in the research or the research questions (a few notable exceptions include the work of Bowker, 1984; Bowker, Arbitell, & McFerron, 1988; Browne & Williams, 1989; Williams & Flewelling, 1988).

Overall, theories of violence, especially lethal violence, have been classified as (a) structural, looking at poverty and racism; (b) cultural and subcultural, focusing on how society gives permission for or encourages violence; and (c) interactional, involving situations that escalate. Structural perspectives often examine economic reasons for violence, such as lack of job opportunities. Cultural explanations concentrate on the values and norms that teach or encourage violence. An interactional perspective addresses how the dynamics of situations can lead to violent acts (Wilson, 1993).

These explanations for lethal violence can be developed at both the macro level (structural and cultural) and the micro level (sociopsychological, such as learning theories and theories on aggression). Much of the sociological literature focuses on the structural conditions of lethal violence, especially homicide (Blau & Blau,

1982; Messner & Golden, 1992; Williams, 1984; Williams & Flewelling, 1988). Other examples of structural and cultural explanations are the distinctions between rural and urban violence and between southern and nonsouthern violence (Huff-Corzine, Corzine, & Moore, 1986, 1991; Loftkin & Hill, 1974).

Researchers have explained homicide theoretically at an aggregate level using cultural factors, inequality, and social disorganization (Bursik & Grasmick, 1993; Kposowa & Breault, 1993; Messner, 1989; Messner & Golden, 1992; Miethe, Hughes, & McDowall, 1991; Warner & Pierce, 1993; Williams, 1984). Other researchers have attempted to explain how these structural conditions contribute to acts of violence (Bernard, 1990; Kennedy & Baron, 1993; Klein, Maxson, & Cunningham, 1991; Luckenbill & Doyle, 1989; Maxson, Gordon, & Klein, 1985; Riedel, 1987).

The study of domestic violence in particular is a fairly recent topic for social scientists (Okun, 1986; Pagelow, 1992; Pleck, 1987). Beginning in the late 1970s, scholars from a variety of disciplines have attempted to explain violence between family members and in intimate relationships. Some structurally oriented researchers have examined the incidence and rate of violence that occurs in families (Gelles, 1993; Gelles & Straus, 1988; Straus & Gelles, 1990), whereas others have considered the societal response to violence against women and children (Bograd, 1988; Dobash & Dobash, 1992; Kurz, 1989). Microperspectives have concentrated on social learning theories and psychological studies of the victims (Blackman, 1986; Walker, 1979, 1984, 1989). Although studies of domestic violence and community violence are plentiful, rarely are these two types of violence included in the same discussion. Domestic violence has consistently been excluded from major criminological theoretical and substantive studies of violence. There is a great need, however, to include both kinds of violence in the same discussion, because these forms often coincide in the everyday lives of people.

The Relationship Between Domestic Violence and Community Violence

Cindy's story, as told by a battered women's shelter worker: Cindy, after a history of battering, left her husband and went to the local shelter. She decided that she didn't want to live with the violence in her home anymore, so she moved into an apartment, got a job, and relocated her children to a different school. After she moved, she was attacked twice by young men in her new neighborhood. After the first attack, she stayed in her new home. After the second attack, she moved back in with her batterer to escape the community violence.

A story of a sexual assault perpetrator, as told by a children's advocate: A man was accused of molesting his three daughters over a period of several years. During the investigation, the Department of Social Services began to hear rumors that he had also molested other children. It was found that he had sexually assaulted other children in his community.

An anecdote of sibling abuse, as told by a high school teacher: A young woman, a high school senior, tells the class about her younger brother. She states that he is crazy, often running around the house threatening other family members with knives. She states that in the community with his friends, he also threatens others. When asked if he has been referred for counseling or any other kind of services, she says that nobody has thought to seek help for him.

An incident of parental abuse, as told by a community activist: A grandfather and grandmother are the victims of violence at the hands of their grandson, who lives with them. They are afraid of him but will not turn him in to the police because they have seen how other young men have returned after spending time in the juvenile justice system.

These four examples illustrate some of the ways in which domestic violence and community violence intersect. When domestic violence and community violence are placed in their social context, their similarities become apparent and the separation between the two more arbitrary. We can draw on research from studies of community violence and domestic violence for insights into different assumptions on which to base prevention and intervention programs.

Social learning theories are considered some of the most salient explanations of the connection between community and family violence. Most versions of social learning theories state that what a child experiences influences his or her cognition and behavior in adulthood (Okun, 1986; Pagelow, 1984; Walker, 1984, 1989). Specifically, some social learning theories support the theory of intergenerational transmission of violence (Gelles & Straus, 1988; Pagelow, 1992; Walker, 1984; Widom, 1992). A central assumption of this perspective is that children who are victims of violence or who witness violence on a regular basis are more likely to use violence as adults or to engage in other forms of criminal activity than are children who are not abused or who do not witness violence. A related premise is that children who witness or experience violence are more likely to be victims of violence than are those who do not.

Although the intergenerational transmission of community and family violence is accepted as common sense (Pagelow, 1992), some recent analyses have shown that this theory does not provide a total explanation of a person's use of violence (Kaufman & Zigler, 1987). For example, Okun (1986) has demonstrated that women who witnessed violence as children are no more likely to be in violent relationships than are women who did not. He also has shown that women who were raised in nonviolent conjugal families are more likely to return to their abusive partners than are women who were raised in violent conjugal families (p. 228).

Other studies confirm that social learning plays a significant part in the continuation of violence. Widom (1992) found in a longitudinal study that "those who had been abused or neglected as children were more likely to be arrested as juveniles (26 percent versus 17 percent), as adults (29 percent versus 21 percent), and for a violent crime (11 percent versus 8 percent)" (p. 2). Of those children in her study who had been physically abused, only 15.8% had been arrested for violent offenses; of those children who had been neglected, 12.5% had been arrested for violent offenses. This indicates that neglect is nearly as important a factor for future violence as physical abuse, and more important than sexual abuse (5.6%). Widom's study quite remarkably underscores that, although experiencing violence in some form in childhood may influence an individual's later behavior, it is only one of several influential factors. Furthermore, it shows that "childhood abuse and neglect [have] no apparent effect on the movement of juvenile offenders toward adult criminal activity" (p. 3).

Several chapters in this book discuss the power of "protective factors" in moderating the effects of living with violence. See especially Chapter 5, by Martin Bloom, for a discussion of the role resilience may play in moderating risk, and Chapter 6, by Aleta Meyer and Linda Lausell, for the role of spirituality as a protective factor.

In the criminology literature, learning theories have been influential in explaining criminal behavior (Gottfredson & Hirschi, 1990). These theories suggest that people learn to commit criminal acts because those acts gain them positive sanctions from significant primary groups, in spite of their cost in terms of negative sanctions from other, less important, primary groups. In that context, these theories are used to examine criminal behavior as part of learning a set of norms or behaviors (Glaser, 1960; Sutherland & Cressey, 1974).

Related to social learning theories are hypotheses about violence based on "learned helplessness." This theory holds that victims' experiences teach them that there is nothing they can do about their situations. They learn, in other words, that their own actions will not stop the violence (Blackman, 1986, 1989; Walker, 1984, 1989). In analyzing street violence, Bernard (1990, 1993) notes that because of structural conditions, such as racism and poverty, an individual may experience a condition he calls "angry aggression," which eventually explodes in violence. Bernard compares this situation with learned helplessness, in that people in some neighborhoods learn that alternatives to violence are not possible.

Fagan and Wexler (1987) believe that a social learning paradigm may unify our understanding of the connections between domestic violence and community violence, moving from microexplanations to larger social and cultural levels. Social learning theories offer partial and important explanations of the links between community violence and domestic violence, but their concentration on the individual rather than the social structure limits research questions and hypotheses and, consequently, the types of prevention programs developed.

Alternative Methods for Linking
Community Violence and Domestic Violence

Social learning theories assert that the dynamics of violence are taught and learned in one setting at a particular time and place and are transferred either to another setting or to another generation. This discussion departs from that perspective to propose that the dynamics of community violence and domestic violence may have other similar patterns. The similarities to be explored are the identification of perpetrators by gender, the relationships between perpetrators and victims, the existence of history between victims and perpetrators, and perpetrators' frequent access to their victims, which may escalate the violence over time. The process of how violence occurs between people who know each other is complex. In both domestic violence situations and community violence situations, identifying perpetrators, attributing motivations, and determining causes are intricate issues.

The identification of the perpetrators of violent crime is gendered. Overwhelmingly, men are involved as perpetrators and as victims of most types of violence in our culture (Dunford, Elliott, & Huizinga, 1990), including violence in the home and in the community (Saunders, 1988). The 1992 national crime statistics published by the U.S. Department of Justice (1993b) show that men (78%) are much more likely than women (21.9%) to be murder victims. Most men are killed by other men (nearly 90%), and 9 of every 10 female victims are murdered by men. Furthermore, in U.S. culture men are mostly in control of the legitimate weapons of violence and are more often the enforcers of the law (e.g., in military or civilian law enforcement). Although there is a debate about the role of women in child and domestic abuse, most researchers agree that the most serious cases of child abuse are perpetrated by men (Bowker et al., 1988; Stark & Flitcraft, 1988). In addition, men are more likely to inflict greater injury on and more likely to kill their wives and girlfriends than women are to kill their abusive partners (Browne & Williams, 1989). Even Straus and Gelles (1990), who have found that women can be as violent as men in the home, state that young men and boys are more likely to use violence in public.

In many violent acts, including homicide, there is some prior relationship between the victim and the perpetrator. Of the 22,540 homicides committed in the United States in 1992, nearly 11,000 were committed by individuals who knew their victims (U.S. Department of Justice, 1993a). In some types of domestic violence, such as spouse and sibling abuse, identities of perpetrators and victims are sometimes unclear. And by definition, domestic violence involves interactions between individuals with intimate ties, such as husbands and wives, children and parents, or siblings.

The criminal justice literature also recognizes that some violent acts are defined by the relationship between the victim and the perpetrator (Wolfgang, 1958). Sometimes the relationship is defined by the neighborhood or community in which people live or by their own criminal or delinquent behavior, which may increase their risk of victimization (Lauritsen, Sampson, & Laub, 1991). Routine activities theory addresses how victims and perpetrators can meet in their everyday lives:

> The probability of victimization increases with the convergence in space and time of motivated offenders, suitable targets and the absence of capable guardians. Choice in turn influences individuals' routines and their actions in convergence. Individuals leading risky lifestyles in dangerous locations increase their likelihood of victimization through their association and contact with other offenders. The nature of offending behavior also increases individuals' vulnerability as circumstances influence outcomes. Finally, risk is increased by the proximity to crime in certain areas. (Kennedy & Baron, 1993, pp. 94-95)

However, Fagan, Piper, and Cheng (1987) point out that the relationship is not necessarily as straightforward as two people with risky lifestyles engaging in mutual or retaliatory violence. They propose that the processes that "produce adolescent victims and offenders may differ substantially" (p. 608). They emphasize the necessity of focusing more on contextual aspects and situational factors rather than on aggregate descriptions of types of neighborhoods or the values of the inner-city youth. The relationship between the victim and the perpetrator may be as central to the understanding of the violent interaction in community violence as in domestic violence.

Along with the violent acts committed between people who know each other, there is usually a history of interaction, some of which is based on coercion and control. This history of the relationship contributes to the meaning of a particular violent act. Understanding the face-to-face violent event entails taking into consideration the relationship and the history of the perpetrator and the victim. Research into instances of domestic violence has provided information about the nature of these relationships (Okun, 1986), but in the literature about community violence, much of the history and face-to-face interaction have not been documented. Horowitz (1987) addresses this:

> While structure may encourage a violent situation and certain types of people are more likely to be in those situations and to be the kind of people for whom violence is more probable, we really do not know enough about the situations or the construction of meaning that may lead to violence. We need to know more about what goes on in the face-to-face violent event and its meanings for the actors. (p. 447)

Between victims and perpetrators who know each other and have a history of interactions, repeated assault is possible and probable. In a violent intimate relationship, the perpetrator attacks the victim systematically over time. Several studies on domestic violence have shown that without intervention, violence escalates over time (Dobash & Dobash, 1979, 1992; Walker, 1979, 1984). Luckenbill (1977) describes situated homicides, in which the violence between acquaintances escalates during the incident. His description of homicide includes not only the behavior of the perpetrator, but the behavior of the victim and of bystanders. Violent perpetrators in the community often find the same victims or similar victims, and access to those victims over time may result in escalation of the violence by the perpetrator. As Block (1993) notes:

> Many expressive violent confrontations begin as an argument in which both parties, and often bystanders as well, participate. Often, similar incidents have occurred between the same participants numerous times in the past, and the history of these events is a silent partner in the current incident. (p. 289)

The dynamics of both community violence and domestic violence share some similarities, including that men are much more frequently the perpetrators of the violence than are women, the perpetrator and the victim know each other, and the victim and perpetrator may have a relationship that contributes to repeated accessibility and escalation of violence over time. However, these are not the only similarities between these two types of violence—the ways in which both types of violence are perceived by others in the community and some of the institutional responses to them may be analogous.

Silence and Knowledge: Community Response to Domestic and Community Violence

A community's responses to domestic violence and community violence are often similar. Silence has been a prevalent community response to domestic violence (Pleck, 1987; Walker, 1979, 1984). Silence about domestic violence is usually described in terms of victims' not speaking of the violence and not asking for help. However, others who know about this violence but choose not to or are unable to help also contribute to the silence. Many manage "not to know about" this violence while being aware that "something" is going on. Preserving family privacy becomes more important than the safety of victims as friends and members of the community turn away (Pleck, 1987). Intimidation by the perpetrator of the victim or others who know about the violence often intensifies the silence. Families make excuses, such as, "He's a good provider" or "He's a good father."

Silence about domestic violence is a complex issue that transcends the victim's own silence. It pervades our culture and provides an excuse for those individuals and institutions who wish not to deal with the problem. As with the need to make the criminal "the other," this silence allows us to make the victim of domestic violence "the other." In the case of domestic violence, until the 1970s the silence was so profound that academicians virtually ignored this behavior.

Silence takes on different forms in the case of community violence. Although we are constantly confronted with the effects of community violence in the media, rarely is it analyzed beyond a few aphorisms, such as *gang related* or *drug related*. The violent perpetrator is often portrayed one-dimensionally as a gang member or drug user. Horowitz (1987) studied family members who were able to separate their sons' and brothers' gang violence from their behavior toward their own families. She describes circumstances in which gang members are part of the community for some occasions, such as birthdays, weddings, and funerals, and are not violent. Yet, in other contexts, these same young men use violence for honor and to prove themselves. Family members may have knowledge about the behavior of gangs, but they are silent about the gang membership of their own family.

Silence can be crippling to law enforcement. People in the community may know who the violent perpetrators are, but will not share their knowledge with law enforcement agencies or other representatives of the criminal justice system. Part of this reluctance stems from fear of reprisal. The silence about both types of violence that exist in the neighborhood provides a form of immunity.

One consequence of silence for both domestic violence and community violence is that policymakers attempt to create programs using incomplete information. For example, the actual number of assaults that occur between people who know each other is unknown. Although victimization studies have helped to provide a clearer and more accurate picture of these crimes than was formerly available, much policy is based on speculation about the dynamics of violent crimes. For example, are there identifiable precipitating events to a violent crime that can be known? If the community's knowledge is not voiced, this silence enables the continuation, escalation, and proliferation of both types of violence.

Institutional Responses to Violence

The lack of systematic exploration of the context of violence reflects and contributes to the institutional responses to both types of violence. Law enforcement represents an example of policy and implementation at the institutional level and is often cited as the most salient contributor to the culture's understanding of acquaintance and domestic violence. Responses to domestic and acquaintance violence constitute a great portion of present police work. Sherman (1992) found that in a single year, more than 8 million domestic dispute calls were recorded through law enforcement dispatchers. On a local level, between one third and one half of all calls were related to domestic disputes.

Police attitudes toward violence between people who know each other have historically been difficult. Police officers have been reluctant to respond to domestic disputes (Ferraro, 1989; Pearce & Snortum, 1983) because of many officers' continuing belief that domestic violence situations are the most dangerous calls they face and that women are potentially as violent toward police officers as are men (Jenkins, Osofsky, & Lewis, in press; Pagelow, 1992). Police also have come under scrutiny for the ways in which they handle violence in certain neighborhoods and communities. Law enforcement is often viewed as a paramilitary activity (Bittner, 1995), and this has caused distrust in many nonaffluent neighborhoods. Much of the distrust experienced by both the police and the community is based on attitudes that both the police and members of the community have about each other (Manning, 1995).

Moreover, violence between people who know each other is still not treated as seriously in terms of prosecution and sentencing (Lundsgaarde, 1977; Stanko, 1988). "Real police work" is thought to be "catching the bad guys," not stopping domestic or neighborhood disputes. The criminal justice system appears to operate under the belief that a stranger committing a violent act should receive more serious consequences, including arrest, prosecution, and sentencing, than should an acquaintance or intimate of the victim (Lundsgaarde, 1977).

Not surprisingly, almost all crime prevention efforts focus on stranger and street crime. Preventive efforts concentrate on teaching potential victims to keep themselves safe, rather than on changing the behavior of the stranger. Neighborhood Watch groups and victims' assistance programs usually are designed to prevent the stranger from coming into the neighborhood and to compensate victims of stranger crime. Moreover, the gun-control debate concentrates on stranger crime rather than on the more common ways guns are used—that is, between or among acquaintances and family members.

Still, some efforts have been made to change police responses to domestic and community violence. For example, the institution of mandatory arrest policies originated with an experimental study known as the Minneapolis Project, which found that the arrest of perpetrators prevented or lessened further calls to police (Sherman & Berk, 1984). These findings led to the creation of mandatory arrest policies across the nation, although results overall have been less than encouraging (Dunford et al., 1990; Sherman, 1992).

In response to the problems of police in neighborhoods, "community policing" has become the new approach for improving relations between police and members of the community (Alpert & Dunham, 1989; Manning, 1989). Community policing generally involves a community-based problem-solving approach that often removes police officers from patrol cars and has them walking regular beats. Also, some police are assigned to specific neighborhoods for relatively long periods of time; in some cases, the officers live in those neighborhoods. As with innovative programs for domestic violence, many of these new initiatives have yet to be evaluated, so their effects are still unknown (Williams & Murphy, 1995).

Finally, the political response to domestic and community violence has been to create new regulations and laws. Efforts to change policies related to domestic violence began as a grassroots campaign (Schechter, 1982). Over the past 20 years, efforts to reduce domestic violence have been made at the local, state, regional, and national levels (Maguigan, 1991). Stalking laws, protective orders, marital rape laws, and mandatory arrest policies have been designed to address the increasing awareness of danger for women. In contrast, the political response to street crime has been increasingly harsh—mandatory sentencing for drug trafficking, "three strikes" sentencing laws for repeat felony offenders, and increasing incarceration of juveniles. Thus, whereas the political response to awareness of domestic violence has been to begin taking steps to protect victims, the response to community violence has been to institute much more punitive law enforcement practices.

Conclusion

Every culture must decide how to understand and respond to acts of violence and, in particular, whether some acts of violence are acceptable. It is much easier for us to think about and fear stranger crime than it is to comprehend the violent criminal as someone we know. In order to respond to violence between people who know each other, we must reframe our understanding of danger and safety. Different questions can be asked: How do we make family members safe from each other? What can a community do to keep children safe in their own neighborhood? How can we help a woman who is battered remain in her home safely? How can a community become safer?

First, we need to understand that the fear of stranger violence is related to domestic violence. Surveys indicate that women and the elderly are constantly more afraid of crime than are men. Yet young men are more likely than women or elderly people to be perpetrators *and* victims in public, street violence; women are much less likely to be assaulted or to assault in a public setting than are men. As Stanko (1988) notes, this fear on the part of women may have more to do with the context of their lives than with fear of what might happen to them in the streets. That is, fear of crime perpetrated by strangers may be a reflection of the violence experienced by victims at the hands of people they know. Consequently, reducing danger in the home may reduce the level of fear in communities.

Given that current efforts have either failed outright or proven to be inadequate, alternative solutions should be explored. Community health models hold that violence between people who know each other is preventable (Bell & Jenkins, 1994; Prothrow-Stith, 1991). Prothrow-Stith (1991) calls for a national campaign to end violence. Such a campaign would be based on the assumption that violence between people who know each other can be understood and prevented. The elements discussed in this chapter can help guide the development of such prevention and intervention programs.

Two major frameworks may be useful in the effort to design programs to prevent domestic and community violence. The technology of primary prevention provides a guide for building on the strengths of the community. This technology includes education, community organization, systems intervention, social support, and the promotion of competence (see the discussion in Chapter 2 of this volume). Reiss and Roth (1993) point out that prevention must occur at many levels: the biological, the psychosocial, the microsocial, and the macrosocial. These efforts, then, can be directed by an understanding of child development issues, neurological and genetic processes, social and community-level intervention, and situational approaches. Both strategies take a structural look at prevention; in the following, I attempt to incorporate prevention and intervention techniques applicable to domestic and community violence.

Understanding the similar dynamics and similar social contexts behind community violence and domestic violence. As discussed above, much of the violence that occurs in a community is not stranger violence, but violence between people who know each other. Because not all neighborhoods have the same rates of domestic or community violence, prevention and intervention programs can be more effective if they are designed and carried out locally. Such community-based programs should address the specific historical conditions of the communities for which they are designed, rather than reflect wider-ranging models, and should build on the strengths of their particular communities. For example, community members may be able to diffuse possible violent situations among gang members (Spergel, 1986). Neighborhood groups may be able to work with local law enforcement personnel to develop trust and to monitor use of force in particular neighborhoods (Osofsky, in press). Such community-based programs would allow victims to remain safely in their neighborhoods and would make communities safer for everyone. "Ownership" of a program by the community provides a way for the community to control the types of services it needs and to hold those who deliver those services accountable (McKnight, 1985).

Community organizing around safety issues goes far beyond Neighborhood Watch programs to include improved living conditions in the neighborhood (Gullotta, 1994), housing policies aimed at reversing the geographic concentration of low-income families, stronger community policing programs, and economic revitalization in urban neighborhoods (Reiss & Roth, 1993).

Understanding the dynamics of community and domestic violence and creating opportunities for prevention and intervention. Community and family members are aware of the violence in their neighborhoods. The knowledge that community members have about this violence can be used to design and implement programs that work toward safety. One possible solution is for neighborhoods to identify particular geographic trouble areas and then work to make them safe spots. Intervention teams made up of social workers, medical personnel, and indigenous neighborhood caregivers can augment these resources and de-escalate potentially violent situations.

Breaking the silence surrounding domestic and community violence. Prevention efforts have at their core breaking the silence—not only the silence of the victims but the silence of their families, friends, law enforcement, and others. Law enforcement may incorporate new police procedures, so that police respond to calls with the techniques of community policing. In other words, police undertake problem solving to defuse the level of anger rather than generate more.

Establishing a new body of knowledge toward prevention of community and domestic violence. By concentrating on the similarities and differences in community violence and domestic violence, we might shift the emphasis away from the less frequent phenomenon of stranger violence. This shift would give community and domestic violence prevention efforts more prominence in policy decisions and may help to emphasize workable alternatives to punishment and incarceration.

Such a shift in focus would show a deeper understanding of community violence and domestic violence, their similarities and differences. There are still many unanswered questions about the relationship between domestic violence and community violence. One of the questions worthy of exploration is whether those neighborhoods plagued by community violence experience more problems with domestic violence than do other communities. Related to this is the question of whether neighborhood residents experience community violence and domestic violence differently or regard the two types of violence differently. Moreover, some neighborhoods may have little community violence but still have frequent incidents of domestic violence. We should also inquire into how silence concerning both types of violence is constructed and maintained and how people survive in the midst of violence. Answers to these questions and others will lead to more appropriate and effective responses to all types of violence. The acquisition of knowledge about violence must be done in coordination and cooperation with the victims of violence. Community members, victims, law enforcement personnel, and others may be able to help each other understand what actually happens in violent situations.

Bringing the community to the table. It is obvious that to understand what happens in violent situations, we need more than experts. The lives of the current victims of violence, especially young men of color, need to be considered a priority. Communities can be full participants in the search for solutions to the problem of violence in their neighborhoods. Many of these communities who are losing their sons to prison and to death are grieving in silence. The collaboration of the community, social service providers, and educational institutions can identify specific strategies for creating safer neighborhoods.

Notes

1. I use the term *rebellion* here specifically because it is the term that many members of the South-Central L.A. community use to describe the events for themselves (Reynolds, 1993).

2. These are arbitrary definitions for both types of violence, and there are certainly conceptual and theoretical reasons to make other distinctions, for example, between spouse abuse and woman abuse. However, for this discussion, these definitions are useful because they allow us to think in different ways about the relationship between domestic violence and community violence.

References

Alpert, G. P., & Dunham, R. G. (1989). Community policing. In R. G. Dunham & G. P. Alpert (Eds.), *Critical issues in policing: Contemporary readings* (pp. 406-424). Prospect Heights, IL: Waveland.

Bell, C., & Jenkins, E. (1994). Community violence and children in Chicago's Southside. *Psychiatry, 56,* 46-54.

Bernard, T. J. (1990). Angry aggression among the "truly disadvantaged." *Criminology, 28,* 73-96.

Bernard, T. J. (1993). The intent to harm. In A. V. Wilson (Ed.), *Homicide: The victim/offender connection* (pp. 23-41). Cincinnati, OH: Anderson.

Bittner, E. (1995). The quasi-military organization of the police. In V. E. Kappeler (Ed.), *The police and society: Touchstone readings* (pp. 173-183). Prospect Heights, IL: Waveland.

Blackman, J. (1986). Potential uses for expert testimony: Ideas toward the representation of battered women who kill. *Women's Rights Law Reporter, 9,* 227-238.

Blackman, J. (1989). *Intimate violence: A study of injustice.* New York: Columbia University Press.

Blau, J. R., & Blau, P. M. (1982). The cost of inequality: Metropolitan structure and violent crime. *American Sociological Review, 47,* 114-129.

Block, C. R. (1993). Lethal violence in the Chicago Latino community. In A. V. Wilson (Ed.), *Homicide: The victim/offender connection* (pp. 267-342). Cincinnati, OH: Anderson.

Bograd, M. (1988). Feminist perspectives on wife abuse: An introduction. In K. Yllö & M. Bograd (Eds.), *Feminist perspectives on wife abuse* (pp. 11-26). Newbury Park, CA: Sage.

Bowker, L. H. (1984). Coping with wife abuse: Personal and social networks. In A. R. Roberts (Ed.), *Battered women and their families: Intervention strategies and treatment programs* (pp. 168-191). New York: Springer.

Bowker, L. H., Arbitell, M., & McFerron, J. R. (1988). On the relationship between wife beating and child abuse. In K. Yllö & M. Bograd (Eds.), *Feminist perspectives on wife abuse* (pp. 158-174). Newbury Park, CA: Sage.

Browne, A., & Williams, K. (1989). Exploring the effect of resource availability and the likelihood of female-perpetrated homicides. *Law and Society Review, 23,* 75-94.

Bursik, R. J., Jr., & Grasmick, H. G. (1993). *Neighborhoods and crime: The dimensions of effective community control.* Lexington, MA: Lexington Books.

Dobash, R. E., & Dobash, R. P. (1979). *Violence against wives: A case against the patriarchy.* New York: Free Press.

Dobash, R. E., & Dobash, R. P. (1992). *Women, violence and social change.* London: Routledge.

Dunford, F., Elliott, D., & Huizinga, D. (1990). The role of arrest in domestic assault: The Omaha Police Experiment. *Criminology, 28,* 183-206.

Fagan, J., Piper, E. S., & Cheng, Y. (1987). Contributions of victimization to delinquency in inner cities. *Journal of Criminal Law and Criminology, 78,* 586-613.

Fagan, J., & Wexler, S. (1987). Crime at home and in the streets: The relationship between family and stranger violence. *Violence and Victims, 2,* 5-23.

Ferraro, K. J. (1989). Policing woman battering. *Social Problems, 36,* 61-74.

Gelles, R. J. (1993). Family violence. In R. L. Hampton, T. P. Gullotta, G. R. Adams, E. H. Potter III, & R. P. Weissberg (Eds.), *Family violence: Prevention and treatment* (pp. 1-24). Newbury Park, CA: Sage.

Gelles, R. J., & Straus, M. A. (1988). *Intimate violence: The causes and consequences of abuse in the American family.* New York: Simon & Schuster.

Glaser, D. (1960). Differential association and criminological prediction. *Social Problems, 8,* 6-14.

Gottfredson, M., & Hirschi, T. (1990). *A general theory of crime.* Stanford, CA: Stanford University Press.

Gullotta, T. P. (1994). The what, who, why, where, when, and how of primary prevention. *Journal of Primary Prevention, 15,* 5-14.

Horowitz, R. (1987). Community tolerance of gang violence. *Social Problems, 34,* 437-450.

Huff-Corzine, L., Corzine, J., & Moore, D. C. (1986). Southern exposure: Deciphering the South's influence on homicide rates. *Social Forces, 64,* 906-924.

Huff-Corzine, L., Corzine, J., & Moore, D. C. (1991). Deadly connections: Culture, poverty, and the direction of lethal violence. *Social Forces, 69,* 715-732.

Jenkins, P., Osofsky, J., & Lewis, M. (in press). Problem solving paradigms for police officers. In J. D. Osofsky (Ed.), *Children, youth and violence: Searching for solutions.* New York: Guilford.

Kaufman, J., & Zigler, E. (1987). Do abused children become abusive parents? *American Journal of Orthopsychiatry, 57,* 186-192.

Kennedy, L. W., & Baron, S. W. (1993). Routine activities and a subculture of violence: A study of violence on the street. *Journal of Research in Crime and Delinquency, 30*(1), 88-112.

Klein, M. W., Maxson, C. L., & Cunningham, L. C. (1991). "Crack," street gangs, and violence. *Criminology, 29,* 623-650.

Kposowa, A., & Breault, K. (1993). Reassessing the structural covariates of U.S. homicide rates: A county level study. *Sociological Focus, 26,* 27-46.

Kurz, D. (1989). Social science perspectives on wife abuse: Current debates and future directions. *Gender & Society, 3,* 489-505.

Lauritsen, J. L., Sampson, R. J., & Laub, J. H. (1991). The link between offending and victimization among adolescents. *Criminology, 29,* 265-291.

Loftkin, C., & Hill, R. H. (1974). Regional subculture and homicide: An examination of the Gastil-Hackney thesis. *American Sociological Review, 39,* 714-724.

Luckenbill, D. F. (1977). Criminal homicide as a situated transaction. *Social Problems, 25,* 176-186.

Luckenbill, D. F., & Doyle, D. P. (1989). Structural position and violence: Developing a cultural explanation. *Criminology, 27,* 419-436.

Lundsgaarde, H. P. (1977). *Murder in space city.* New York: Oxford University Press.

Maguigan, H. (1991). Battered women and self-defense: Myths and misconceptions in current reform proposals. *University of Pennsylvania Law Review, 140,* 379-486.

Manning, P. K. (1989). Community policing. In R. G. Dunham & G. P. Alpert (Eds.), *Critical issues in policing: Contemporary readings* (pp. 395-405). Prospect Heights, IL: Waveland.

Manning, P. K. (1995). The police: Mandate, strategies, and appearances. In V. E. Kappeler (Ed.), *The police and society: Touchstone readings* (pp. 97-125). Prospect Heights, IL: Waveland.

Maxson, C. L., Gordon, M. A., & Klein, M. W. (1985). Differences between gang and nongang homicides. *Criminology, 23,* 209-222.

McKnight, J. (1985). A reconsideration of the crisis of the welfare state. *Social Policy, 16*(1), 27-30.

Messner, S. F. (1989). Economic discrimination and societal homicide rates: Further evidence of the cost of inequality. *American Sociological Review, 54,* 597-611.

Messner, S. F., & Golden, R. M. (1992). Racial inequality and racially desegregated homicide rates: An assessment of alternative theoretical explanations. *Criminology, 30,* 421-447.

Miethe, T., Hughes, M., & McDowall, D. (1991). Social change and crime rates: An evaluation of alternative theoretical approaches. *Social Forces, 70,* 165-185.

Okun, L. (1986). *Woman abuse: Facts replacing myths.* Albany: State University of New York Press.

Osofsky, J. D. (Ed.). (in press). *Children, youth and violence: Searching for solutions.* New York: Guilford.

Pagelow, M. D. (1984). *Family violence.* New York: Praeger.

Pagelow, M. D. (1992). Adult victims of domestic violence: Battered women. *Journal of Interpersonal Violence, 7,* 87-120.

Pearce, J. B., & Snortum, J. R. (1983). Police effectiveness in handling disturbance calls: An evaluation of crisis intervention training. *Criminal Justice and Behavior, 10,* 71-92.

Pleck, E. (1987). *Domestic tyranny: The making of American social policy against family violence from colonial times to the present.* New York: Oxford University Press.

Prothrow-Stith, D. (1991). *Deadly consequences: How violence is destroying our teen-age population and a plan to begin solving the problem.* New York: HarperCollins.

Reiss, A. J., Jr., & Roth, J. A. (Eds.). (1993). *Understanding and preventing violence.* Washington, DC: National Academy Press.

Reynolds, B. (1993, April 23). GOP senators just don't get the message about jobs. *USA Today,* p. A11.

Riedel, M. (1987). Stranger violence: Perspectives, issues and problems. *Journal of Criminal Law and Criminology, 78,* 223-258.

Rojek, D. G., & Williams, J. L. (1993). Interracial vs. intraracial offenses in terms of the victim/offender relationship. In A. V. Wilson (Ed.), *Homicide: The victim/offender connection* (pp. 249-265). Cincinnati, OH: Anderson.

Saunders, D. G. (1988). Other "truths" about domestic violence: A reply to McNeely and Robinson-Simpson. *Social Work, 33,* 179-183.

Schechter, S. (1982). *Women and male violence: The visions and struggles of the battered women's movement.* Boston: South End.

Sherman, L. W. (1992). *Policing domestic violence.* New York: Free Press.

Sherman, L. W., & Berk, R. A. (1984). The specific deterrent effects of arrest for domestic assault. *American Sociological Review, 49,* 261-272.

Spergel, I. A. (1986). The violent gang problem in Chicago: A local community approach. *Social Service Review, 60,* 94-131.

Stanko, E. A. (1988). Fear of crime and the myth of the safe home: A feminist critique of criminology. In K. Yllö & M. Bograd (Eds.), *Feminist perspectives on wife abuse* (pp. 52-75). Newbury Park, CA: Sage.

Stark, E., & Flitcraft, A. H. (1988). Women and children at risk: A feminist perspective on child abuse. *International Journal of Health Services, 18*(1), 97-108.

Straus, M. A., & Gelles, R. J. (Eds.). (1990). *Physical violence in American families: Risk factors and adaptations to violence in 8,145 families.* New Brunswick, NJ: Transaction Books.

Sutherland, E. H., & Cressey, D. R. (1974). *Criminology.* Philadelphia: J. B. Lippincott.

U.S. Department of Justice. (1993a). *Bureau of Justice Statistics sourcebook of criminal justice statistics.* Washington, DC: Government Printing Office.

U.S. Department of Justice. (1993b). *Crime in the United States, Uniform Crime Reports.* Washington, DC: Government Printing Office.

Walker, L. E. A. (1979). *The battered woman.* New York: Harper & Row.

Walker, L. E. A. (1984). *The battered woman syndrome.* New York: Springer.

Walker, L. E. A. (1989). *Terrifying love: Why battered women kill and how society responds.* New York: HarperCollins.

Warner, B., & Pierce, G. L. (1993). Reexamining social disorganization theory using calls to the police as a measure of crime. *Criminology, 31,* 493-517.

Widom, C. S. (1992, October). The cycle of violence. *National Institute of Justice: Research in Brief,* pp. 1-6.

Williams, H., & Murphy, P. V. (1995). The evolving strategy of police: A minority view. In V. E. Kappeler (Ed.), *The police and society: Touchstone readings* (pp. 29-52). Prospect Heights, IL: Waveland.

Williams, K. R. (1984). Economic sources of homicide: Reestimating the effects of poverty and inequality. *American Sociological Review, 49,* 283-289.

Williams, K. R., & Flewelling, R. L. (1988). The social production of criminal homicide: A comparative study of desegregated rates in American cities. *American Sociological Review, 53,* 421-431.

Wilson, N. K. (1993). Gendered interaction in criminal homicide. In A. V. Wilson (Ed.), *Homicide: The victim/offender connection* (pp. 43-62). Cincinnati, OH: Anderson.

Wolfgang, M. E. (1958). *Patterns of criminal homicide.* New York: John Wiley.

CHAPTER 4

Violence in Communities of Color: Where We Were, Where We Are, and Where We Need to Be

ROBERT L. HAMPTON

BETTY R. YUNG

Where We Were

Despite the growing literature on family violence, significant deficits remain in our research, theory, and practice. Violence in families and communities of color has been neither adequately explored nor appropriately explained. This omission limits the development of accurate knowledge about the prevalence and characteristics of violence among these groups. Consequently, practitioners frequently lack pertinent information on which to base the development of culturally sensitive intervention and prevention programs.

Unfortunately, where we were—that is, where we have been until recently—in learning about and addressing violence among ethnic minority groups had limitations. We did not fully recognize the problem, knew little about it beyond its very broadest patterns, and frequently oversimplified or misinterpreted what was known. In fact, it may be safe to argue that researchers and practitioners discovered family violence in communities of color only in the 1980s. As knowledge of the extent of the problem increased, so did the demands for prevention and control. One explanation for this growing concern is the realization that the disproportionate mortality

and morbidity experienced by some minorities is a direct consequence of violence.

A primary contributor to the perception of minority violence as
a public health problem came from the Task Force on Black and
Minority Health of the U.S. Department of Health and Human
Services (U.S. DHHS) (1985). Assaultive injuries, or interpersonal
violence, were clearly identified as a major factor accounting for
the disparity in death and illness that blacks and Hispanics face in
the United States.[1] For instance, black males and Hispanic males
appear to account for a major share of the elevated risk experienced
in their communities (Mercy, 1988).

An increased interest in violence among minorities exists because
people of color constitute a growing proportion of the population
of the United States. Whereas minorities were 11.4% of the population (20.6 million) in 1960, in the 1990 census they constituted
24.7% (62 million), or roughly one of every four persons. Census
bureau projections suggest that by the year 2050, their proportion
within the population will be one half (McKenney & Bennett,
1994). In many of our large urban areas, people of color are already
in the majority. Demographic conditions are an important factor
that will continue to increase our awareness that we live in a
multiracial society.

In the rest of this chapter, we describe where we are now in
understanding and preventing violence in communities of color. We
begin with a brief discussion of methodological constraints hinder-
ing research on violence and the role of cultural assumptions in
interpreting research results and developing explanatory theory. We
summarize data on violence experienced by African Americans,
Hispanics, Native Americans, and Asian Americans, noting the
numerous gaps in our present knowledge. We close the chapter with
recommendations on where we need to be with regard to this
violence. We stress the need for focused research that will (a) yield
a more accurate understanding of the extent and nature of the
problem of violence in communities of color and (b) create an
ecological perspective that recognizes the role of both interpersonal
and environmental factors in supporting or discouraging acts of
violence. Finally, we advocate the development and testing of
culturally relevant approaches to violence prevention and intervention and highlight promising trends in this direction.

Where We Are:
Research on Violence in Families of Color

General Methodological Issues

Our knowledge about violence among ethnic minorities is hampered by overall limitations in data about violence among all Americans, particularly with regard to the incidence and prevalence of nonfatal violence. Although both health and criminal justice data sources provide some indications of national patterns, their methodological shortcomings in presenting a true picture of the prevalence of assaultive violence have been widely recognized (Christoffel, 1990; Flowers, 1988; National Committee for Injury Prevention and Control, 1989; Rodriguez, 1990). There are two major national statistical systems, both administered by the U.S. Department of Justice, for measuring victimization and violent offending. Each year, the National Crime Survey (NCS) collects data on personal crimes of rape, robbery, and assault based on interviews with individuals 12 years of age and older. Like all self-report measures, the NCS is considered to be subject to underreporting or overreporting due to such phenomena as memory failure, lying, miscoding, misinterpretation, and reluctance to self-identify as a victim (Flowers, 1988). The other data system is the Uniform Crime Reporting (UCR) program, which captures law enforcement agency reports. Problems noted with the UCR database include definitional problems in measuring crime, reliability of reporting, incorrect data entry, and law enforcement agency manipulation of statistics (Flowers, 1988; Rokaw, Mercy, & Smith, 1990). In addition, the UCR program does not obtain data on crime that fails to receive official attention, and thus excludes a vast number of violent episodes known through other sources to have occurred (Elliott, Huizinga, & Morse, 1986). For example, the 1991 NCS found that close to 1.2 million violent crimes against adolescents were not reported to the police (U.S. Department of Justice, 1991).

Not surprisingly, the NCS and UCR data sets yield entirely different pictures of violent crime in the United States. Whereas analyses based on UCR reports would support a conclusion that the numbers of violent crimes have never been higher, NCS results suggest that violent crime has declined consistently since 1975 (Barham, 1992; Menard, 1992).

Measurement of specific types of violence, particularly intrafamily spouse/partner abuse and child abuse, has comparable problems of validity. Clinical studies have been criticized for using samples that are not representative and often for lacking appropriate comparison groups (Gelles, 1993). Official records are subject to different recording and reporting practices and omit the vast quantity of unreported victimization (Finkelhor & Dziuba-Leatherman, 1994). Self-report surveys carry the inherent threat of misreporting (Gelles, 1993). Furthermore, methodological limitations of the national data collection system for child abuse make it impossible to compare across states (Finkelhor & Dziuba-Leatherman, 1994). In general, family violence research has not provided the critical data needed to answer key research, practice, and policy questions (Gelles, 1993).

Methodological Issues Related to Ethnic Minorities

Most national surveillance systems that report on violence collect data on race and ethnicity; however, they frequently aggregate these data into categories of black, white, and other (Flowers, 1988; U.S. DHHS, 1990). This is true for homicides reported in the UCR, for mortality reports of the National Center for Health Statistics, and for the victimization self-reports of the NCS. Thus, national estimates of the magnitude of lethal and nonlethal violence among Hispanics, Native Americans, and Asian Americans are virtually unavailable. Some data can be found on the incidence of Hispanic and Native American violence, but this information has limitations. Although the Federal Bureau of Investigation's Supplemental Homicide Report System has included a Hispanic identifier since 1980, information on this identifier is missing for a high percentage of victims (Mercy, 1988). Similarly, the Bureau of Justice periodically publishes special reports on Hispanic victimization as identified in the NCS. However, infrequent publication of these data impairs their usefulness; for example, 9 years elapsed between a supplemental report on Hispanic victimization appearing in 1981 and a later update (U.S. Department of Justice, 1991). Data on Native American homicides are gathered and reported by the Indian Health Service (e.g., Ogden, Spector, & Hill, 1970; Wallace, Kirk, Houston, Annest, & Emrich, 1993). Unfortunately, these data include only Native Americans living on or near reservations who are being served by the Indian Health Service, excluding the more sizable off-reservation population—now estimated to be about three quarters of all Native Americans (Gruber, DiClemente, & Anderson, in press).

There are special difficulties in gathering information on smaller ethnic minority groups through national surveys. In order to make reliable estimates for smaller subgroups such as Asian Americans and Native Americans, sample size would have to be expanded to a degree that would make surveys prohibitively expensive to administer (U.S. DHHS, 1990). Oversampling (i.e., the modification of random probability samples to include greater numbers of members of underrepresented groups than would have been selected based on their proportion within the general population) has been used in order to survey less numerous groups (Sugarman, Brenneman, LaRoque, Warren, & Goldberg, 1994). Although this technique is helpful in shedding light on general trends for the ethnic group, it fails to capture the enormous diversity and risk-factor variations within racial and ethnic populations. For example, homicide patterns among Native Americans vary by tribal affiliation (Young, 1990), and certain Asian American ethnic subgroups have significant problems with violent youth gangs whereas others do not (Conly, Kelly, Mahanna, & Warner, 1993).

Ensuring accuracy in methods of collecting data on race and ethnicity is quite complex. For example, *Hispanic* is defined in differing ways, making it confusing for those who are asked to self-identify (Zahn, 1988). In other cases, classification of ethnicity may be based on surname or may be designated by an observer. Different methods for obtaining information on race and ethnicity can yield substantially different results, particularly for those typically designated as "other race" (McKenney & Bennett, 1994). Sugarman, Soderberg, Gordon, and Rivara (1993) found a 68% underestimate in annual injury rates among Native Americans in Oregon when hospital data (determined either by patient self-report or observation by hospital staff) were matched with Indian Health Service records that use formal documentation of tribal memberships or American Indian heritage for determining ethnicity.

Conducting survey or interview research with Southeast Asian refugee and immigrant groups presents unique challenges. For those who have fled from political persecution, there may be fear of the effects of their responses on their personal or family safety;

the need to sign consent forms may be a source of particular anxiety, as may be any tape-recording of responses. Interviews may require the use of an interpreter, who may alter the communication according to his or her own emotional and intellectual filters. Furthermore, the use of an interpreter who is a community member may generate concerns about confidentiality. Respondents to a survey or interview who are unfamiliar with social science research may give answers that reflect politeness or desire to please the interviewer rather than make accurate disclosures. Finally, cooperation with the research agenda may be helped or hindered by researchers' adherence to or ignorance of cultural etiquette in such areas as gaining entry into the community by approaching its formal and informal leaders and interviewer behavior in accepting ritual drinks or gifts (Frye & D'Avanzo, 1994; Pernice, 1994).

Interpretation of Violence Research: Cultural Perspectives

Not only is our measurement of violence among ethnic minorities fraught with problems of accuracy, researchers' own viewpoints about culture present other possible sources of distorted information. Cultural perspectives play a key role in the interpretation of research on a particular problem, the development of etiological theories to explain it, and the selection of approaches to prevent or ameliorate it. For example, in the social science literature, differences between white middle-class families and African American families are often explained from varying perspectives, which may be labeled cultural deviant, cultural equivalent, and cultural variant perspectives (Allen, 1978; Fine, Schwebel, & James-Myers, 1987). These perspectives are useful in the study of other families of color as well.

The *cultural deviant perspective* recognizes that families of color are different from families belonging to the majority group, and views these differences as pathological or deviant. Virtually ignoring the positive features of African American, Native American, and Hispanic families, this perspective has contributed to the development of stigmatizing explanations of etiology such as the "subculture of violence" theory, which asserts that violence in the African American community results from a permeating value system that condones acts of aggression as legitimate, justifiable responses to provocation (Sampson, 1987).

The *cultural equivalent perspective* assumes that there are no clear cultural distinctions between families of European ancestry and families of color. Advocates of this perspective argue that differences in socioeconomic status, especially higher rates of poverty among many minority groups, explain differences between groups. This perspective may lead researchers to fail to measure or consider aspects of environmental conditions that potentially exacerbate family problems and to advocate for the application of "universal" solutions to problems that in fact may "make services so ethnocentric as to render them virtually useless to all but the most assimilated people of color" (Cross, Bazron, Dennis, & Isaacs, 1989, p. 23).

The *cultural variant perspective* argues that differences in family life can be attributed to culture rather than economics. This perspective is similar to an ecological perspective in that it recognizes that the environment has an impact on family in both its structure and its functioning and that the individual or family has a reciprocal influence on the environment. From this perspective, family patterns are often seen as necessary (but not always positive) adaptations of a group to various environments (Daniel, 1985). This broader perspective enhances the probability of making accurate assessments of complex problems and finding effective solutions for them.

Cultural perspectives not only affect the conclusions drawn from research findings, they can potentially influence any aspect of violence research, including decisions concerning what population to study, formulation of hypotheses, and the choice of survey and sampling methods. For example, those who hold the view that Asian Americans are a "model minority" unlikely to experience violence (Chen & True, 1994) may not choose to include this group in surveys on victimization. Recognition of the role of cultural perspectives or biases is an important step toward needed advances in what we know about violence in families and communities of color.

Lethal Violence in Communities of Color

What we know now about violence among ethnic minority groups is far from complete. More is known about homicide than about other forms of violence. Because of the standard practices for collecting and reporting violent death rates, reliable data on homicide victimizations are available only for whites and African Americans. These data persistently demonstrate a risk disparity for African Americans, with homicide rates across all age and gender groups far exceeding those for whites and for members of other ethnic minorities (National Center for Health Statistics, 1990, 1992; National Committee for Injury Prevention and Control, 1989). The most vulnerable population is young African American men, ages 15 to 24, who are murdered at rates 9 to 11 times higher than those for their same-age white male peers (Centers for Disease Control, 1990; National Center for Health Statistics, 1990, 1992). Inner-city residence further increases the risk of homicide. A study of pediatric deaths in Detroit between 1980 and 1988 indicated that urban African American males ages 15 to 18 had homicide rates more than 16 times greater than those of white males of the same age (Ropp, Visintainer, Uman, & Treloar, 1992).

The epidemic proportions of the African American male homicide problem have tended to overshadow the significant risk for African American women. Since 1978, homicide has been the leading cause of death for African American men *and* African American women ages 15 to 34. African American women are in fact the second most vulnerable group, with their murder rates surpassing those of white males within the same age range (National Center for Health Statistics, 1990, 1992).

The available data on homicide among Hispanics suggest that their homicide rates are lower than for African Americans but three to four times higher than for non-Hispanic whites (Becker, Samet, Wiggins, & Key, 1990; Mercy, 1988; Smith, Mercy, & Rosenberg, 1986; U.S. DHHS, 1990). Homicide is a leading cause of death for Hispanics. However, this elevated risk appears to apply only to males; regional studies have found rates for Hispanic females roughly comparable to those of white non-Hispanic women, who are generally considered to be a comparatively low-risk group (Becker et al., 1990).

Homicide rates for Native Americans generally have been found to be one and a half to three times higher than for whites, lower than for African Americans, and about comparable to those of Hispanics (Kahn, 1986; Kettl, 1993; Leyba, 1988; U.S. DHHS, 1990; Wallace et al., 1993). However, exceptions have been reported. Sloan and colleagues (1988) determined that Native Americans in Seattle, Washington, and Vancouver, British Columbia, had higher homicide rates than whites or individuals of any other ethnic group. Becker et al. (1990), who studied homicide in New Mexico over a 30-year period, found substantially higher rates for both male and female Native Americans than for Hispanic and non-Hispanic men and women. Findings from these studies may not be generalizable because of small sample sizes and unique demographic patterns.

Neither national nor regional studies have focused on homicide among Asian Americans. Homicide is not among the leading causes of death for Asian Americans and appears not to be considered a major health risk for this group (U.S. DHHS, 1990). However, it may well be that some subgroups within this population are at elevated risk. There are significant cultural distinctions and unique adverse health and social conditions among subgroups of Asian Americans, particularly Southeast Asian refugees and immigrants. Health risks vary widely according to socioeconomic and acculturation levels and community of residence. Many of the newer waves of refugee groups, such as Laotians, Cambodians, Vietnamese, and Hmong, experience extreme poverty, isolation, high stress levels, culture shock and disruption, problems with family role changes, and traumatic memories that contribute to higher-than-average rates of adjustment and psychiatric disorders (Cerhan, 1990; Frye & D'Avanzo, 1994; U.S. DHHS, 1994). Particularly when combined with residence in high-crime inner-city areas, these personal problems may place some Southeast Asian groups at higher levels of risk for fatal violence. Present methods of aggregating all such individuals into the generic category of Asian/Pacific Islander may conceal disparities of health status and mortality risk.

Lethal Violence in Families of Color

From 1976 through 1985, the spouse homicide rate in the United States was 1.6 per 100,000 married persons, with wives being at 1.3 times the risk of husbands (Mercy & Saltzman, 1989). African Americans accounted for 45.4% of all spouse homicide victims and had a rate of spouse homicides that was 8.4 times higher than that for whites.

There is virtually no comparative information on the incidence of lethal violence occurring among Asian American and Native

American couples. Two studies suggest lesser incidence for Native American families, finding that Native American homicides most frequently affect single men and are usually committed by other Native American males in the friend or acquaintance category (Kahn, 1986; Kettl, 1993). However, the sample sizes in these studies were too small to permit the drawing of definitive conclusions.

Comparisons of intrafamily homicide patterns can be made, however, among Hispanics, African Americans, and whites. Several studies have shown that Hispanic homicide victims are less likely than others to have been killed by family members (Block, 1988; Leyba, 1988; Rodriguez, 1988; Valdez & Nourjah, 1988; Zahn, 1988).

In a study of homicide data from nine cities, killings within Hispanic families were found to be much less concentrated on spouses than were killings within African American or non-Hispanic white families (Zahn, 1988). Some 47% of whites who killed within the family killed a spouse, compared with 56% of African Americans and only 18% of Hispanics. Although the number was small, Hispanic intrafamilial homicides had a higher percentage involving parent-child relations. Hispanics also had a higher percentage of killing other family members than did African Americans or non-Hispanic whites (Zahn, 1988).

Not only is the home the place where female victims are more likely to be killed, it is also the place where they are more likely to kill their marital partners (Goetting, 1991; Jurik & Winn, 1990; Rose & McClain, 1990). When women kill, it is frequently during situations of domestic conflict or in retaliation for previous abuse (Browne, 1987; Goetting, 1991; Jurik & Winn, 1990; Mann, 1991). Several studies have shown that African Americans are overrepresented among female perpetrators (Block, 1988; Jurik & Winn, 1990; McClain, 1982-1983; Valdez & Nourjah, 1988).

Researchers have suggested that what appear to be racial differences may actually be differences in socioeconomic status, because race is highly correlated with poverty, which in turn is correlated with homicide between family members and friends (Smith & Parker, 1980). Some argue that socioeconomic factors are more important than race in explaining variations in homicide rates (Hawkins, 1990; Loftin & Hill, 1974; Williams, 1984). Although African Americans and Hispanics share relatively low socioeconomic status, there may be some aspects of Hispanic culture that serve to reduce the risk of spousal homicide (Rodriguez, 1988). It can be argued that Hispanic norms about family solidarity may intervene to attenuate the potential danger of family conflicts that are only intensified by the stresses of poverty (Rodriguez, 1988).

Nonlethal Violence

Violence Toward Children

There are several good reviews available of the literature on violence toward children; consequently, we do not attempt to provide such a review here (see, e.g., Gelles, 1992; Hampton, 1991; Milner & Crouch, 1993; National Research Council, 1993). Examinations of the relationship between ethnicity and family violence dating back to the early 1980s have yielded mixed results (Gelles, 1982; Hampton, 1987; Showers & Bandman, 1986; Spearly & Lauderdale, 1983). Although many researchers acknowledge the potential bias of differential labeling in accounting for ethnic differences in violence toward children, some suggest that cultural factors may influence differences in rates for particular types of maltreatment. Caution must be exercised in attempting any explanation, because it may easily be construed as the mere restatement of a simplistic stereotype (Garbarino & Ebata, 1983).

Many of the early studies of violence toward children were based on analyses of cases reported to child protective services. Several studies have shown that in some instances children from poor and minority families are more vulnerable to receiving the label of *abused* than are children from more affluent households (Gelles, 1982; Hampton & Newberger, 1985; Newberger, Reed, Daniel, Hyde, & Kotelchuck, 1977; Zellman, 1992). Hampton and Newberger (1985), using a sample of cases from the First National Study of the Incidence and Severity of Child Abuse and Neglect (U.S. DHHS, 1981), found that hospitals tend to overreport African Americans and Hispanics and underreport whites for possible abuse. For African American and Hispanic families, recognition of alleged child maltreatment almost guaranteed reports to child protective services. Additional empirical evidence suggests that socioeconomic factors and race are associated with child maltreatment reporting as strongly as or more strongly than the nature and severity of the child's injury. Zellman (1992) found that socioeconomic status and race appear to influence report-relevant decisions. When families of lower socioeconomic status and African American families were involved, professionals generally judged the cases to be more serious and were more likely to define them as abuse; they regarded the law as more clearly requiring a report. In such cases, the outcomes of reports were also judged to be better for lower-status families, and in every case respondents were more likely to report them (Zellman, 1992).

Because of the limitations associated with official data, the Second National Family Violence Survey provides us with a better measure of the incidence and prevalence of parent-to-child violence among African American and Hispanic families.[2]

In their analysis of parent-to-child violence among Hispanics, Straus and Smith (1990) used two measures of child abuse. The first measure, Child Abuse 1, was confined to acts by parents that are almost universally regarded as abusive: kicking, biting, punching, beating up, scalding, and attacking with weapons. They found that the rate of such indisputably abusive violence was 48 per 1,000 Hispanic children in 1985. When this rate was applied to the 6.1 million Hispanic children living in the United States in 1985, it resulted in an estimate of 288,000 severely assaulted Hispanic children.

The second measure, Child Abuse 2, adds hitting with an object, such as a stick or belt, to the items used in the first measure of child abuse. Because hitting a child with an object involves a greater risk of injury than spanking or slapping with the hand, this may be a better measure of child abuse (Straus & Smith, 1990). In 1985, 134 out of every 1,000 Hispanic children were assaulted by a parent severely enough to be classified as abused. When this rate is applied to the number of Hispanic children living in the United States in 1985, it results in an estimate of 804,000 abused children per year.

Comparing the rate of violence used by African American parents to violence used by white parents, Hampton and Gelles (1991) found that African American parents were more likely to report throwing things at their children and hitting or trying to hit them with objects. This is consistent with other studies of disciplinary techniques in African American families that report African American parents' use of belts, cords, switches, sticks, and straps to discipline their children (Hampton, 1987; Johnson & Showers, 1985; Lassiter, 1987; Showers & Bandman, 1986). Hampton, Gelles, and Harrop (1989) found African American parents to be more likely to use severe and very severe violence toward their children. The rates for Child Abuse 1 and Child Abuse 2 for African American families in 1985 were 40 per 1,000 African American children and 197 per 1,000 African American children, respectively.

The rates of parent-to-child violence were higher for Hispanic and African American families than for white families. Because no comprehensive comparative analysis of these group differences has been conducted to date on these data, it is difficult to assess the extent to which these differences may be related to income, education, employment status, or other factors.

Few published data have specifically addressed physical child abuse in Native American families. Variations in reporting practices among different tribes and lack of data on off-reservation incidents contribute to the difficulties in estimating prevalence of child physical abuse among Native Americans (DeBruyn, Hymbaugh, & Valdez, 1988; DeBruyn, Lujan, & May, 1992; Lujan, DeBruyn, May, & Bird, 1989). Studies of physical abuse and neglect among Native American and Alaska Native children reviewed by the Office of Technology Assessment (1990) suggest rates ranging from 5.7 to 26 per 1,000. Native American adolescents in a statewide survey in Minnesota reported higher rates of physical abuse than African American or white respondents. Native American boys and girls were, respectively, 1.4 and 2.4 times more likely to report being beaten by an adult in their households than were their white same-age/same-gender peers (Yung & Gruber, 1995).

Still fewer data are available on child physical abuse in Asian American families. However, it has been noted that Southeast Asian refugee children may receive accidental injury from practices rooted in folk medicine that, by U.S. standards, may be deemed abusive. One study cited several case reports of children with burn injuries resulting from a practice of burning herbs (or, as an available alternative, cigarettes) or hard rubbing of coins to a surface area of the body representing an illness or dysfunction (Feldman, 1984). This practice, deemed by parents to be health restoring, can easily result in official reports of child abuse.

Couple Violence

Families of color have been victims of benign neglect in community-based studies of spousal violence. The First National Family Violence Survey (Straus, Gelles, & Steinmetz, 1980) was constrained by the small sample of African American families ($n = 147$) and limited sampling frame. The survey did not include Hispanic families in sufficient numbers for comparative analyses.

Violence Among African American Couples

The Second National Family Violence Survey was designed to address many of the shortcomings of previous research. A comparison of data from the two surveys revealed that overall husband-to-wife violence was unchanged between 1975 and 1985. Severe violence, or "wife beating," declined by 43.4% (Hampton et al., 1989).[3]

Although there was a decline in wife beating, this research revealed that African American women were 1.23 times more likely to experience minor violence and were more than twice as likely to experience severe violence compared with white women. Young age, low socioeconomic status, short length of time residing in the community, and unemployment or part-time employment of the husband were risk factors for violence toward African American women. The findings support a structural-cultural theory of intimate violence; that is, it arises out of structural pressures and dysfunctional adaptation to those pressures.

Violence Among Hispanic Couples

Data collected as part of the Los Angeles Epidemiologic Catchment Area survey provide us with some of our best information on couple violence among Hispanics. To avoid problems associated with generalizing across Hispanic subgroups, analyses were limited to persons of Mexican descent. The sample included 1,243 Mexican American and 1,149 non-Hispanic whites (Sorenson & Telles, 1991).

There were no significant differences between non-Hispanic white and Mexican American families in lifetime rates of self-reported violence toward a spouse. Spousal violence rates for

Mexican Americans born in Mexico and non-Hispanic whites born in the United States were virtually equivalent (20.0% and 21.6%, respectively); rates were highest for Mexican Americans born in the United States (30.9%) (Sorenson & Telles, 1991).

Perhaps the most important finding that emerged from this study was that rates of spousal violence among Mexican Americans varied according to immigration status. Mexican Americans born in the United States reported rates 2.4 times higher than those born in Mexico. It is suggested that this may be related to cultural conflicts in which members of subsequent generations of immigrant families are exposed to discrepancies between their familial culture of origin and the dominant culture in which they reside (Sorenson & Telles, 1991).

The Second National Family Violence Survey provides us with an opportunity to compare rates of couple violence for African Americans, non-Hispanic whites, and Hispanics. African American and Hispanic families had comparable rates (174 per 1,000 and 173 per 1,000, respectively) of husband-to-wife violence. Whites reported lower rates of overall husband-to-wife and severe violence. The rates of severe assaults on wives in African American and Hispanic families, which can be considered a measure of wife beating, were more than double that of non-Hispanic white families.

Straus and Smith (1990) found that, compared with white families, the higher rate of spouse abuse in Hispanic families reflects the economic deprivation, youthfulness, and urban residence of Hispanics. When these factors are controlled, there is no statistically significant difference between Hispanics and non-Hispanic whites. Although income inequalities are a factor in explaining differences in rates of violence between African American and white families, controlling for income does not exclusively account for the racial disparity (Hampton & Gelles, 1991; Hampton et al., 1989).

Violence Among Native American and Asian American Couples

Data are quite limited on the incidence of domestic violence among Native American and Asian American couples. Lack of accessible resources, combined with the attitude that these problems are private family matters, contributes to underreporting, making it difficult for researchers to determine prevalence in either group (DeBruyn, Wilkins, & Artichoker, 1990; Durst, 1991; Frye & D'Avanzo, 1994). There are some indicators of a widespread problem with interspousal violence in some Native American communities. One study of physical violence affecting women in the 12 months preceding childbirth reported rates of battering among Native American women that were twice as high as those of white women and about one and a half times higher than those among African American women (U.S. DHHS, 1994). Also, Native American adolescents in a statewide Minnesota health survey reported seeing family members beaten by other family members at rates slightly higher than African American youth (26.6% and 25.2%, respectively) and two times higher than the 13.1% reported by white adolescents. The Native American adolescents in this survey also reported a high degree of dating relationship violence, a pattern of concern as a precursor to later patterns of physical abuse within spouse or partner relationships. Their rates of being hit by a date in anger were 1.4 times higher than those reported by their white peers (Yung & Gruber, 1995).

There are only descriptive and anecdotal reports of violence in Asian American families, and most report only on the problem within Southeast Asian families of lower socioeconomic status (Chen & True, 1994; Frye & D'Avanzo, 1994). The limited data available suggest that Southeast Asian women tend to keep battering problems within the family, either out of the notion that physical abuse by husbands is "normal" (Chen & True, 1994) or because they lack information and resources. In the words of one Cambodian woman interviewed on family stress and violence, "Most Khmer [Cambodian] men, they hit their wives but the women don't know who can help" (quoted in Frye & D'Avanzo, 1994, p. 72).

Community Violence and Living in War Zones

Family violence and other violent behaviors have been investigated separately by sociologists and criminologists. Many widely cited theories of family violence build directly on the premise that violence in the home is highly contextual and is largely unaffected by the outside world except insofar as external frustrations and anger may be displaced onto the family setting (Shields, McCall, &

Hanneke, 1988). More recent thinking and research suggest that violence in the home and violence outside the home may be related (Fagan & Wexler, 1987; Hampton, 1986; Hotaling, Straus, & Lincoln, 1990; Sampson, 1987; Shields et al., 1988). For example, one study of African American adolescents found that the three factors most closely correlated with their perpetration of violence were exposure to violence and victimization in the community, degree of witnessing family conflict, and severity of corporal punishment used at home (DuRant, Cadenhead, Pendergrast, Slavens, & Linder, 1994).

Violence is a common part of the urban experience for African American and Hispanic youth (Garbarino, Kostelny, & Dubrow, 1991). One study conducted at a Baltimore clinic revealed that among the 168 teen respondents (80% of whom were females), 24% had witnessed a murder and 72% knew someone who had been shot. On average, each had been victimized 1.5 times by some sort of violence, and each had witnessed five serious crimes taking place. One out of five had had his or her life threatened, and one in eleven had been raped.

What we have in many cities is what the military calls a low-intensity conflict. In recent years there has been a resurgence of youth gangs in many major urban centers in the United States. In most cities these gangs are overwhelmingly made up of African American and Hispanic youth. Although youth gangs are very different from one another—varying from one time to another, from one place to another, and from one group to another, even in the same city— they often form quasi-institutional structures within poor minority communities (Moore, 1988a, 1988b). Gangs have contributed to a rapid increase in the numbers of homicides, aggravated assaults, rapes, and other kinds of interpersonal violence committed in the United States (Seever, 1990).

The gang problem is particularly acute in Los Angeles. Between 1970 and 1979, gang killings in that city accounted for 16% of all Hispanic homicides (but no more than 7% of homicides in other ethnic groups) (Moore, 1988b). The Los Angeles Police Department estimates that there are at least 400 different gangs, with total gang membership of more than 100,000. Of these members, about 58% are Hispanic, 27% are African American, 3% are Asian American (primarily Chinese and Vietnamese), and 2% are white. In a 1991 study, gang-related drive-by shootings were found to be a significant cause of early mortality for children and adolescents. Of the 2,222 people shot at in these incidents, 38% were victims under the age of 18. A total of 36 child and adolescent victims (78% Hispanic and the remainder African American) died as a result of this gang violence (Hutson, Anglin, & Pratts, 1994). The growth of Vietnamese gangs in Los Angeles has also been recognized as a problem contributing to nonlethal criminally motivated assault in Vietnamese communities. Certain Vietnamese cultural practices (e.g., distrust of banks and the resulting tendency to keep cash and gold bars in the home) make these neighborhood residents vulnerable to muggings and assaults by young gang members (Huff, 1993).

Gang violence can be used to achieve real and symbolic gains (Majors & Billson, 1992). For many African American and Hispanic males who have been locked out of the social and economic mainstream, running with a gang or engaging in fortuitous violence can be a form of social achievement. Drive-by shootings, assaults, raids, gun battles, and other violent episodes become the means through which many males can demonstrate their masculinity.

Gangs maintain powerful images in many communities and threaten not only citizens but the police and other law enforcement officials as well. One of the major differences between gangs today and the gangs of 30 years ago is in weaponry. One study of urban gangs found that nearly half of the African American males interviewed possessed at least one firearm, usually a handgun (Hagedorn & Macon, 1988).

Gangs represent only one form of community violence seen and experienced by ethnic minority children and adolescents. The present wave of youth violence is not confined to large U.S. cities with established high-crime reputations and large gang populations but is spilling over to smaller metropolitan, suburban, and rural areas as well. Pervasive community violence affects children too young to be gang members and cities with no notable concentration of gangs (Fitzpatrick & Boldizar, 1993; Osofsky, Wewers, Hann, & Fick, 1994). Even in Los Angeles, non-gang-related violence and homicides are roughly four times more common than gang-related murders (Rogers, 1993).

Unfortunately, at present we know much more about the prevalence of community violence than we do about its effects on young victims and witnesses. For example, much of the research on violence victimization does not clearly distinguish among the effects of witnessing and the effects of experiencing violence, the levels of severity of violence exposure, and the age of the observer or victim, nor does it always compare the impact of within-family victimization or witnessing versus exposure to community violence (Hammond & Yung, 1994). There is abundant evidence, however, of damaging emotional consequences following *any* type of experience with violence, particularly for children and adolescents (Fitzpatrick, 1993; Fitzpatrick & Boldizar, 1993; Lorion & Saltzman, 1994; Martinez & Richters, 1994). Behaviors correlated with both victimization and exposure to violence (e.g., increased fighting, the carrying of weapons, gang involvement, and other health risk behaviors such as substance abuse, school failure, and school suspensions) may in fact contribute to a continuing cycle of violence (Cotten et al., 1994; DuRant et al., 1994; Kulig, Valentine, & Steriti, 1994; Webster, Gainer, & Champion, 1993). Some research suggests that the dual risk-factor combination of both experiencing and witnessing family violence results in the most severe consequences in terms of subsequent emotional distress and behavior problems (Miller, Handal, Gilner, & Cross, 1991).

Where We Need to Be

Although there are many unanswered questions about violence in families and communities of color, it is clear that the disproportionate risk for violent victimization and offending is at epidemic levels for at least some subgroups within this growing population. The directions in which we need to move are also evident.

First, we simply need to know more about the problem. Lack of resources, including the absence of research, has limited the ability of many to respond appropriately to violence in ethnic minority communities. Especially needed are studies of ethnic, cultural, subcultural, age, and gender variations in the prevalence, distribution, correlates, precipitators, and consequences of violence. The general methodological problems surrounding violence research as well as those specifically applying to ethnic minorities must be addressed so that we can begin to close the many gaps in our present knowledge. Prevention and intervention programs must be established on an appropriate base of knowledge about the issues and the communities. Scholars and practitioners from communities of color must be in the forefront of designing, collecting, and analyzing research data that will serve as the basis for new approaches.

Research efforts need to focus on risk factors at both interpersonal and environmental levels. For example, it is important to examine the range of personal responses available to African Americans and Latinos to the structurally induced circumstances that produce elevated levels of violence. A concept known as "cool pose" has been identified as one such response. As articulated by Majors and Billson (1992), it is

> a ritualized form of masculinity that entails behaviors, scripts, physical posturing, impression management, and carefully crafted performances that deliver a single, critical message: pride, strength and control. . . . It is a distinctive coping mechanism that serves to counter, at least in part, the dangers that African American males encounter on a daily basis. (p. 4)

Poussaint has related the adoption of "cool pose" as a dysfunctional response to a lack of strong male role models and the need to demonstrate masculinity (see Goleman, 1992). When translated to behavior on the street, this personal style may make it difficult for a male to be able to walk away from a fight or apologize to a girlfriend (Majors & Billson, 1992). Although the concept emerged from a study of African American teenagers in Boston, it can be applied to many young males in the inner city. It allows these young men to appear in control, whether through a style of walking, facial expression, clothes, haircuts, gold chains, or music. It is meant to show all that they are proud and strong in spite of their status in American society (Majors & Billson, 1992). Research is needed to explicate more fully the role of this and other subcultural styles, attitudes, values, and norms in interspousal violence.

In searching for interventions to address violence among ethnic groups, we need to acknowledge and take into account the impact of certain social and economic influences or conditions. The widespread acceptance of violence as an appropriate dispute resolution technique is a strong factor in the maintenance of our violent culture. The concentration of poverty in particular geographic areas may contribute to an accumulation of frustration and anger for many individuals. Violence and male joblessness are strongly associated. Men of color have historically had higher rates of unemployment than majority males, and intimate violence often arises out of dysfunctional adaptations to such economic and personal pressures (Sampson, 1987).

To improve the nationwide response to the critical problem of violence in the United States, we need to work diligently in our research and practice to ensure that sensitivity to the race, ethnicity, and culture of the minority target population is taken into account in the design of programs for prevention or intervention. Language, communication styles, behaviors, customs, attitudes, beliefs, values, social structures, and institutions vary widely among ethnic/cultural minority groups and subgroups. Recognizing and responding to these differences in culturally sensitive programming represents an especially promising trend that may improve the effectiveness and efficiency of violence prevention efforts.

Culturally Sensitive Prevention and Intervention Programs

Cultural sensitivity is a concept that is receiving increased attention in social services, health, and mental health practice in communities of color. It is generally defined as an ability to balance consideration of universal, specific group, and individual norms in interactions with members of a particular racial/ethnic/cultural group (Lopez et al., 1989; Soriano, 1993). Although there is little disagreement on the basic meaning of the term, there are diverse ways of operationalizing and practicing it.

At the lowest level, cultural sensitivity simply involves making a traditional prevention or treatment program more accessible to a target ethnic or cultural group. Increasing accessibility might involve locating a program within a minority agency or neighborhood school, employing ethnic minority staff, doing outreach to generate a broad level of community buy-in, and (if applicable) using the community's first or preferred language (Isaacs & Benjamin, 1989; Prinz & Miller, 1991; Rogler, Malgady, Costantino, & Blumenthal, 1987; Sue, Fujino, Hu, Takeuchi, & Zane, 1991; Yeh, Takeuchi, & Sue, 1994). Improving access to services for minority groups is a prerequisite of culturally sensitive practice, but if improved accessibility is the

only discernible difference in a program, and intervention procedures are applied to the minority group in virtually the same ways
they are used with the mainstream population (Prinz & Miller,
1991), the program does not meet the higher standard of *cultural
competence* or *cultural proficiency* (Cross et al., 1989). Exclusive
emphasis on enhanced accessibility with no cultural modifications
to the intervention would appear to be based on the cultural
equivalent perspective (Fine, Schwebel, & James-Myers, 1987),
which assumes that color or culture makes no difference and that
helping approaches are universally applicable (Cross et al., 1989).
Culturally competent agencies and service providers, on the other
hand, recognize and demonstrate an acceptance of differences
among ethnic groups and cultures. They work in partnership with
communities of color to develop collaborative solutions to meet
family and community needs, based on principles of self-determination and empowerment. Their responsiveness to cultural differences is evident in specific policies and practices that stress "the
importance of culture, the assessment of cross-cultural differences,
the expansion of cultural knowledge, and the adaptation of services
to meet culturally-unique needs" (Cross et al., 1989, p. 13).

Agencies and programs striving for this higher level of cultural
sensitivity may put effort into selecting treatment approaches that
match the features to cultural characteristics (Rogler et al., 1987).
For example, a therapeutic program serving low-income ethnic
minority clients may choose to avoid insight-oriented therapies
(seen as irrelevant to the context of inner-city realities) in favor of
behavior-oriented interventions and hands-on teaching/learning methods. Often a case management system is also introduced as a means
of addressing multiple problems consumers may be experiencing
(Damond, Breuer, & Pharr, 1993; Isaacs & Benjamin, 1989; Rogler
et al., 1987). Life-skills training programs may center on traditional
cultural values such as self-reliance (Bobo, Gilchrist, Cvetkovich,
Trimble, & Schinke, 1988).

Alternatively, instead of (or in addition to) selecting an intervention method that is culturally compatible with the consumers'
culture, program designers may adapt particular aspects of the
intervention (Rogler et al., 1987). Such adaptations might include
incorporating traditional healing practices, folktales, and rites-of-
passage ceremonies into programs of prevention and intervention
(Costantino, Malgady, & Rogler, 1994; Office of Substance Abuse

Prevention, 1990; Wilson-Brewer & Jacklin, 1990). In some cases there may be a collaborative or cotherapist relationship between folk practitioners and conventional treatment providers (Manson, Walker, & Kivlahan, 1987; Tharp, 1991). The community itself—grassroots leaders, families, churches—is a primary force in shaping the focus and techniques of culturally sensitive service programs.

Cultural adaptations of intervention methods of course presuppose that the provider has an adequate base of knowledge about the group he or she is serving. It is often assumed (a) that members of the ethnic group automatically have this cultural knowledge base; (b) for nonminority individuals, that it is easy to transmit such knowledge though brief programs of cultural sensitivity training; and (c) that having a cultural knowledge base is equivalent to being culturally sensitive (Soriano, 1993). None of these assumptions is a given. The acquisition of culturally appropriate knowledge and skills is a complex process that needs to be ongoing. Ideally, individuals would have repeated exposure to a variety of training experiences and would be encouraged to self-monitor and self-evaluate their cross-cultural knowledge, skills, attitudes, and values (Cross et al., 1989). It is critically important for cultural sensitivity training programs to incorporate examination of the participants' own cultural biases in addition to the mere provision of cultural information. Both minority and nonminority staff should be included in such training (Cross et al., 1989; Isaacs & Benjamin, 1989; Lopez et al., 1989; Soriano, 1993).

Soriano (1993) has challenged the "ethnic homogeneity assumption," which is grounded in the view that all members of an ethnic group have common experiences, norms, beliefs, and values. Similarly, Sue (1988) has noted that ethnic membership (emphasizing similar geographic, racial, or national origin) may be quite different from cultural membership (related more to identification with a particular group and commonalities of life experiences and value systems). Finally, cultural sensitivity must also take into account the individual characteristics and backgrounds of service consumers as well as the cultural influences of their gender and age groups (Hammond & Yung, 1993).

There is little specific guidance in the professional literature on developing and implementing culturally sensitive violence prevention programs. An exception is the work of Hammond and Yung (1991), which reports on a prosocial skill development and anger management intervention for African American adolescents at high risk for violence victimization and perpetration. Detailed how-to instructions for improving the cultural sensitivity of preventive interventions of this type have been outlined in a practitioner manual designed to assist others who wish to establish similarly focused groups (Yung & Hammond, 1995).

In spite of the scarcity of writing on cultural sensitivity in violence prevention programming, there is a growing body of general literature on the attainment of cultural competence that can be extremely helpful to those wishing to design and implement programs specifically addressing the problem of violence. This literature includes guidelines and recommendations (Cross et al., 1989; Isaacs & Benjamin, 1989), theoretical perspectives (Rogler et al., 1987; Tharp, 1991), individual studies (e.g., Bobo et al., 1988; Costantino et al., 1994; Damond et al., 1993; Schinke, Moncher, Palleja, Zayas, & Schilling, 1988), and program inventories and summaries (Isaacs & Benjamin, 1989; Office of Substance Abuse Prevention, 1990; Wilson-Brewer & Jacklin, 1990).

Of particular benefit are descriptions that provide an in-depth look at cultural adaptations that have been made in prevention and intervention methods. For example, Bobo and her colleagues (1988) describe a process in which curricular modifications were made to a standard substance abuse prevention program in order to make it more relevant for Native American youth. Lengthy reviews of program materials were made by Native American community gatekeepers, tribal elders, adolescents, parents, and program staff. Among other outcomes, this review resulted in changes in the content and language of vignettes used to introduce skills as well as modifications in teaching methods because of Native American adolescent cultural norms against self-disclosure.

Also helpful are summary descriptions of the characteristics of programs based on principles of cultural competence. Isaacs and Benjamin (1989) conclude that programs founded on these precepts carefully consider issues of accessibility in broader ways than neighborhood location and hours of service. They give particular attention to building a positive reputation for collaborative work throughout the community and to reducing any stigma associated with program participation, avoiding an identity of "problem prevention." They frequently select names that have positive cultural connotations, and they adapt services, delivery methods, curricula, and outreach methods to the unique cultural values, customs, and community environment of their service consumers. Service programs are provided by staff who are well trained in cultural sensitivity. Staff typically reflect the ethnic makeup of the consumer community, and service providers accept family systems that might include multiple generations, coparenting, and extended families, often making use of these kinship networks as part of interventions. There is a similar reliance on natural helpers in the community for brokering and reinforcement of intervention components.

We are now beginning to understand how to make the concept of cultural sensitivity operational so that families and communities of color—the most vulnerable segment of our population—can begin to reduce their disproportionate risk for violent injury and death.

Conclusion

Clearly, we are not yet where we need to be. There are still too many questions about violence in communities and families of color for which we do not have answers. Foremost among these is our lack of a very basic understanding of the relationship between ethnic minority status and the tangled web of social, cultural, structural, situational, and interpersonal factors that can interact to suppress or support violence. We do appear to be moving in the right direction, however. There is greater awareness than formerly of the problem of violence in ethnic minority communities. Violence research is becoming more inclusive and is beginning to examine trends affecting diverse populations and subgroups. Simultaneously, there is a growing recognition of opportunities for prevention. The call to prevent violence is being taken up by the communities most damaged by its aftermath.

Communities of color are not paralyzed, existing in a state of "learned helplessness."[4] People who are in such a state give up, are psychologically immobilized, and blame themselves for their predicament (Gondolf & Fisher, 1988). The members of communities of color are survivors, and many are involved in grassroots programs designed to reduce violence. Working with consultants and collaborators, they must use primary prevention's technology of education, competence promotion, community organization/systems intervention, and natural caregiving to encourage the growth of functional behaviors (Gullotta, 1994).

No single initiative will eliminate violence, but we believe that efforts to prevent violence are preferable to the alternatives: building more prisons for violent offenders, developing harsher penalties for perpetrators, and dealing with the consequences of violence for the lives of victims and witnesses. We have described in this chapter where we were, where we are, and where we need to be with respect to violence in communities of color. We hope that the larger society will move forward collaboratively with communities of color to construct opportunities for prosocial behaviors and to develop community-based approaches to primary prevention.

Notes

1. Within this category one finds individuals from a number of different sociocultural environments and with varying degrees of acculturation.

2. For a complete discussion of the survey methodology, see Gelles and Straus (1988).

3. The comparison was based on the more limited version of the Conflict Tactics Scale.

4. The concept of learned helplessness has been applied to the study of battered women. Lenore Walker (1979) has used this concept to describe women who become "psychologically paralyzed" as a result of the violence to which they are constantly exposed.

References

Allen, W. R. (1978). The search for applicable theories of black family life. *Journal of Marriage and the Family, 40,* 117-129.

Barham, J. (1992, July). *Has violent crime really increased? A comparison of violence rates reported by the two U.S. Department of Justice data sets.* Paper presented to the American Psychological Association Commission on Youth and Violence (based on testimony given to the U.S. General Accounting Office, April 19, 1990).

Becker, T., Samet, J., Wiggins, C., & Key, C. (1990). Violent death in the West: Suicide and homicide in New Mexico, 1958-1987. *Suicide and Life-Threatening Behavior, 20,* 324-334.

Block, C. (1988). Lethal violence in the Chicago Latino community, 1965 to 1981. In J. F. Kraus, S. B. Sorenson, & P. D. Juarez (Eds.), *Proceedings from the Research Conference on Violence and Homicide in Hispanic Communities* (pp. 31-65). Los Angeles: UCLA Publication Services.

Bobo, J., Gilchrist, L., Cvetkovich, G., Trimble, J. & Schinke, S. (1988). Cross-cultural service delivery to minority communities. *Journal of Community Psychology, 16,* 263-272.

Browne, A. (1987). *When battered women kill.* New York: Free Press.

Centers for Disease Control. (1990). Homicide among young black males: United States, 1978-87. *Morbidity and Mortality Weekly, 39,* 869-873.

Cerhan, J. (1990). The Hmong in the United States: An overview for mental health professionals. *Journal of Counseling and Development, 69,* 88-92.

Chen, S. A., & True, R. H. (1994). Asian/Pacific Island Americans. In L. D. Eron, J. H. Gentry, & P. Schlegel (Eds.), *Reason to hope: A psychosocial perspective on violence and youth* (pp. 145-162). Washington, DC: American Psychological Association.

Christoffel, K. (1990). Violent death and injury in U.S. children and adolescents. *American Journal of Diseases of Childhood, 144,* 697-706.

Conly, C., Kelly, P., Mahanna, P., & Warner, L. (1993). *Street strategies—gangs: Current knowledge and strategies.* Washington, DC: National Institute of Justice.

Costantino, G., Malgady, R., & Rogler, L. (1994). Storytelling through pictures: Culturally sensitive psychotherapy for Hispanic children and adolescents. *Journal of Clinical Child Psychology, 23,*13-20.

Cotten, N., Resnick, J., Browne, D., Martin, S., McCarraher, D., & Woods, J. (1994). Aggression and fighting behavior among African-American adolescents: Individual and family factors. *American Journal of Public Health, 84,* 618-622.

Cross, T., Bazron, B., Dennis, K., & Isaacs, M. (1989). *Towards a culturally competent system of care.* Washington, DC: CASSP Technical Assistance Center.

Damond, M., Breuer, N., & Pharr, A. (1993). The evaluation of setting and a culturally specific HIV/AIDS curriculum: HIV/AIDS knowledge and behavioral intent of African American adolescents. *Journal of Black Psychology, 19,* 169-189.

Daniel, J. H. (1985). Cultural and ethnic issues: The black family. In E. H. Newberger & R. Bourne (Eds.), *Unhappy families* (pp. 145-153). Littleton, MA: PSG.

DeBruyn, L., Hymbaugh, K., & Valdez, N. (1988). Helping communities address suicide and violence: The Special Initiatives Team of the Indian Health Service. *American Indian and Alaska Native Mental Health Research, 1,* 56-65.

DeBruyn, L., Lujan, C., & May, P. (1992). A comparative study of abused and neglected American Indian children in the Southwest. *Social Science and Medicine, 35,* 305-315.

DeBruyn, L., Wilkins, B., & Artichoker, K. (1990, November 30). *"It's not cultural": Violence against Native American women.* Paper presented at the 89th annual meeting of the American Anthropological Association, New Orleans.

DuRant, R., Cadenhead, C., Pendergrast, R., Slavens, G., & Linder, C. (1994). Factors associated with the use of violence among urban black adolescents. *American Journal of Public Health, 84,* 612-617.

Durst, D. (1991). Conjugal violence: Changing attitudes in two northern native communities. *Community Mental Health Journal, 27,* 359-373.

Elliott, D., Huizinga, D., & Morse, B. (1986). Self-reported violent offending: A descriptive analysis of juvenile violent offenders and their offending careers. *Journal of Interpersonal Violence, 1,* 472-513.

Fagan, J., & Wexler, S. (1987). Crime at home and in the streets: The relationships between family and stranger violence. *Violence and Victims, 2,* 5-24.

Feldman, K. (1984). Pseudoabusive burns in Asian refugees. *American Journal of Diseases of Children, 138,* 768-769.

Fine, M., Schwebel, A. I., & James-Myers, L. (1987). Family stability in black families: Values underlying three different perspectives. *Journal of Comparative Families Studies, 18,* 1-23.

Finkelhor, D., & Dziuba-Leatherman, J. (1994). Victimization of children. *American Psychologist, 49,* 173-183.

Fitzpatrick, K. (1993). Exposure to violence and presence of depression among low-income African-American youth. *Journal of Consulting and Clinical Psychology, 61,* 528-531.

Fitzpatrick, K., & Boldizar, J. (1993). The prevalence and consequences of exposure to violence among African-American youth. *Journal of the American Academy of Child and Adolescent Psychiatry, 32,* 424-430.

Flowers, R. (1988). *Minorities and criminality.* Westport, CT: Greenwood.

Frye, B., & D'Avanzo, C. (1994). Cultural themes in family stress and violence among Cambodian refugee women in the inner city. *Advances in Nursing Science, 16*(3), 64-77.

Garbarino, J., & Ebata, A. (1983). The significance of ethnic and cultural differences in child maltreatment. *Journal of Marriage and the Family, 45,* 773-783.

Garbarino, J., Kostelny, K., & Dubrow, N. (1991). *No place to be a child.* Lexington, MA: Lexington Books.

Gelles, R. J. (1982). Child abuse and family violence: Implications for medical professionals. In E. H. Newberger (Ed.), *Child abuse* (pp. 25-42). Boston: Little, Brown.

Gelles, R. J. (1992). Poverty and violence toward children. *American Behavioral Scientist, 35,* 258-274.

Gelles, R. J. (1993). Family violence. In R. L. Hampton, T. P. Gullotta, G. R. Adams, E. H. Potter III, & R. P. Weissberg (Eds.), *Family violence: Prevention and treatment* (pp. 1-24). Newbury Park, CA: Sage.

Gelles, R. J., & Straus, M. A. (1988). *Intimate violence: The causes and consequences of abuse in the American family.* New York: Simon & Schuster.

Goetting, A. (1991). Patterns of marital homicide: A comparison of husbands and wives. In R. L. Hampton (Ed.), *Black family violence: Current research and theory* (pp. 147-160). Lexington, MA: Lexington Books.

Goleman, D. (1992, April 21). Black scientists study the "pose" of the inner city. *New York Times,* pp. C1, C7.

Gondolf, E. W., & Fisher, E. R. (1988). *Battered women as survivors: An alternative to treating learned helplessness.* Lexington, MA: Lexington Books.

Gruber, E., DiClemente, R., & Anderson, M. (in press). Risk-taking among Native American adolescents in Minnesota public schools: Comparisons with black and white adolescents. *Ethnicity and Disease.*

Gullotta, T. P. (1994). The what, who, why, where, when, and how of primary prevention. *Journal of Primary Prevention, 15,* 5-14.

Hagedorn, J. M., & Macon, C. (Eds.). (1988). *People and folks: Gangs, crime and the underclass in a Rustbelt city.* Chicago: Lake View.

Hammond, W. R., & Yung, B. (1991). Preventing violence in at-risk African-American youth. *Journal of Health Care for the Poor and Underserved, 2*, 359-373.

Hammond, W. R., & Yung, B. (1993). Psychology's role in the public health response to assaultive violence among young African-American men. *American Psychologist, 48*, 142-154.

Hammond, W. R., & Yung, B. (1994). African Americans. In L. D. Eron, J. H. Gentry, & P. Schlegel (Eds.), *Reason to hope: A psychosocial perspective on violence and youth* (pp. 103-118). Washington, DC: American Psychological Association.

Hampton, R. L. (1986). Family violence and homicide in the black community: Are they linked? In U.S. Department of Health and Human Services, *Report of the Secretary's Task Force on Black and Minority Health: Vol. 5. Homicide, suicide, and unintentional injuries* (pp. 69-97). Washington, DC: Government Printing Office.

Hampton, R. L. (1987). Violence against black children: Current knowledge and future research needs. In R. L. Hampton (Ed.), *Violence in the black family: Correlates and consequences* (pp. 3-20). Lexington, MA: Lexington Books.

Hampton, R. L. (1991). Child abuse in the African American community. In J. E. Everett, S. Chipungu, & B. R. Leashore (Eds.), *Child welfare: An Afrocentric perspective* (pp. 200-246). New Brunswick, NJ: Rutgers University Press.

Hampton, R. L., & Gelles, R. J. (1991). A profile of violence toward black children. In R. L. Hampton (Ed.), *Black family violence: Current research and theory* (pp. 21-34). Lexington, MA: Lexington Books.

Hampton, R. L., Gelles, R. J., & Harrop, J. W. (1989). Is violence in black families increasing? A comparison of 1975 and 1985 national survey rates. *Journal of Marriage and the Family, 51*, 969-980.

Hampton, R. L., & Newberger, E. H. (1985). Child abuse incidence and reporting by hospitals: The significance of severity, class, and race. *American Journal of Public Health, 75*, 56-60.

Hawkins, D. F. (1990). Explaining the black homicide rate. *Journal of Interpersonal Violence, 5*, 151-163.

Hotaling, G. T., Straus, M. A., & Lincoln, A. J. (1990). Intrafamily violence and crime and violence outside the family. In M. A. Straus & R. J. Gelles (Eds.), *Physical violence in American families: Risk factors and adaptations to violence in 8,145 families* (pp. 431-470). New Brunswick, NJ: Transaction Books.

Huff, R. (1993). Gangs in the United States. In A. Goldstein & R. Huff (Eds.), *The gang intervention handbook* (pp. 3-20). Champaign, IL: Research Press.

Hutson, R., Anglin, D., & Pratts, M. (1994). Adolescents and children injured or killed in drive-by shootings in Los Angeles. *New England Journal of Medicine, 330*, 324-327.

Isaacs, M., & Benjamin, M. (Eds.). (1989). *Towards a culturally competent system of care: Programs which utilize culturally competent principles, II.* Washington, DC: CASSP Technical Assistance Center, Center for Child Health and Mental Health Policy, Georgetown University Child Development Center.

Johnson, C. F., & Showers, J. (1985). Injury variables in child abuse. *Child Abuse and Neglect, 9*, 207-216.

Jurik, N. C., & Winn, R. (1990). Gender and homicide: A comparison of men and women who kill. *Violence and Victims, 5*, 227-242.

Kahn, M. (1986). Psychosocial disorders of aboriginal people of the United States and Australia. *Journal of Rural Community Psychology, 7,* 45-59.

Kettl, P. (1993). Homicide in Alaska Natives. *Alaska Medicine, 35,* 168-172.

Kulig, J., Valentine, J., & Steriti, L. (1994). A correlational analysis of weapon-carrying among urban high school students: Findings from a cross-sectional survey [Abstract of a paper presented at the annual meeting of the Society for Adolescent Medicine, March 16-20, 1994]. *Journal of Adolescent Health, 15,* 90.

Lassiter, R. F. (1987). Child rearing in black families: Child-abusing discipline. In R. L. Hampton (Ed.), *Violence in the black family: Correlates and consequences* (pp. 3-20). Lexington, MA: Lexington Books.

Leyba, C. (1988). Homicide in Bernalillo County: 1978-1982. In J. F. Kraus, S. B. Sorenson, & P. D. Juarez (Eds.), *Proceedings from the Research Conference on Violence and Homicide in Hispanic Communities* (pp. 101-118). Los Angeles: UCLA Publication Services.

Loftin, C., & Hill, R. H. (1974). Regional subculture and homicide. *American Sociological Review, 39,* 714-724.

Lopez, R., Grover, P., Holland, D., Johnson, M., Kain, C., Kanel, K., Mellins, C., & Rhyne, M. (1989). Development of culturally sensitive psychotherapists. *Professional Psychology: Research and Practice, 20,* 369-376.

Lorion, R., & Saltzman, W. (1994). Children's exposure to community violence: Following a path from concern to research to action. *Psychiatry, 56,* 55-65.

Lujan, C., DeBruyn, L., May, P., & Bird, M. (1989). Profile of abused and neglected American Indian children in the Southwest. *Child Abuse and Neglect, 13,* 449-461.

Majors, R., & Billson, J. M. (1992). *Cool pose: The dilemmas of black manhood in America.* Lexington, MA: Lexington Books.

Mann, C. R. (1991). Black women who kill their loved ones. In R. L. Hampton (Ed.), *Black family violence: Current research and theory* (pp. 129-146). Lexington, MA: Lexington Books.

Manson, S., Walker, D., & Kivlahan, D. (1987). Psychiatric assessment and treatment of American Indians and Alaska Natives. *Hospital and Community Psychiatry, 38,* 165-173.

Martinez, P., & Richters, J. (1994). The NIMH community violence project: II. Children's distress symptoms associated with violence exposure. *Psychiatry, 56,* 22-35.

McClain, P. D. (1982-1983). Black females and lethal violence: Has time changed the circumstances under which they kill? *Omega, 13*(1), 3-25.

McKenney, N., & Bennett, C. (1994). Issues regarding data on race and ethnicity: The Census Bureau experience. *Public Health Reports, 109,* 16-25.

Menard, S. (1992). Residual gains, reliability, and the UCR-NCS relationship: A comment on Blumstein, Cohen, and Rosenfeld. *Criminology, 30,* 105-113.

Mercy, J. A. (1988). Assaultive injury among Hispanics: A public health problem. In J. F. Kraus, S. B. Sorenson, & P. D. Juarez (Eds.), *Proceedings from the Research Conference on Violence and Homicide in Hispanic Communities* (pp. 1-13). Los Angeles: UCLA Publication Services.

Mercy, J. A., & Saltzman, L. E. (1989). Fatal violence among spouses in the United States. *American Journal of Public Health, 79,* 595-599.

Miller, T., Handal, P., Gilner, F., & Cross, J. (1991). The relationships of abuse and witnessing violence on the Child Abuse Potential Inventory with black adolescents. *Journal of Family Violence, 6,* 351-363.

Milner, J. S., & Crouch, J. L. (1993). Physical child abuse. In R. L. Hampton, T. P. Gullotta, G. R. Adams, E. H. Potter III, & R. P. Weissberg (Eds.), *Family violence: Prevention and treatment* (pp. 25-55). Newbury Park, CA: Sage.

Moore, J. (1988a). Introduction: Gangs and the underclass—a comparative perspective. In J. M. Hagedorn & P. Macon (Eds.), *People and folks: Gangs, crime and the underclass in a Rustbelt city* (pp. 3-17). Chicago: Lake View.

Moore, J. (1988b). Variations in violence among Hispanic gangs. In J. F. Kraus, S. B. Sorenson, & P. D. Juarez (Eds.), *Proceedings from the Research Conference on Violence and Homicide in Hispanic Communities* (pp. 213-230). Los Angeles: UCLA Publication Services.

National Center for Health Statistics. (1990). Prevention profile. In *Health, United States, 1989* (DHHS Publication No. PHS 90-1232). Hyattsville, MD: Author.

National Center for Health Statistics. (1992). *Vital statistics of the United States, 1989* (Vol. 2, Pt. A). Hyattsville, MD: Author.

National Committee for Injury Prevention and Control. (1989). *Injury prevention: Meeting the challenge.* New York: Oxford University Press.

National Research Council. (1993). *Understanding child abuse and neglect.* Washington, DC: National Academy Press.

Newberger, E. H., Reed, R., Daniel, J. H., Hyde, J., & Kotelchuck, M. (1977). Pediatric social illness: Toward an etiologic classification. *Pediatrics, 60,* 178-185.

Office of Substance Abuse Prevention. (1990). *Breaking new ground for American Indian and Alaska Native youth at risk: Program summaries* (OSAP Technical Report 3, DHHS Publication No. ADM 90 1705). Washington, DC: Government Printing Office.

Office of Technology Assessment. (1990). *Indian adolescent mental health* (OTA-H-446). Washington, DC: Government Printing Office.

Ogden, M., Spector, M., & Hill, C. (1970). Suicides and homicides among Indians. *Public Health Reports, 85,* 75-80.

Osofsky, J., Wewers, S., Hann, D., & Fick, A. (1994). Chronic community violence: What is happening to our children? *Psychiatry, 56,* 36-45.

Pernice, R. (1994). *Methodological issues in research with refugees and immigrants. Professional Psychology: Research and Practice, 25,* 207-213.

Prinz, R., & Miller, G. (1991). Issues in understanding and treating childhood conduct problems in disadvantaged population. *Journal of Clinical Child Psychology, 20,* 379-385.

Rodriguez, J. (1990). Childhood injuries in the United States. *American Journal of Diseases of Childhood, 144,* 627-646.

Rodriguez, O. (1988). Hispanics and homicide in New York City. In J. F. Kraus, S. B. Sorenson, & P. D. Juarez (Eds.), *Proceedings from the Research Conference on Violence and Homicide in Hispanic Communities* (pp. 67-84). Los Angeles: UCLA Publication Services.

Rogers, C. (1993). Gang-related homicides in Los Angeles County. *Journal of Forensic Sciences, 38,* 831-834.

Rogler, L., Malgady, R., Costantino, G., & Blumenthal, R. (1987). What do culturally sensitive mental health services mean? The case of Hispanics. *American Psychologist, 42,* 565-570.

Rokaw, W., Mercy, J., & Smith, J. (1990). Comparing death certificate data with FBI crime reporting statistics on U.S. homicides. *Public Health Reports, 105,* 447-455.

Ropp, L., Visintainer, P., Uman, J., & Treloar, D. (1992). Death in the city: An American childhood tragedy. *Journal of the American Medical Association, 267,* 2905-2910.

Rose, H. M., & McClain, P. D. (1990). *Race, place and risk: Black homicide in urban America.* Albany: State University of New York Press.

Sampson, R. J. (1987). Urban black violence: The effect of male joblessness and family disruption. *American Journal of Sociology, 93,* 348-382.

Schinke, S., Moncher, M., Palleja, J., Zayas, L., & Schilling, R. (1988). Hispanic youth, substance abuse, and stress: Implications for prevention research. *International Journal of the Addictions, 23,* 809-826.

Seever, F. (1990). *Report to the MacArthur Foundation.* Unpublished manuscript.

Shields, N. M., McCall, G. J., & Hanneke, C. R. (1988). Patterns of family and nonfamily violence: Violent husbands and violent men. *Violence and Victims, 3*(2), 83-97.

Showers, J., & Bandman, R. L. (1986). Scarring for life: Abuse with electric cords. *Child Abuse and Neglect, 10,* 25-31.

Sloan, J., Kellermann, A., Reay, D., Ferris, J., Koepsell, T., Rivara, F., Rice, C., Gray, L., & LoGerfo, J. (1988). Handgun regulation, crime, assaults, and homicides. *New England Journal of Medicine, 319,* 1256-1262.

Smith, J., Mercy, J., & Rosenberg, M. (1986). Suicide and homicide among Hispanics in the Southwest. *Public Health Reports, 101,* 265-270.

Smith, M. D., & Parker, R. N. (1980). Type of homicide and variation in regional rates. *Social Forces, 59,* 614-624.

Sorenson, S. B., & Telles, C. A. (1991). Self-reports of spousal violence in a Mexican-American and non-Hispanic white population. *Violence and Victims, 6*(1), 3-15.

Soriano, F. (1993). Cultural sensitivity and gang intervention. In A. Goldstein & R. Huff (Eds.), *The gang intervention handbook* (pp. 441-461). Champaign, IL: Research Press.

Spearly, J., & Lauderdale, M. (1983). Community characteristics and ethnicity in the prediction of child maltreatment rates. *Child Abuse and Neglect 7,* 91-105.

Straus, M. A., &. Smith, C. (1990). Violence in Hispanic families in the United States: Incidence and structural interpretations. In M. A. Straus & R. J. Gelles (Eds.), *Physical violence in American families: Risk factors and adaptations to violence in 8,145 families* (pp. 341-368). New Brunswick, NJ: Transaction Books.

Straus, M. A., Gelles, R. J., & Steinmetz, S. K. (1980). *Behind closed doors: Violence in the American family.* Garden City, NY: Anchor/Doubleday.

Sue, S. (1988). Psychotherapeutic services for ethnic minorities. *American Psychologist, 43,* 301-308.

Sue, S., Fujino, D., Hu, L., Takeuchi, D., & Zane, N. (1991). Community mental health services for ethnic minority groups: A test of the cultural responsiveness hypothesis. *Journal of Consulting and Clinical Psychology, 59,* 533-540.

Sugarman, J., Brenneman, G., LaRoque, W., Warren, C., & Goldberg, H. (1994). The urban American Indian oversample in the 1988 National Maternal and Infant Health Survey. *Public Health Reports, 109,* 243-250.

Sugarman, J., Soderberg, R., Gordon, J., & Rivara, F. (1993). Racial misclassification of American Indians: Its effect on injury rates in Oregon, 1989 through 1990. *American Journal of Public Health, 83,* 681-684.

Tharp, R. (1991). Cultural diversity and treatment of children. *Journal of Consulting and Clinical Psychology, 59,* 799-812.

U.S. Department of Health and Human Services. (1981). *National study of the incidence and severity of child abuse and neglect: Study findings* (Publication No. OHDS 81-03026). Washington, DC: Government Printing Office.

U.S. Department of Health and Human Services. (1985). *Report of the Secretary's Task Force on Black and Minority Health.* Washington, DC: Government Printing Office.

U.S. Department of Health and Human Services. (1990). *Healthy people 2000: National health promotion and disease prevention objectives* (DHHS Publication No. PHS 91-50212). Washington, DC: Government Printing Office.

U.S. Department of Health and Human Services. (1994). Physical violence during the 12 months preceding childbirth: Alaska, Maine, Oklahoma, and West Virginia, 1990-91. *Morbidity and Mortality Weekly Report, 43,* 133-137.

U.S. Department of Justice. (1991). *Criminal victimization, 1990* (Bureau of Justice Statistics Special Report No. NCJ-122743). Washington, DC: Government Printing Office.

Valdez, R. B., & Nourjah, R. (1988). Homicide in Southern California, 1966-1985: An examination based on vital statistics data. In J. F. Kraus, S. B. Sorenson, & P. D. Juarez (Eds.), *Proceedings from the Research Conference on Violence and Homicide in Hispanic Communities* (pp. 85-100). Los Angeles: UCLA Publication Services.

Walker, L. E. A. (1979). *The battered woman.* New York: Harper & Row.

Wallace, D., Kirk, M., Houston, B., Annest, J., & Emrich, S. (1993). *Injury mortality atlas of Indian Health Service areas, 1979-87.* Atlanta, GA: Centers for Disease Control and Prevention, National Center for Injury Prevention and Control.

Webster, D., Gainer, P., & Champion, H. (1993). Weapon carrying among inner-city junior high school students: Defensive behavior vs. aggressive delinquency. *American Journal of Public Health, 83,* 1604-1608.

Williams, K. R. (1984). Economic sources of homicide: Reestimating the effects of poverty and inequality. *American Sociological Review, 49,* 283-289.

Wilson-Brewer, R., & Jacklin, B. (1990). *Violence prevention strategies targeted at the general population of minority youth.* Background paper prepared for the Forum on Youth Violence in Minority Communities: Setting the Agenda for Prevention. Newton, MA: Education Development Center.

Yeh, M., Takeuchi, D., & Sue, S. (1994). Asian-American children treated in the mental health system: A comparison of parallel and mainstream outpatient service centers. *Journal of Clinical Child Psychology, 23,* 5-12.

Young, T. (1990). Poverty, suicide, and homicide among Native Americans. *Psychological Reports, 67,* 1153-1154.

Yung, B., & Gruber, E. (1995). [The experience of violence among Native American adolescents: Minnesota public schools, 1988]. Unpublished raw data.

Yung, B., & Hammond, R. (1995). *PACT: Positive Adolescents Choices Training: A model for violence prevention groups with African-American youth. Program Guide.* Champaign, IL: Research Press.

Zahn, M. A. (1988). Homicide in nine American cities: The Hispanic case. In J. F. Kraus, S. B. Sorenson, & P. D. Juarez (Eds.), *Proceedings from the Research Conference on Violence and Homicide in Hispanic Communities* (pp. 13-30). Los Angeles: UCLA Publication Services.

Zellman, G. L. (1992). The impact of case characteristics on child abuse reporting decisions. *Child Abuse and Neglect, 16,* 57-74.

CHAPTER 5

Primary Prevention and Resilience:
Changing Paradigms and Changing Lives

MARTIN BLOOM

R*esilience* refers to the fact, as Garmezy (1971, p. 114) so neatly expresses it, that sometimes healthy children emerge from unhealthy settings. Our current understanding of resilience stems from a large body of empirical evidence coming from independent researchers working in many places around the world—England, Hawaii, Minnesota, Berkeley, St. Louis, Rochester, and elsewhere (Anthony, 1977; Garmezy, 1991; Rutter, 1987; Werner & Smith, 1992; Wyman, Cowen, Work, & Parker, 1991). Although they have differed in target problems, populations, and methods of study, they have produced generally similar results, namely, that some proportion of young people living in various stressful psychosocial and physical environments grow up to become apparently healthy adults.

The Paradox of Resilience

This astonishing set of findings appears to be contrary to conventional wisdom. Isn't it only common sense to believe that people who are exposed to severe and chronic stresses throughout their childhoods would likely exhibit some kind of dysfunction as adults? Fortunately, for reasons we are now seeking to understand, some people appear more adaptable then many believed was ever possible. But it is equally well established by these same studies, and many others, that another sizable proportion of people growing up in the same stressful circumstances do not become healthy and effective adults. Why this differential outcome occurs is a paradox that scientists are seeking to understand. Perhaps if we can understand why some people surmount their disadvantaged and destructive childhood years to become happy and effective citizens, we might be able to help the majority of such citizens living in similar circumstances.

Presupposition 1

Scientists use conceptual ideas and empirical facts in various combination in order to understand some portion of the world. However, it is important to recognize that they also begin their fact-finding and idea generating with certain presuppositions about the way the world works. In this chapter, I will present a series of presuppositions, along with the concepts and empirical facts that were generated in the course of trying to solve this significant paradox (Werner, 1990). This series of historical efforts also reflects the nature of social science in trying to come to terms with a complex reality.

To understand the excitement the findings on resilience have generated from various studies around the world, we have to go back to the 1950s and 1960s, when conventional wisdom held that high levels of stress cause problems. This idea was a reflection of some dominant paradigms of that era. Kuhn (1970) characterized a paradigm as a pervasive worldview for a given domain that establishes the kinds of questions that can be asked and determines which types of answers are acceptable within this perspective. Seligman (1991, p. 8) has noted the paradigmatic power that the behavioral and psychoanalytic perspectives held at this time (the 1950s). People were viewed as the products of their environments, either because of external reinforcements or because of internal urges.

In addition, the helping professions (clinical psychology, psychiatry, and social work especially) were guided by another paradigm, the medical model, which claimed that some underlying pathology was producing the visible problems. Solutions required specialists using high technology; the recipients of this service had to be "patient" and had to follow the "doctor's orders." This underlying pathology may have been a physical or psychical one; in either case, it required the skilled efforts of physician or psychiatrist, often operating in institutions and involving high costs, to get at the root of the matter.

Let's begin this historical reconstruction in the development of the resilience concept with a first presupposition that I infer to have been operating as a given in the early 1960s:

1. High levels of biopsychosocial stress operating on a vulnerable individual would naturally produce high levels of dysfunction.

In the behavioral or psychoanalytic view of reality, the "vulnerable individual" was practically ignored in this equation because the strength of either external reinforcements or internal unconscious conflicts was so great as to overwhelm any "free will" on the part of the individual. Essentially, some powerful external or internal force ensured that its stressful events would produce dysfunction in the individual. Institutions and specialists providing treatment or rehabilitation services for the unhappy and dysfunctional end products of these events flourished.

There are endless examples. Anthony (1977) summarized thinking in genetics regarding the children of psychotics:

A certain percentage—the figure varying with different investigators—were apparently doomed to develop psychosis during adult life. (p. 165)

(Anthony later went on to refute this finding with his own research.) Vance (1977) wrote in the same vein:

Siblings of drug users, for example, are likely to be at higher risk for drug use and alcohol than other children. Also, as a number of studies consistently demonstrate, there is a strong association between parental conflict and psychiatric disorder in children (Rutter, 1974; Fontana, 1966; Wynne & Singer, 1963 a & b). (p. 210)

Spring and Zubin (1977) expressed this common understanding this way:

[It is] well documented [that] life event stressors [precipitate] physical but especially psychosocial disorders (Rahe, 1964; Brown, 1968; Dohrenwend, 1972). (p. 266)

Thus, whether on a biological or a psychosocial level, there was widespread agreement with what I have called Presupposition 1. There was agreement for the very good reason that there was an enormous amount of research data corroborating that relationship.

However, just when we believe that we know something for sure, anomalies often emerge that throw our certainty into question and stimulate new discoveries in science (Kuhn, 1970, p. 52). These anomalies may be of a factual or a conceptual nature, but they are serious enough to require some response. In the case of Presupposition 1, empirical evidence emerged or, perhaps more accurately, was eventually recognized, even though it was not an acceptable kind of information, that some people living in stressful conditions emerged as healthy adults. The numbers involved were well beyond what could have happened by chance alone. The concept of the vulnerable person as one at the mercy of internal or external forces also came under fire. It did not seem to reflect the adaptive nature of the human organism that social-cognitive theorists such as Piaget and Bandura were describing.

Presupposition 2

The growing awareness that some healthy people were emerging from high-stress situations provoked consternation among the defenders of the then-existing paradigms, because the new presupposition was describing a scientifically untenable situation:

2. High levels of stress, operating on a vulnerable individual, will sometimes lead to functional social behavior and other times to dysfunctional social behavior.

Such statements were no way to run a science, especially within the dominant paradigm of that time. We had to know what the terms of the presupposition meant, and what led to what. So scientists began to dissect the equation by doing further research and reconceptualization.

This task was not easy to do, because of the varieties of people ("patients") involved, even though in each research study, some disadvantaged population was presumed to be at risk for developmentally dysfunctional behaviors. Many specific kinds of problems were being studied. The specific disadvantages that put individuals at risk included biological insults to infants such as perinatal complication and congenital heart defects (Werner & Smith, 1982). Or disadvantages might stem from serious caregiving deficits in the immediate family, such as parents who were divorced (Hetherington, Cox, & Cox, 1982), psychotic parents (Garmezy, 1987), alcoholic parents (Werner, 1986), and parents prone to child abuse (Farber & Egeland, 1987). Or disadvantages might have been more general, such as poverty, racial oppression, and war conditions that required the relocation of young children.

The defining characteristic of these early studies was that some proportion of the children exposed to unhealthy developmental conditions came out in positive and healthy ways. But this proportion varied in different studies. For example, Werner (1989b) identified 30% of the children in her Hawaiian sample as being at high risk, defined as having four or more serious risk factors occurring before the age of 2. Yet in follow-up studies 18 to 30 years later, one in three of these children at high risk had developed into competent and caring adults. Werner's (1989a) description of one high-risk child gives the flavor of the situation:

> The son of teen-age parents, Michael was born prematurely. . . . He spent his first three weeks of life in a hospital, separated from his mother. Immediately after his birth, his father was sent with the U.S. Army to Southeast Asia, where he remained for two years. By the time Michael was eight years old, he had three siblings, and his parents were divorced. His mother had deserted the family and had no further contact with her children. His father raised Michael and his sibling with the help of their aging grandparents. (p. 108)

However, by age 18, Michael turned out to be a healthy, happy young man. He exhibited high self-esteem and a sound set of values. He was successful in school, was liked by his peers, and looked forward to the future.

Anthony (1977) studied a sample of children in St. Louis who were presumed to be at high risk for schizophrenia or manic-depression, like their parents. Yet his results showed that about 30% seemed "normally adjusted," another 30% had minor adjustment problems but did not require psychiatric intervention, and the remaining 40% manifested "significant maladjustment" (p. 165). I want to note for later discussion that Anthony observed that 10% of the first group in fact were credited as having "superior adjustment."

Robins (1966) found that 60% of her control group who grew up in the slums of St. Louis were found to be well adjusted as adults. Rutter and Madge (1976) reported that half of the disadvantaged children in their study moved up from this status as adults.

In summary, considerable evidence was generated by different research groups that a sizable proportion of children at high risk for a variety of problems nonetheless developed into effective adults. The concept of *vulnerability* did not seem like the right term to apply to this healthy portion of the disadvantaged population. What was there about these individuals in the context of their severely stressful lives that enabled them to avoid maladjustment? The options scientists saw at that time were to reconsider the environmental stress and to revise their view of the nature of the vulnerable individual. What they chose to do once again reflected the dominant paradigms of the times, but the times, they were a-changing. I want to mention briefly two important changes.

The first, in the field of psychology, was the emergence of cognitive theory. Long in coming to the United States, these ideas (from theorists such as Piaget, Bandura, and Chomsky) led to a general reconsideration of the nature of the individual. What happens inside a person's head finally was recognized as a part of the set of events that leads to behaviors. What people think, wish, expect, and idealize affects what they do—along with internal forces (perhaps growing less insistent with the shrinking of psycho-analytic influence) and external forces (perhaps growing less insistent with the shrinking of radical behaviorism) (Bandura, 1986). These cognitive ideas took root within a context of rigorous scientific effort and a variety of practice applications (such as Ellis's rational-emotive therapy).

Also, in the 1960s, the community mental health movement was gaining momentum in the context of a massive societal change promoting human rights. Collective structures and forces could be reorganized to face problems and attempt humane solutions of them. As Albee (1983) so eloquently expressed the underlying principle: Massive social problems would never be resolved by treating their victims one by one. Some form of collective action was needed, before the problems were manifested.

Presupposition 3

In the face of these societal changes and the anomaly of healthy adults emerging from unhealthy environments, the scientific community reacted cautiously. Presupposition 3 is an exaggerated summary of my view of how the social science community initially responded:

3. High levels of stress, operating on invulnerable individuals, will not interfere with the expression of functional social behavior.

I interpret the history of this period to show that the first response to the challenge to Presupposition 2 was to make a conceptual change regarding the host person. In effect, a whole new entity was conceived, the "invulnerable individual" (Garmezy, 1971, p. 114), an unsinkable individual who would not succumb to high levels of stress. This option required less change for society than would identifying causal conditions in the stressful environment. The magical quality of children who were "invincible" (Werner & Smith, 1982, p. 3) and "stress resistant" (Hauser, Vieyra, Jacobson, & Wertleib, 1985, p. 82) in the face of serious, often chronic, social stresses seemed to be irresistible to researchers and theorists at that time. But that time was to end soon.

Note that *invulnerability* is essentially an absolute term: One is either invulnerable or vulnerable. Of course, the empirical data did not support the all-or-nothing character of invulnerability. There were degrees of competence exhibited. Some traits that were characteristic of one group of competent children were absent in another group. One individual might show signs of competence in one situation, but not in another. Moreover, some investigators found that people may be competent in some areas (especially external, task-oriented areas), but have problems in other parts of their lives (such as having emotional difficulties) (Luthar, 1991). Clearly, another concept was needed to describe the protean nature of the individual. And this is when the term *resilience* entered the scene.

Presupposition 4

Another way in which the individual was conceptually changed was by the identification of "protective factors," some underlying conditions that were used to explain the pattern of observed events. Werner (1990) describes the process this way: "Variables associated with subsequent positive outcomes suggested possible protective factors" (p. 99). Indeed, this is how concepts are inductively constructed. But what we see "associated with subsequent positive outcomes" depends on our own presuppositions. Those who view the world through individualistic glasses see resilience in individual terms, or in individual interactions (Rutter, 1987, pp. 317, 327; Werner, 1990, p. 98). Those who view the world developmentally in a family context see resilience as emerging in a protective family structure (Hauser et al., 1985). Others see the sociophysical environment as having powerful influences, such as neighborhood schools that reach out to connect with parents and children (Comer, 1988, p. 42). A few researchers consider multiple perspectives, and have discovered that "the individual organism, the immediate family, and the larger social context" (Werner, 1990, p. 100) are all intimately involved in the resilience seen in adults.

Such were the ingredients at work to produce the fourth presupposition, one reflecting an expanded view of the person and the environment. The conceptual nature of the person—now viewed as resilient and having certain protective factors, in contrast to being invulnerable—is combined with an enlarged sense of the system of stresses—now viewed as involving person, primary groups, and secondary groups.

4. High levels of stress coming differentially from personal, familial, and social environments, affecting an individual who is viewed as resilient because of the operation of certain protective factors, may optimally result in a healthy, well-functioning adult when the balance of protective factors outweighs stress factors.

Various commentators have noticed that there are three kinds of protective factors: the individual, familial, and social types—not surprisingly, the same three factors discussed in relation to personal/environmental stresses (e.g., Werner, 1986). These protective factors are somehow connected with the observed healthy outcome. What the actual mechanisms are that produce the healthy outcome in the face of severe and chronic stress are unclear (Rutter, 1987, p. 317). For example, some writers think that protective factors somehow buffer or protect the resilient person from stressors, as when children engage in hobbies that presumably take their minds off of their difficult life conditions. This explanation involves circular reasoning, because we would not have identified hobbies unless they were correlated with resilience. Correlation does not necessitate causation, and so we need more information about how, for example, the "protective factors" emerging from research—such as doing chores, having a best friend in school, and having the ability to seek out adults for assistance—are specifically related to the outcome, resilient behavior. We have to think about what buffering means in the context of a resilient child—does it involve complete protection, gradual exposure that builds up some psychological immunity to stresses, or what? This is important to know, but it is only a first step for changing empirical data into practice methods and policies.

Presupposition 4 is more complex than the preceding ones, but it may begin to reflect the complexities of the reality it seeks to explain. This is essentially where matters stand today. We have expanded on the nature of stress, and we have recognized the adaptability of people stemming from at least some protective factors that buffer the stresses of social life. It is also well recognized that we need greater clarity on the actual mechanisms by which protective factors protect and, beyond that, how they also promote resilience. However, some new developments in the concept of primary prevention may help us to see resilience in a new light as well.

Presupposition 5

I believe that a fifth presupposition is coming into view, clarified by the lens of what may be a new paradigm, a positive form of primary prevention. As ancient as folk sayings (e.g., "A stitch in time saves nine") and as modern as the most recent pronouncement of the surgeon general, primary prevention is an idea "whose time has come" (Klein & Goldston, 1977) and keeps on emerging in every aspect of social life as the realities of limited resources and exploding populations become clear.

Primary prevention may be briefly defined in terms of planned actions that seek to prevent some predictable problem, to protect some existing state of health or healthy functioning, and to promote

some desired health objective. Thus, a full-formed primary prevention involves all three elements—prevention, protection, and promotion—within a systems perspective where each element affects
and is affected by every other significant element. The conceptual
world of primary prevention is three-dimensional and optimistic.
It demands of us that we see the world in a new light, in contrast
to the paradigms of pathology (the medical model) and single
sovereign understandings of human behavior (psychoanalysis or
radical behaviorism) (Albee, 1983; Bond & Joffe, 1982).

It follows from the definition that primary prevention is concerned with states of health as well as problematic states. This
means that primary preventers work with the strengths of client
groups (usually designated as *participants,* not patients) as well as
with their weaknesses or limitations. In fact, two of the three
component activities involve protecting and promoting healthy
states, and only one seeks to prevent predictable problems from
overtaking a (healthy) person. This, too, is a radical shift from a
pathological view of people as patients.

Another implication of the definition of primary prevention is
that it involves action taken before some "at-risk" condition becomes a problem. This is the meaning of acting before some
predictable problem has a chance to occur, or acting so as to reduce
its untoward potency. Moreover, primary prevention is equally
concerned with taking actions with regard to people's "potentials."
One seeks to promote some strength that does not yet currently
exist in the target person or group, as well as to protect existing
states of health or healthy functioning. Thus, primary prevention
intrinsically operates in a triadic mode, dealing with problems for
which the target group is at risk as well as the strengths that
currently exist (which may need protection) and those desired states
that may "potentially" come into existence for that target group.
Often, in the actual programming of primary prevention services,
we have to remove the at-risk condition by means of interjecting
the "with-potential" condition, using the existing states of health
as our basis of effort. To put this another way, we add a strength to
take the place of a weakness, rather than leave a psychosocial-physi-
cal vacuum.

There are a lot of things that have to be done to remove at-risk
conditions and also introduce with-potential conditions. Fortunately, primary prevention is a multidisciplinary endeavor, and

there are many sciences and professions that take part in its activities. Psychologists, psychiatrists, caseworkers, and physicians, among others, may deal with individuals in the context of primary prevention. Group workers, educators, recreation agency personnel, and others may deal with small groups in the context of primary prevention. Community psychologists, community social workers, reformers, and social activists of all sorts are often involved with large-scale groups, neighbors, and whole communities in primary prevention efforts.

A major contribution of primary prevention to the considerations of resilience relates to this configuration of interrelated social systems. Resilience may be found in resilient individuals, resilient families, and resilient neighborhoods, schools, and whole communities. Indeed, one may argue that this systems perspective gives a three-dimensional meaning to the term *resilience*. No longer can we view one individual as resilient independent of some context. As we discover what portions of their worlds resilient children explore and incorporate into their helping environments, we will discover new constructive situations that other disadvantaged children might use. Indeed, it may be possible that all children can benefit from this exploration of growth-promoting experiences. It may be that promoting development in advantaged children may produce what Anthony (1977) calls "superior adjustment" as well as children who are what he calls "normally adjusted." This extension of the use of resilience training may benefit all walks of society and, thereby, society itself. A question that we will have to explore carefully in the near future is, What is the nature of resilience?

What is emerging with increasing clarity is that there may be some uniformities in growth-promoting experiences that represent the context for the "resilient individual." By focusing too much on that "individual," rather than on individuals in social, cultural, and environmental contexts, we may lose sight of options for preventive/promotive services. I propose that we should use the term *resilience* to refer to systems properties, rather than in relation to an exclusive focus on a resilient individual. This is the spirit of Werner's (1990) discussion, which I take to be a bellwether for the future of this concept.

Given this brief description of a full-spectrum primary prevention, what does this have to contribute to the discussion of resilience, and what does resilience have to contribute to primary prevention?

Reconsider the four presuppositions discussed above. From the perspective of primary prevention, some important observations may be made. First, all of the former presuppositions involve stress as the major independent variable, affecting some types of people, resulting in some combination of functional or dysfunctional behaviors. If we think in terms of stress as a pathological agent, then we inevitably focus on "protective factors" to reduce the unpleasant or harmful stimuli. We think in terms of buffering the stress. Yet many of the correlates with resilience are not of the protective, buffering kind, but rather involve an outgoing curiosity and optimism. We tend not to see these proactive behaviors, however, because we have asked stress questions and expect to find stress-buffering answers. The newer version of primary prevention offers a radically different perspective (Bond & Joffe, 1982). Indeed, the primary prevention that emphasizes promotion or enhancement essentially opposes the basic presupposition of the stress model and the medical model, both of which look for underlying pathology-producing events or conditions.

Many years ago, Hollister (1967, p. 197) introduced the term *strens* to mean growth-producing experiences. It was a term that was intended to be parallel to the concept of stress. Poser and King (1975) introduced the term *salutogenesis*. Both these terms refer to the same important phenomenon, that there exist in nature and society many growth-promoting experiences, some of which may be intentionally introduced to target groups.

Thus, one major shift in the way we look at reality, including the reality of children growing up in disadvantaged environments where they face chronic and severe stress, is to try to identify the strens in their lives. It is likely that these strens, in balance with the stresses, are the significant experiences influencing what we call resilient behavior. Resilient children may be hypothesized to have more strens than stresses on balance.

If we consider strens and stresses as the two classes of independent variables and begin to seek for specificity in what particulars cause each for given persons in certain contexts, then we will be constructing an affecting systems context that permits us many more avenues to make changes. In general, we should promote strens and reduce stresses to manageable size. It is as important to be aware of and to activate strens as it is to be aware of and neutralize overwhelming stresses. Indeed, it may be more important to emphasize strens than to deal with stresses because we may more effectively capture the motivation of participants by focusing on their strengths than by focusing on their limitations. This is another contribution of primary prevention to resilience research—the promotion of strengths that engage or empower participants to achieve their own potentials.

Another contribution primary prevention may make to the stress presupposition concerns the so-called protective factors that are emerging from the empirical correlates with documented resilience. If one's model calls for stress to affect people, then, logically, one's model should call for some defense reaction—that is, protective factors. However, if the model is enlarged to consider both strens and stresses, then the response should be enlarged as well to include proaction as well as reaction. The helping professions should be empowered by these equations to deal with the full range of human experiences, not merely the problematic, stressful ones.

So, paralleling the components of primary prevention itself, I would suggest, we should consider preventive factors, protective factors, and promotive factors, so that we broaden the spectrum of service programs (see Rutter, 1987, pp. 317-318). If we look again at the list of correlates of resilience from this expanded conceptual perspective, we might begin to see underlying conditions that call for differential action—prevention, protection, and promotion.

For example, in dealing with preventive factors, we would have to foresee predictable problems in a target group and offer the various technologies of primary prevention (Gullotta, 1987)—to change the individuals involved, to change the agent that might produce the problem, or to change the environment in which agent and host might meet. As an instance of preventive factors in resilience, consider teaching problem-solving skills to preschoolers (Shure & Spivack, 1988). Teaching such skills anticipates the difficulties impulsive or overly shy children have in negotiating effectively in a social context, as well as the basic lessons in problem solving that all children need to learn. By providing these skills in advance, we can help children avoid predictable problems.

Likewise, some of the correlates of resilience are essentially protective in nature; that is, they act to sustain existing states of health—which may need support to remain healthy, vital parts of some target group. Consider the range of activities that may take place in schools to sustain the natural curiosity and motivation of students as they start their formal education. From Head Start to Follow Through programs, we are essentially protecting existing states of healthy functioning. (Yes, some Head Start programs do involve preventive and promotive elements too. Conceptual boundaries are clearer in these pages than on the street. See Zigler & Styfco, 1993.)

Instances of the third category, promotive factors, can be found among the correlates of resilience. For example, we can promote experiences that we believe will have positive outcomes. We can give assertiveness training to passive or impulsive individuals to make it possible for them to respond within a desired range of behaviors, rather than with passive or aggressive responses. We can set up chores for children in disadvantaged situations so that they are a part of the family, an element that is correlated with resilience. We can introduce significant adult role models and confidants for such children, where experiences with such vital supports may be lacking in their own lives.

It may be very important to praise the unknown people who step into the breach and make highly significant contributions to the growth of disadvantaged individuals. The unpaid volunteers, the extended family members (like Michael's aging grandparents), the favorite schoolteacher—these and many like them may be making the critical difference between an overall strens balance or a stressful one. I would hypothesize that it is the overall positive strens balance that produces the complex outcome that we currently describe as being a resilient individual in a disadvantaged environment. Viewed from the inside perspective (i.e., the personal weighing of factors in oneself and one's environment), the disadvantages are outweighed by the constructive efforts of those around the child, as well as the personal characteristics he or she possesses. What these personal weighings are remains unknown—perhaps it is the optimistic personality (Seligman, 1991) who interprets whatever stimuli impinge as being potentially constructive, and thereby helps to build such a helpful environment even in the midst of familial, social, and economic chaos.

We can construct strens-like environments of all sizes, and even though we cannot guarantee that every particular element will be growth promoting to every individual, we can begin to make some progress in setting up individualized cafeterias of strens experiences. Although we may not be able to make large system changes of stresses, we probably have more opportunities to scale sizes of strens. For example, constructed play environments offer an array of defensible spaces and open spaces for social and physical engagement. Children may be encouraged to move in and out of these spaces as particular circumstances require.

In general, if we think more broadly than in terms of mere reaction to stress, if we consider ways to be proactive with regard to potential strengths of target groups, then we may expand the numbers of would-be resilient individuals. Indeed, we may not merely move disadvantaged children to some level of normal functioning, we may also be able to move some to extraordinary levels of functioning, as Anthony found in his study of the children of psychotic or manic-depressive parents. We will need all the extraordinary individuals we can get to be able to survive—no, not merely survive, but, as Faulkner said, to prevail—in the contemporary world.

With regard to the complexity of contemporary social problems and the fact that people have both at-risk and with-potential conditions, I believe that the contribution of primary prevention will come in the form of collaborative team projects rather than single-profession projects. We will need the professional and scientific services of people at the individual level, at the primary and secondary group levels, and at the levels of the neighborhood, community, society, and subculture—as well as the physical environment itself. We need these essentially all at once and with coordination among them.

We have few guidelines to coordinate many professions working in harmony toward the solution of some complex social problems. I think about the complexities in designing and carrying out planned communities of a few thousand people, compared with the complexities of dealing with millions in large urban areas (Klein, 1977).

Some beginning working models are present in some large-scale and long-term primary prevention projects, such as Kellam's Woodland project in Chicago, which mapped the correlations between types of families and the mental health of children (Kellam, Ensminger, & Turner, 1977). (For example, whereas mother-alone families were at highest risk in terms of social maladjustment of children, the presence of certain second adults, such as a mother-grandmother combination, was nearly as effective as mother-father families.) This is another task for the future, but that future begins now as we are able to presume that systemic actions can introduce strens into the lives of the disadvantaged while reducing or neutralizing stresses to whatever degree possible. (We should also frame a picture of the Pruitt-Igoe public housing project being blown up as a reminder of bad urban planning and unanticipated negative consequences. However, that photograph will be as much a reminder of the constructive uses of dynamite as it is of the fallibility of human enterprises.)

Theorists in primary prevention have not yet put together in one grand theory the concepts of stress and strens, but I predict that this will likely be the concern of the next wave of theorists grappling with increasingly complicated social problems. I think we can see some fuzzy images of this coming theory—it will probably include elements of what we call ecological theory today, in which we make a serious attempt to see how each major element influences and is influenced by every other major element in a common social and physical space. I believe that the theories guiding primary prevention, such as George Albee's (1983) equation on the factors involved in mental health and illness, may be a preview of coming attractions.

To present a general model of Albee's equation, we could say that any significant social behavior is some function of the following ingredients: the strengths of persons, primary and secondary groups, the society, and subcultures, as these operate in some physical environment and historical time, and as these strengths are reduced by the weaknesses of persons, primary and secondary groups, the society, and subcultures, as these operate in some physical environment and historical time. That is a mouthful, but it does combine all of the active ingredients we need to be aware of with regard to the strengths and limitations of persons and collectives. Lacking are the specific ways these interact and how the resulting action emerges. Determining these, too, is a task for the future.

Review of the Literature on Resilience

Several scholars, especially Werner (1990), but also Cowen and Work (1988), Garmezy (1991), Hauser et al. (1985), Luthar and Zigler (1991), Rutter (1987), Watt, David, Ladd, and Shamons (1992), Wyman et al. (1991), and others have provided important reviews of the literature on correlates of resilience, generally in the context of their own research. They have also discussed numerous methodological and conceptual issues.

It is important to report some major findings from these reviews so as to give a sense of the scope of the problems facing those who would make sense of, and use, this literature in the service of primary prevention. But it is difficult to present a simple summary or a tabular listing because such presentations necessarily remove the particular research contexts from the correlates of resilience, and we are left with only abstract terms. Yet there is considerable consistency in the correlates that have emerged, so it is worth the gamble to summarize this rich database so as to get a brief overview of the totality of current knowledge (see Table 5.1).

Some general observations are in order concerning the material presented here in Table 5.1. The most common feature across most studies is the lower socioeconomic status of the participants. Many are members of ethnic minorities living in more or less oppressive cultural contexts. But beyond these features, there are many different types of problems facing these people, as the table indicates.

First, the table presents a brief overview of various characteristics of resilient adults when they were children growing up in highly stressful environments. The table is divided by age stages of the individual, by the inner and outer circles of the family, and by the three social settings beyond the family: peers, school, and the community at large. Second, for the age stages of the individual, the table lists the protective factors under two columns, so as to emphasize two distinct components of resilience; one deals with intrapersonal characteristics, the other with interpersonal or what might be called *extrapersonal* characteristics (those dealing with the social environment as it affects the individual). Third, the family variable is divided into intrafamily factors (the child's relationship to the family) and overall family characteristics, as both are correlated with resilience as presented in adulthood.

The social variables are less often studied, and are presented here as simple correlations between these factors and resilience. In general, the list in Table 5.1 is to be interpreted only as a point of departure; researchers should return to the original studies for contextual understanding of the variables and then translate these into hypotheses to be tested in new settings.

Table 5.1 Correlates of Resilience: Individual, Family, and Social Characteristics

Individual Organism	Intraindividual Qualities Associated With Resilience	Interpersonal or Extrapersonal Qualities Associated With Resilience
Infant	active, vigorous (Werner, 1990, p. 100)	affectionate, cuddly, good-natured (Werner, 1990, p. 100)
	regular feeding and sleeping habits (Werner, 1990, p. 100)	elicits attention from others (Rutter, 1987, p. 326; Werner, 1990, p. 100)
	high energy level (Garmezy, 1991, p. 421)	easy to deal with temperament (Cowen & Work, 1988, p. 601; Wyman et al., 1991, p. 422)
		firstborn son, with sibs born several years apart (Werner, 1990, p. 101)
		female protected from family discord more than male (Luthar, 1993, pp. 449-450)
		"securely attached" infant (Rutter, 1987, p. 327)
Preschool	autonomous (Cowen & Work, 1988, p. 601; Werner, 1990, p. 101)	socially oriented (Werner, 1990, p. 101)
	alert (Werner, 1990, p. 102)	responsive (Garmezy, 1991, p. 421)
	cheerful (Cowen & Work, 1988, p. 601; Werner, 1990, p. 102)	adaptable in new situations (Earls et al., 1987; Garmezy, 1991, p. 421)
	self-confident; has good self-esteem (Garmezy, 1991, p. 424; Rutter, 1987, p. 327)	highly involved in play activities (Earls et al., 1987)
	seeks out novel experiences; curious (Cowen & Work, 1988, p. 601; Rutter, 1987, p. 326; Werner, 1989a, p. 108)	fearless and socially at ease (Halverson & Waldrup, 1974)
	self-reliant, does not need reassurance (Werner, 1989a, p. 108)	responds positively to environmental stress (Earls et al., 1987)
	self-initiating (Earls et al., 1987)	

Table 5.1 Continued

Individual Organism	Intraindividual Qualities Associated With Resilience	Interpersonal or Extrapersonal Qualities Associated With Resilience
	easy temperament (Rutter, 1987, pp. 321, 326)	
	intelligent (Garmezy, 1991, p. 424; Luthar, 1993, p. 449; Masten, 1988)	
	persevering (Cowen & Work, 1988, p. 601)	
Middle childhood	alert, cheerful (Werner, 1990, p. 102)	has good verbal development; communication skills (Werner, 1990, p. 102)
	shows advanced locomotion skills (Werner, 1990, p. 102)	socially at ease; socially mature; possesses social skills (Cowen & Work, 1988, p. 601; Garmezy, 1991, p. 424; Werner, 1990, p. 103)
	autonomous; independent; has self-help skills (Werner, 1990, p. 103)	knows how to ask for support when needed (Werner, 1989a, p. 108)
	competent (Werner, 1990, p. 103)	sociable (Werner, 1990, p. 103)
	shows perceived self-efficacy (Rutter, 1987, p. 327; Werner, 1990, p. 103)	well liked by peers and adults (Garmezy, 1991, p. 424; Werner, 1990, p. 103)
	displays problem solving (Werner, 1990, p. 103)	compassionate but detached from problem people in family (Anthony, 1977)
	shows reflective cognitive style (not impulsive) (Garmezy, 1991, p. 424)	employs hobbies as diversions to stressful conditions (Werner, 1990, p. 103)
	has internal locus of control (Luthar, 1993, p. 450; Werner, 1990, p. 103; 1990, p. 77)	does chores, representing connection to family (Clark, 1983; Elder, 1974; Rutter, 1987, p. 328)
	displays flexible coping style (Rutter, 1987, p. 326; Werner, 1990, p. 103)	displays androgynous competence, including caring and risk taking, and in play (Werner, 1990, pp. 103-104)

continued

Table 5.1 Continued

Individual Organism	Intraindividual Qualities Associated With Resilience	Interpersonal or Extrapersonal Qualities Associated With Resilience
	shows sense of humor (Masten, 1986)	
	intelligent, not particularly gifted but uses talents effectively (Luthar, 1991, p. 611; Werner, 1989a, p. 108)	
Adolescent	achievement oriented (Werner, 1990, p. 104)	responsible (Werner, 1990, p. 104)
	prefers structure in life; has purposeful life goals (Garmezy, 1971, p. 114; 1991, p. 424)	appreciative (Werner, 1990, p. 104)
	internalizes positive set of values; sees meaning in life (Werner, 1990, p. 104; Werner, 1989a, p. 110)	socially perceptive (Werner, 1990, p. 104)
	gentle (Werner, 1990, p. 104)	socially mature; possesses social skills
	shows coping skills (Werner, 1990, p. 104)	nurturant (Werner, 1990, p. 104)
	autonomous (Werner, 1990, p. 104)	planful of long-term decisions (Rutter, 1987, p. 326)
	has internal locus of control (Werner, 1990, p. 104)	prefers structure in life (Werner, 1990, p. 104)
	intelligent (Garmezy, 1991, p. 424; Werner, 1990, p. 105)	
	has perceived self-efficacy (Werner, 1990, p. 105)	
	shows strong ego development (Luthar, 1991, p. 612)	
Adult	has internal locus of control (Werner, 1989b, p. 77; but not Watt et al., 1992)	has education beyond high school (Werner, 1989b, p. 76)

Table 5.1 Continued

Individual Organism	Intraindividual Qualities Associated With Resilience	Interpersonal or Extrapersonal Qualities Associated With Resilience
	happy with current life situation and self, even with financial stress, family stress, and health problems (Werner, 1989a, p. 110; Werner, 1989b, pp. 76-77)	married (women only), with young children
	assertive (Watt et al., 1992)	working full-time (both men and women) (Werner, 1989b, p. 76)
	decisive (Watt et al., 1992)	(men) in professions or skilled trades and technical jobs (Werner, 1989b, p. 76)
	determined to transcend adversity (Watt et al., 1992)	(women) mainly in semi-professional or managerial positions (Werner, 1989b, p. 76)
	has strong feelings of self-worth (Watt et al., 1992)	has androgynous expectations of own children; resilient women expect high achievement, resilient men consider caring
	strongly autonomous (Watt et al., 1992)	most important in parenting (Werner, 1989b, p. 77)

Family	Intrafamily Factors (Relating Child to Family) Associated With Resilience	Family Factors (Characteristics of the Family Per Se) Associated With Resilience
Immediate family	opportunity for close bonding with at least one family member (including sibling) (Rutter, 1987, p. 321; Werner, 1990, pp. 106-107)	"good enough nurturing" (Werner, 1990, p. 106; and others)
	formation of secure attachment as infant, as basis of trust (Rutter, 1987, p. 327)	less physical crowding (Garmezy, 1991; Werner & Smith, 1982)
	having chores (productive roles of responsibility) (Werner, 1990, p. 108; and others)	household cleaner and less cluttered (Garmezy, 1991, p. 424)

continued

Table 5.1 Continued

Family	Intrafamily Factors (Relating Child to Family) Associated With Resilience	Family Factors (Characteristics of the Family Per Se) Associated With Resilience
	having religious faith, sense of rootedness, sense of a meaningful future (Werner, 1990, p. 108)	home has consistently enforced rules, good supervision, and well-balanced discipline (Rutter, 1987, p. 326; Werner & Smith, 1982; Wyman et al., 1991, pp. 421-423)
		parents who are competent, loving, and share values; marital support by spouse (Block & Block, 1980; Clark, 1983; Rutter, 1987, p. 321; Wyman et al., 1991, p. 422)
		healthy communication pattern within family (Rutter, 1987, p. 326; Wyman et al., 1991, p. 421)
		family cohesion; well-defined parent and child roles (Garmezy, 1991, p. 424)
		family with four or fewer children, spaced 2 or more years apart (Werner, 1989a, p. 108)
		mother whose coping and compensating style redeems father absence (Garmezy, 1991)
		parents optimistic about child's future (Wyman et al., 1991, p. 421)
Extended family	some provision of stable care and positive models of identification from extended family members (Garmezy, 1991; Rutter, 1987; Werner, 1990, p. 108; Wyman et al., 1991, 421)	mother-grandmother family nearly as effective as two-parent families (Kellam et al., 1977)

Table 5.1 Continued

Family	Intrafamily Factors (Relating Child to Family) Associated With Resilience	Family Factors (Characteristics of the Family Per Se) Associated With Resilience
	able to recruit surrogate parents, even from baby-sitters, house mothers in orphanages, etc., and develop social ties (Rutter, 1987, p. 327; Werner, 1990, p. 107)	(resilient girls) homes have emphasis on risk taking and independence, plus absence of overprotection; working mother strong model of identification (Garmezy, 1991, p. 424; Werner, 1990, p. 107)
	warmth, cohesion, and caring adult in absence of caring parent (Garmezy, 1991, p. 421)	(resilient boys) homes have greater structure, parental supervision, male model for identification (Werner, 1990, p.107)
	surrogate parent who encourages hope (Garmezy, 1971, p. 106)	

Social Setting Beyond Family: Factors Associated With Resilience

Peers	good peer relations, with at least one close friend (Garmezy, 1971, p. 114; Werner, 1990, pp. 103, 109)
	girls tend to keep childhood friends longer than boys (Werner, 1990, p. 108)
	makes friends of the parents of friends from stable families (as supplements to, not substitutes for, own family) (Werner, 1990, p. 108)
School	enjoyment of school; engagement with school (Garmezy, 1991; Werner, 1990, p. 108)
	school may become refuge from disordered home (Garmezy, 1991, pp. 424-425; Werner, 1990, p. 108)
	stress on academic achievement and commitment to education (Garmezy, 1971, p. 114)
	"successful schools" (i.e., those with high proportions of resilient children—Rutter et al., 1979) characterized by (a) setting of high standards, (b) availability of positive incentives as feedback, (c) positions of trust and responsibility for pupils (see also Garmezy, 1991, pp. 426-427)
	responsive and nurturant atmosphere (Werner, 1990, p. 110)

continued

Table 5.1 Continued

Social Setting Beyond Family: Factors Associated With Resilience

	organized and predictable environment with clear rules, etc. (Werner, 1990, p. 110): control and structured support more salient for boys, for bright children from divorced homes, and for talented minority children from poor homes; nurturance more salient for girls
	teachers may be role models and confidants; "favorite teacher" frequently associated with resilience (Garmezy, 1991, p. 421; Werner, 1990, p. 110)
	participation in extracurricular activities provided by school (Werner, 1989a, p. 110)
Community	viewed with optimism as a place congenial to young people, and as a place to work (Garmezy, 1991, p. 420; Long & Vaillant, 1984)
	opportunities for personal growth in structured situations (Elder, 1974)
	connection to some institutional support, caring agency, or church (Garmezy, 1991, p. 421); resilient women draw on larger number of sources of support than do resilient men (Werner, 1989b, p. 77)
	cooperative community as protective factor in high-risk situation (wartime) (Bloom & Halsema, 1983)

Conclusions

What are we to make of this array of optimistic correlates? How are we to combine these positive attributes of persons, groups, and environments in some personally and socially useful way? It is strange to be thinking these kinds of thoughts, because we have been educated in a contrary paradigm, one that looks for pathology—and finds it. Although these particular facts may not hold up in later research, it is likely that the general patterns among them will become clearer over time. We literally have to turn ourselves around and look to these strengths (in the context of the varied limitations) among the several social spheres and environmental contexts. This kind of ecological or systems thinking is difficult and yet exhilarating, because we appear to be getting closer to the full reality of clients' lives and with some reasonable degree of rigor and objectivity.

The bad news is that we have a long way to go. Rutter (1987) and Luthar (1993) have raised many difficult questions about the nature of our presumed knowledge of resilience and the many questions yet unanswered. Luthar (1991, p. 602), for example, notes that some erstwhile invulnerable adults may be carrying some emotional burdens (depression and anxiety) that have been overlooked in the happy search for the behavioral measures of competence.

There are significant questions about how the many spheres of experience interact. Luthar (1991), Rutter (1987), and others question whether the impact of strens is direct or interactive. My conceptual bias is to assume that all facets affect and are affected by every other relevant factor, so that we would see evidence of additive impact or threshold effects where one factor begins to take effect only after other factors have reached a certain intensity. Yet the mechanisms of influence are essentially unknown. How is it that any of the correlates of resilience influence the outcome? This requires the long process of research in which each factor (or set of factors) is teased out to observe its effect in real-world situations.

Looking at Table 5.1, we can observe that a large number of these correlates are directly or indirectly amenable to social influence. The very fact that so many are accessible to experimental manipulation means that we have an embarrassment of riches that researchers and practitioners rarely have. Which should be tried first, in what order, in what combinations? The hints provided by correlational evidence give us little instruction in changing lives. Just the fact that there are many individual attributes correlated to resilience tells us nothing about their internal relationships or the contexts in which they operate. Experimental manipulations (such as that carried out by Blau, Whewell, Gullotta, & Bloom, 1994) are the beginning of a new phase in the applied social sciences: making primary prevention changes specifically in the resilience context.

References

Albee, G. W. (1983). Psychopathology, prevention, and the just society. *Journal of Primary Prevention, 4,* 5-40.

Anthony, E. J. (1977). Preventive measures for children and adolescents at high risk for psychosis. In G. W. Albee & J. M. Joffe (Eds.), *Primary prevention of psychopathology: Vol. 1. The issues* (pp. 164-174). Hanover, NH: University Press of New England.

Bandura, A. (1986). *Social foundation of thought and action: A social cognitive theory*. Englewood Cliffs, NJ: Prentice Hall.

Blau, G. M., Whewell, M. C., Gullotta, T., & Bloom, M. (1994). The prevention and treatment of child abuse in households of substance abusers: A research demonstration progress report. *Child Welfare, 73,* 83-94.

Block, J., & Block, J. (1980). The role of ego control and ego resiliency in the organization of behavior. In W. A. Collins (Ed.), *Minnesota Symposium on Child Psychology* (Vol. 13). Hillsdale, NJ: Lawrence Erlbaum.

Bloom, M., & Halsema, J. (1983). Survival in extreme conditions. *Journal of Suicide and Life-Threatening Behavior, 13,* 195-206.

Bond, L. A., & Joffe, J. M. (Eds.). (1982). *Facilitating infant and early childhood development*. Hanover, NH: University Press of New England.

Clark, R. M. (1983). *Family life and school achievement: Why poor black children succeed or fail*. Chicago: University of Chicago Press.

Comer, J. P. (1988). Educating poor minority children. *Scientific American, 250*(5), 42-48.

Cowen, E. L., & Work, W. C. (1988). Resilient children, psychological wellness, and primary prevention. *American Journal of Community Psychology, 16,* 591-607.

Earls, F., Beardslee, W., & Garrison, W. (1987). Correlates and predictors of competence in young children. In E. J. Anthony & B. Cohler (Eds.), *The invulnerable child* (pp. 70-83). New York: Guilford.

Elder, G. H. (1974). *Children of the Great Depression: Social change in life experience*. Chicago: University of Chicago Press.

Farber, E. A., & Egeland, B. (1987). Invulnerability among abused and neglected children. In E. J. Anthony & B. Cohler (Eds.), *The invulnerable child* (pp. 253-288). New York: Guilford.

Garmezy, N. (1971). Vulnerability research and the issue of primary prevention. *American Journal of Orthopsychiatry, 41,* 101-116.

Garmezy, N. (1987). Stress, competence, and development: Continuities in the study of schizophrenic adults, children vulnerable to psychopathology, and the search for stress resilient children. *American Journal of Orthopsychiatry, 57,* 159-174.

Garmezy, N. (1991). Resiliency and vulnerability to adverse developmental outcomes associated with poverty. *American Behavioral Scientist, 34,* 416-430.

Gullotta, T. P. (1987). Prevention's technology. *Journal of Primary Prevention, 8,* 4-24.

Halverson, C. F., & Waldrup, M. P. (1974). Relations between preschool barrier behaviors and early school measures of coping, imagination, and verbal development. *Developmental Psychology, 10,* 716-720.

Hauser, S. T., Vieyra, M. A. B., Jacobson, A. M., & Wertleib, D. (1985). Vulnerability and resilience in adolescence: Views from the family. *Journal of Early Adolescence, 5,* 81-100.

Hetherington, E. M., Cox, M., & Cox, R. (1982). Effects of divorce on parents and children. In M. Lamb (Ed.), *Non-traditional families* (pp. 223-285). Hillsdale, NJ: Lawrence Erlbaum.

Hollister, W. (1967). The concept of strens in education: A challenge to curriculum development. In E. Bower & W. Hollister (Eds.), *Behavioral science frontiers in education*. New York: John Wiley.

Kellam, S. G., Ensminger, M. E., & Turner, R. J. (1977). Family structure and the mental health of children: Concurrent and longitudinal community-wide studies. *Archives of General Psychiatry, 34,* 1012-1022.

Klein, D. C. (Ed.). (1977). *Psychology of the planned community: The new town experience.* New York: Human Sciences Press.

Klein, D. C., & Goldston, S. E. (1977). *Primary prevention: An idea whose time has come* (DHEW Publication No. ADM 77-447). Washington, DC: Government Printing Office.

Kuhn, T. S. (1970). *The structure of scientific revolutions* (2nd ed.). Chicago: University of Chicago Press.

Long, J. V. F., & Vaillant, G. E. (1984). Natural history of male psychological health: XI. Escape from the underclass. *American Journal of Psychiatry, 141,* 341-346.

Luthar, S. S. (1991). Vulnerability and resilience: A study of high-risk adolescence. *Child Development, 62,* 600-616.

Luthar, S. S. (1993). Annotation: Methodology and conceptual issues in research on childhood resilience. *Journal of Child Psychology, 34,* 441-453.

Luthar, S. S., & Zigler, E. (1991). Vulnerability and competence: A review of research on resilience in childhood. *American Journal of Orthopsychiatry, 61,* 6-22.

Masten, A. S. (1986). Humor and competence in school-aged children. *Child Development, 57,* 461-473.

Poser, E. G., & King, M. C. (1975). Strategies for the prevention of maladaptive fear response. *Canadian Journal of Behavioural Science, 7,* 279-294.

Robins, L. N. (1966). *Deviant children grow up.* Baltimore: Williams & Wilkins.

Rutter, M. (1987). Psychological resilience and protective mechanisms. *American Journal of Orthopsychiatry, 57,* 316-331.

Rutter, M., & Madge, N. (1976). *Cycles of disadvantage: A review of research.* London: Heinemann.

Rutter, M. et al. (1979). *Fifteen thousand hours: Secondary schools and their effects on children.* Cambridge, MA: Harvard University Press.

Seligman, M. K. P. (1991). *Learned optimism.* New York: Alfred A. Knopf.

Shure, M. B., & Spivack, G. (1988). Interpersonal cognitive problem solving. In R. H. Price, E. L. Cowen, R. P. Lorion, & J. Ramos-McKay (Eds.), *14 ounces of prevention: A casebook for practitioners* (pp. 69-82). Washington, DC: American Psychological Association.

Spring, B., & Zubin, J. (1977). Vulnerability to schizophrenic episodes and their prevention in adults. In G. W. Albee & J. M. Joffe (Eds.), *Primary prevention of psychology: Vol. 1. The issues.* Hanover, NH: University Press of New England.

Vance, E. T. (1977). A typology of risks and the disabilities of low status. In G. W. Albee & J. M. Joffe (Eds.), *Primary prevention of psychology: Vol. 1. The issues* (pp. 207-237). Hanover, NH: University Press of New England.

Watt, N. F., David, J. P., Ladd, K. L., & Shamons, S. (1992, April 29-May 2). *The life course of psychological resilience: A phenomenological perspective on deflecting life's slings and arrows.* Paper presented at the Research Conference on Coercion and Punishment, Philadelphia.

Werner, E. E. (1986). Resilient offspring of alcoholics: A longitudinal study from birth to age 18. *Journal of Studies on Alcohol, 47,* 34-40.

Werner, E. E. (1989a, April). Children of the garden island. *Scientific American,* pp. 106-111.

Werner, E. E. (1989b). High-risk children in young adulthood: A longitudinal study from birth to 32 years. *American Journal of Orthopsychiatry, 59,* 72-81.

Werner, E. E. (1990). Protective factors and individual resilience. In S. J. Meisels & J. P. Shonkoff (Eds.), *Handbook of early childhood intervention* (pp. 97-116). Cambridge, MA: Cambridge University Press.

Werner, E. E., & Smith, R. S. (1982). *Vulnerable but invincible: A longitudinal study of resilient children and youth.* New York: McGraw-Hill.

Werner, E. E., & Smith, R. S. (1992). *Overcoming the odds: High risk children from birth to adulthood.* Ithaca, NY: Cornell University Press.

Wyman, P. A., Cowen, E. L., Work, W. C., & Parker, G. R. (1991). Developmental and family milieu correlates of resilience in urban children who have experienced major life stress. *American Journal of Community Psychology, 19,* 405-426.

Zigler, E., & Styfco, S. J. (1993). *Head Start and beyond: A national plan for extending childhood intervention.* New Haven, CT: Yale University Press.

CHAPTER 6

The Value of Including a "Higher Power" in Efforts to Prevent Violence and Promote Optimal Outcomes During Adolescence

ALETA L. MEYER

LINDA LAUSELL

In recent history, efforts to optimize adolescent outcomes have often fallen into two categories: programs designed to *prevent* problem behaviors (e.g., Botvin & Tortu, 1988; Flay et al., 1989; Johnson et al., 1990) and programs designed to *promote* competent behaviors (e.g., Danish et al., 1992; Harder, 1990). This separation between prevention and promotion in applied settings has had its complement in the academic world, where discussion has often focused primarily on risk factors (e.g., Hawkins, Lishner, Jenson, & Catalano, 1987; Petersen & Ebata, 1986) or on optimizing development (Danish, Petispas, & Hale, 1990; Task Force on Education of Young Adolescents, 1989). In both settings, applied and academic, there has been an encouraging paradigm shift that rises above this seeming dichotomy to a discussion of the relationship *between* risk factors and protective factors and their combined impact on adolescent outcomes (Bernard, 1991; Hawkins, 1990; Perry & Jessor, 1985). This discussion is characterized by the resilience literature (Bernard, 1991; Dugan & Coles, 1989; Hawkins, 1990), in which youth are viewed as having both resilient and risky characteristics, whereas families, communities, and schools are

115

characterized by protective and risk factors. Individual outcomes are seen as the result of unique interplays between people and their multiple environments.

An important component of this shift is how it facilitates more than theory about how youth live within an ecological system made up of families, schools, communities, and a larger society and culture (Bronfenbrenner, 1974). It has facilitated programmatic *action* that acknowledges this reality. In the past, most practitioners in prevention and promotion have made individual adolescents the focus of intervention efforts that were characterized by skill building, knowledge acquisition, and attitude change. When these programs were not as successful as initially hoped, the lack of long-term effects was often attributed to the day-to-day environments within which youth live (e.g., How can we expect a 16-week program of hour-long sessions to make a difference, given all the influences in the lives of youth?) (Meyer, 1994). By viewing youth and their environments as having both resilient and risky characteristics, we can see that problems and solutions do not reside solely within the individual—they reside within the larger environment as well. Therefore, future efforts may be more successful.

Another benefit of the current shift is how fluid the boundaries between research and applied settings are becoming. Through the language of resilience and risk factors, these settings are able to inform each other. Yet another benefit is how youth are viewed in terms of their potential contributions. These changes—acknowledgment of the ecology of human development, the practice of communication between research and application, and the positive recognition of youth—are bold and promising.

As violence has increased in our society, numerous programs have been developed that have attempted to prevent and reduce violence. As with other prevention programs for adolescents, program designs have moved from a deficiency model to a model that intends to identify conditions and competencies that enable children to resist adverse circumstances (Barbarin, 1993; Bernard, 1991). Whichever lens is used to look at the problem of violence, the approaches to violence prevention and the promotion of prosocial behavior are usually educational, psychological, environmental, or a combination thereof. Few would argue against the merits of educating young people about healthier behavior and nonviolent conflict resolution, of dealing with individual psychological problems, or of strengthening the environment of youth to make it more conducive to health and social competence. But what has been lacking in the professional discourse about violence prevention and social competence promotion among adolescents is an examination of the role of spirituality.

In other words, the movement from focusing on what we do not like about youth to focusing on what we *do* like requires another bold move: Adults who work with youth need to step away from attempting to be objective about value-laden issues. For example, the Task Force on Education of Young Adolescents (1989), which was organized to address the impending crisis of future generations of young adults being ill prepared for future work situations and the demands of adult life, describes its desired 15-year-old with a high dose of subjectivity: (a) an intellectually reflective person, (b) a person en route to a lifetime of meaningful work, (c) a good local and global citizen, (d) a caring and ethical individual, and (e) a healthy person. People who work with youth (or do research on adolescence, for that matter) must be willing to utilize the current crisis of youth violence purposefully as an opportunity to identify optimal means for youth to transition into adulthood, instead of unconsciously allowing the crisis of youth violence to turn into an alarmist campaign against teenagers.

Moreover, when adults avoid mentioning their values by being objective about value-laden issues, they may inadvertently teach *valuelessness* as the primary value. When adults do allow discussion of issues about which youth disagree (e.g., values, beliefs, and faith), they promote the dialectical process. This process promotes change within individuals, because the validity of two opposing viewpoints must be acknowledged and then synthesized to create a higher form of truth. Hegel has described this as the essence of history making and of the adolescent transition: "History is made only in those periods in which the contradictions of reality are being resolved by growth, as the hesitations and awkwardness of youth pass into the ease and order of maturity" (on Hegel, see Durant, 1961, p. 297). Therefore, in order for youth to develop into responsible adults, they must be encouraged to address issues of values, beliefs, and faith.

Cox (1986) describes a similar process when he discusses what needs to occur in the promotion of peace. Peace is not a passive state; it is the "activity of cultivating agreements" (p. 11). According to Cox, peace-seeking activity requires more energy over a longer period of time than does violent activity. Consequently, by not taking the time to teach youth how to engage in a dialectic, adults may be increasing the possibility that youth will turn to violence when confronted.

In addition to contributing to the creation of peaceful solutions, participation in the dialectical process develops and enhances cognitive functioning. Improved cognitive functioning entails the ability to comprehend abstract ideas, to understand the possible consequences of one's actions, to take on the perspective of others, and to see that what is understood to be true is often relative, rather than absolute (Keating, 1990). In other words, through the dialectical process one can consider differing opinions about issues such as God and the implications of those opinions (i.e., the realization that people have different ideas about what is true, consideration of abstract ideas, contemplation of the consequences of those ideas, and empathy for others' ideas). Therefore, the dialectical process has the potential to promote moral development (Haan, 1989; Kohlberg, 1976) and a personal spiritual belief system.[1]

Unfortunately, the picture drawn by the Task Force on Education of Young Adolescents (1989) is all too accurate: "Millions of these young people [American adolescents] fail to receive the guidance and attention they need to become healthy, thoughtful, and productive adults" (p. 13). When the dialectical process is denied, not only do youth lose out on the value of hearing the viewpoints of others, they may determine that being value-free is optimal and never develop their own spirituality. Perhaps our hesitation to discuss such crucial issues with adolescents has contributed to the increase in violent behavior among them by decreasing their capacity for empathy and an understanding of consequences.

In this chapter, we argue that an adolescent's understanding of his or her own spiritual belief system makes a unique contribution to that person's development on both personal and societal levels. In order to do this, we first describe common themes within spiritual belief systems and then present a preliminary consideration of the role of spirituality in adolescence. We follow this with a review of research directly related to spirituality in adolescence. Finally, we discuss future possibilities for the role of promoting personal spiritual belief systems in preventing violence and optimizing adolescent outcomes.

Common Themes in Religion and Spirituality

Spirituality, whether manifested by specific religious beliefs, denominational affiliations, or a set of guiding principles, seems to emerge as individuals seek to answer basic yet profound questions regarding meaning and purpose in life, identity, and relations to others in the world and the world itself. It is manifested as individuals seek to grapple with the mysteries in life reflected in such questions as, Why and how did the world come about? What happens after death? Determining what spiritual beliefs do for people and the emotionally supportive functions they serve depends on the perspectives of the belief system itself and the degree to which one ascribes to the belief. For the purposes of this chapter, we define a spiritual belief system as containing three common themes. The first concerns *the existence of some kind of higher power* (whether a personal deity or an impersonal force) to which one turns to in faith for inspiration, guidance, replenishment, and comfort. This includes the concept of having a soul (or spirit) in addition to a mind and a body. The second theme concerns *a framework for answering the big questions in life* regarding origin (Where did I come from?), identity (Who am I?), and relations to others (What is my purpose?) and the world itself (What is the meaning of life itself?). The third theme is that *a code for attitude and behavior* (personal or collective) emerges from the process of surrender to a higher power and the answers this provides. This surrender may be individual or it may have been done by important figures in a religion's history. A person's ability to uphold these convictions is directly related to the strength of his or her relationship to this higher power and/or to a religious institution.

Preliminary Thoughts About How Spiritual Themes Relate to Adolescence

As youth move through adolescence, many changes occur within and around them. According to Hill's (1983) framework, the three fundamental changes of adolescence are those related to puberty, cognition, and role transitions. For example, as a result of changes in physical appearance (puberty) and the ability to perceive life through the eyes of others (cognition), adolescents are given responsibilities more like those of adults than those of children (role transitions). These changes occur within the primary contexts of family, peers, school, and work. In addition, Hill identifies important psychosocial areas in which development occurs during adolescence. These areas are identity, autonomy, intimacy, achievement, and sexuality:

Psychosocial Area	*Primary Issues*
Identity	sense of self; self-esteem; sense of purpose in life
Autonomy	priorities; self-directed behavior
Intimacy	bonding; disclosure
Achievement	accomplishment; status
Sexuality	sexual orientation; choices about sexual behavior

Spiritual belief systems affect these fundamental changes, the contexts in which they occur, and psychosocial development in a number of ways. In terms of identity, a spiritual belief system addresses questions of purpose and meaning in life. When a belief system gives an explanation or a framework for addressing one's origins, it can provide a grounding sense of identity above and beyond that provided by name, ethnicity, and family history. A spiritual belief system can contribute to self-esteem, depending on what it says about who you are. For example, it may tell you that you are a unique creation; that you have purpose; and that you have all the skills, talents, and abilities you need to achieve your purpose. Therefore, such a belief system may help an individual to maintain his or her self-esteem in the face of degradation.

For many adolescents, a spiritual belief system can enable them to set goals with respect to their personal development. Personal goals are part of identity, autonomy, and achievement. In terms of identity, the dialectic allows exploration of values and a sense of self during the psychosocial moratorium (Erikson, 1968). A psychosocial moratorium occurs when adolescents are relieved from adultlike responsibilities and obligations. They can then think seriously about options for their future before making commitments to specific life goals. After they have explored their options, their religious beliefs may assist them in keeping the commitments they have made. On the other hand, certain religious beliefs can contribute to identity foreclosure, which happens when an adolescent makes a commitment to a sense of self *without* exploring alternatives.

In terms of intimacy and identity, adolescents who have a relationship of comfort and disclosure with a higher power may be better able than those who do not to cope with the fundamental questions of life. For example, most spiritual belief systems attempt to explain what happens at the time of death. There may be beliefs relating to the concepts of heaven and hell, reincarnation, or returning to a cosmic soup of souls. For adolescents and adults contending with the constant threat of death through violence, such beliefs can create a sense of security against the fear of death (intimacy) and can represent the prospect of a better life in the afterlife or the next life (identity). The belief that a higher power has control over things that we do not can help people cope with feeling alone. For a weary parent trying to survive economically and raise teens in a violent world, it may be very comforting to know that he or she can communicate with a higher power and petition for relief. Such a belief system may also provide emotional replenishment, direction, and hope.

At a time when adolescents are moving from being focused primarily on their families to being focused on their peer groups (Crockett & Petersen, 1993), a spiritual belief system may provide a sense of community among believers. It can even create a feeling of enfranchisement and belonging (e.g., the Christian concept of brothers and sisters in Christ, or the Hindu ashram). This can be a source of emotional support for adolescents who are members of groups that have been traditionally disenfranchised within the U.S. culture (e.g., African Americans, Latinos, newly arrived immigrants).

Many spiritual belief systems provide principles that govern relationships with others as well as personal behaviors. In some cases, these guiding principles are specifically delineated (e.g., the Judeo-Christian Ten Commandments, the Four Noble Truths of Buddhism, Hindu's *niyamas* and *yamas* [dos and don'ts]). Often these principles are internalized in the form of a personal moral code or method for decision making around important issues (e.g., sexuality). For example, some belief systems, including Christianity and many New Age philosophies, instruct followers to forgive those who have harmed them. Forgiveness is also promoted as a form of healing because of the belief that it allows the victim to release psychological wounds of the past.

Research on Spirituality in Adolescence

Given all these areas where spirituality appears to have an important role in adolescent development, has spirituality in adolescence been a topic of exploration in research? According to Thomas and Carver's review of the literature in 1990, little research has linked the concept of spirituality with adolescent development. What little research has been undertaken on adolescence and religion has tended to emphasize the social control aspect of religion as opposed to its socially supportive or motivational role (Jessor & Jessor, 1977). The premise behind social control theory is that the motivation for antisocial behavior is part of human nature, yet most people do not engage in antisocial behavior because of the restraining and controlling forces imposed on them.

Instead of viewing religious beliefs as a controlling force, Thomas and Carver (1990) propose that religion performs two functions: (a) It is a supporting and motivating force, and (b) it is a controlling and guiding force. Their review of the literature linking religious involvement and commitment to various dimensions of social competence shows that religious involvement and commitment are consistently related to increases in the abilities and skills required for adequate functioning in society and to decreases in the likelihood of participating in activities that are devalued in society. To the degree that controls and restrictions are balanced with emotional support and encouragement, Thomas and Carver propose that both religion and family can be combined effectively to assist the adolescent in achieving socially competent skills, attitudes, and behaviors.

In their own research on the role of the Mormon faith among adolescent boys, Thomas and Carver (1990) found that the mentor relationship provided by young adult men in Mormon youth groups assisted the boys they studied in making positive transitions from being family focused to being peer focused and in setting prosocial goals. These findings relate to our third theme concerning a code of behavior. It appears that because these youth were involved with the Mormon Church through a supportive relationship to their mentors and youth groups, their conformity to the institution's expectations was high.

Since the time Thomas and Carver undertook their review, other research has appeared that indicates others find the topic of spirituality in adolescence compelling. Bahr, Hawks, and Wang (1993) have developed a theoretical model concerning substance abuse and religion that is based on social control theory and social learning. They hypothesized that the intervening variable between bonds to religion and the abuse of substances is social learning through friends. In other words, friendships partially determine the strength of adolescents' conformity to religious tenets concerning drug use. The researchers tested their hypothesis by predicting that religious importance would be negatively related to adolescent substance abuse and that this relationship would be moderated by peer drug use. They collected their data through interviews with adolescents. They determined religious importance by asking each respondent how important it was to him or her to conform to specified religious tenets. Their analyses reveal that although the strongest predictor of adolescent drug use in their sample was peer drug use, this relationship did not moderate the impact of conformity to religious tenets concerning drug use. In fact, they found no relationship between religious conformity and drug use.

Unfortunately, Bahr et al.'s (1993) conceptual model of the relationship between religion and substance abuse addresses only our third theme (a code of behavior) and part of our second theme (a sense of identification). It does not address our first theme, which has to do with the existence of a higher power. Perhaps some youth use drug-related experiences as a substitute for what a relationship with a higher power might provide (e.g., comfort, feelings of compassion, inspiration, expansion of one's view of the universe). In other words, substance use and abuse may be a substitute for spirituality when an individual desires the intrinsic value of spirituality as a personal experience. This may be especially true if the adolescent is actively rejecting authority and institutions.

Research undertaken at the Search Institute in Minneapolis supports this idea that adolescents pursue religion for its intrinsic value as well as for more pragmatic reasons, as previously mentioned (see, e.g., Benson, Donahue, & Erickson, 1989; Benson, Williams, & Johnson, 1987; Williams, 1989). Benson et al. (1987) conducted a poll of adolescents in an attempt to determine the nature of their religious beliefs and attitudes. They found interesting gender and racial differences. Boys were more likely to have beliefs and attitudes about religion that viewed religion as a set of rules and guidelines that one followed to achieve particular rewards. Benson et al. refer to this as "extrinsic" religious belief. In contrast, girls were more likely to see religious belief as an end in itself, to find more of a sense of freedom in their beliefs, and to report a more intimate relationship to God and others through their faith. This type of belief the authors refer to as "intrinsic" religious belief. In terms of racial differences, blacks reported more intrinsic religious beliefs than whites. In their discussion of these results, Benson et al. mention that intrinsic beliefs, compared with extrinsic beliefs, are generally viewed as indicative of greater maturity on the part of the believer.

Another area of inquiry that researchers at the Search Institute have investigated is that of parents' influence on the values of their children. Williams (1989) concludes that when parents act in ways that are congruent with their stated beliefs and provide a warm, supportive atmosphere for their youth at home and in the church, youth are likely to develop values similar to those of their parents. Williams emphasizes that both *discussion* of values and *consistent demonstration* are necessary for this transfer to occur.

When Caplan, Choy, and Whitmore (1992) examined the question of why Indochinese refugees performed well academically in urban schools where other minority youth were failing, they uncovered two important correlates to the Buddhist faith. The first was that when youth valued the collective good over the individual good (a Buddhist principle the families interviewed identified), they achieved for the purpose of supporting their families in the future. Second, because of this family focus, families organized in a way that supported academic achievement: Parents relieved children of housework so that they could study every night, and older siblings provided tutoring for their younger siblings.

Although not explicitly tied to adolescence, research on achievement indicates that the identification of spiritual goals may be very important to the success of individuals who have those goals as a priority. Ford and Nichols (1991) have found that although different individuals may have the same intended life outcome (e.g., becoming a doctor), achievement of that outcome may serve very different goals for them. Ford and Nichols have created a taxonomy of goals made up of the following categories: entertainment, tranquillity, bodily sensations, physical well-being, exploration, understanding, intellectual creativity, positive self-evaluations, unity, transcendence, individuality, self-determination, superiority, resource acquisition, belongingness, social responsibility, equity, and resource provision. If an adolescent wants to become a doctor because of an expressed desire for material wealth (e.g., resource acquisition, superiority), that youth may not perform well in important schoolwork because of the changing economic climate, which indicates that doctors may have much lower incomes in the future. However, if the youth wants to be a doctor primarily to help others (e.g., social responsibility, resource provision) and is interested in the human body (e.g., understanding, intellectual creativity), he or she may be more able to achieve in the needed classes even when the economic world changes. According to Ford and Nichols, if individuals are aware of their personal goals, they can much more effectively utilize their resources for achievement. Because youth have multiple goals, individuals' awareness of their own goals can provide the motivation they need to stay on track when obstacles arise. Therefore, if adults assist youth in identifying their spiritual goals, youth may be better able to uphold their personal standards when they are challenged.

Another area of research not directly tied to spirituality in adolescence that applies here is that of the precursor components to violent behavior. Friedlander (1994) describes how individual factors set the stage for violence when specific situational factors are present. For example, a youth may be an impulsive person who has been exposed to many models of violent behavior in his or her family (individual factors), but this youth will not be violent until certain situational factors are present, such as the availability of a weapon, some type of provocation, or disinhibition through substance use. According to Friedlander, our country is full of situational factors that promote violence (e.g., advertisements specialize in disinhibiting people to buy products by provoking them to think they need more than they currently have). Perhaps the intrinsic quality of religious beliefs could change individual factors and reduce vulnerability to such situational factors as messages in the media.

This possibility is supported by Langer's (1987) work on mindfulness and her research on premature cognitive commitments. Premature cognitive commitments occur when people respond to new situations based on decisions made in the past, *without* taking into consideration all the available pertinent information. For example, if a youth says something bad about another's mother, the insulted youth may strike back to save face without taking into consideration what his mother would really want him to do. Langer suggests that mindfulness—that is, being open to multiple perspectives and to all available data—can prevent such reactions. Her definition of mindfulness describes a state similar to many Eastern religious spiritual states in which the individual seeks oneness with all (e.g., Taoism, Buddhism). Perhaps a person's being mindful could prevent his or her use of violence through an acknowledgment of interconnectedness with all other beings.

Although Coles's (1990) qualitative research on spirituality has focused on children, his findings have significant implications for adolescence because adolescents are more mature than children. Coles discusses how the children he interviewed repeatedly and spontaneously brought up spiritual issues; the topic apparently had great intrinsic value to them. In the following example, in which he quotes an 8-year-old black girl's description of a call to her higher power, Coles demonstrates how a child's faith in God and her response to a larger question in life led to a code of behavior for herself and another:

> I was all alone and those [segregationist] people were screaming, and suddenly I saw God smiling and I smiled. . . . A woman was standing there [near the school door], and she shouted at me "Hey you little nigger, what you smiling at?" I looked right at her face and I said, "At God." Then she looked up at the sky, and then she looked at me, and she didn't call me any more names. (pp. 19-20)

Barbarin (1993) discusses similar ways in which rich inner lives have supported black youth and family in this country. He describes how a religious upbringing can promote resilient characteristics:

> Religiosity might influence socialization styles toward firmer control, higher maturity demands, and greater acceptance of personal responsibility for one's behavior. . . . For example, parents who are religious might teach children to cope with emotional arousal by stoically accepting the situation as it is or reach out to others (e.g., a Supreme Being) for help or through prayer. (p. 489)

Clearly, such responses to stress are desirable for youth in the United States today.

Opportunities for Spiritual Development
That Adults Can Provide

The types of opportunities for spiritual development that adults can provide for adolescents take many forms. They can occur in traditional religious settings, community service settings, rites of passage, outdoor adventure programs, and the arts. In order to illustrate the range of possibilities, we present below brief descriptions of some of them.

Traditional settings such as churches, synagogues, and mosques can expand their services to help meet the needs of today's youth. For example, Rubin, Billingsley, and Caldwell (1994) found that less than a third of black churches offer programs for youth. They suggest that in addition to currently popular programs, such as those promoting support, sports, and substance abuse counseling, churches ought to provide (a) programs for pregnant adolescents and adolescent fathers (and potential fathers) in prenatal care and parenting; (b) programs related to parenting, sexuality, and delinquency; (c) programs that include parents in substance abuse prevention; and (d) programs that create educational and vocational opportunities for black adolescents. Other traditional settings could also purposefully open their doors to youth with such programs.

More nontraditional settings may be able to attract youth who are not interested in the structure of traditional institutions by offering structured rites-of-passage programs, such as that described by Blumenkrantz and Gavazzi (1993). These authors detail a program that is designed to link youth to their community and the community to its youth by providing developmental milestones. In their three-phase program, which spans the years from middle school to high school, youth engage in a 21-hour intervention based on physical and cognitive challenges, participate with adults in community-based activities, and provide service to the community, with a focus on working with children. Each phase is concluded with a specific communitywide ceremony.

Other structured rites-of-passage programs ought to be pursued as well, especially because many youth create their own rites of passage that may not teach the values and knowledge of the adult culture. In an essay titled "The Uninitiated," family therapist Robert Taibbi (1991) describes how youth take dangerous risks in an effort to provide themselves with challenges. Activities such as excessive drinking can symbolize a passage to adulthood that makes a boy "feel like a man." Taibbi argues that U.S. society does not have a place for adolescents: "They can consume, but not produce; they can be educated, but not apply the education; they have increasing independence, but often no greater responsibilities than getting their homework done and keeping their rooms clean" (p. 33). If we can assist them in finding a meaningful place in our culture, youth otherwise labeled as rebellious may amaze us.

One method that may attract "thrill-seeking" youth is to offer outdoor adventure (e.g., rock climbing, ropes courses, backpacking). In addition to providing risks and challenges that are positive, outdoor adventure can provide a sense of humility in the face of the awesomeness of nature or what one might call a "cosmic perspective." Many outdoor programs also provide opportunities for participants to make group decisions, to learn about safety, to cooperate with new people, and to concentrate completely on a task (K. Jones, personal communication, November 1993). Therefore, although outdoor adventure may attract youth because of its challenging nature, the outcomes of a successful program may include increased commitment to others, increased autonomy, and awareness of new dimensions concerning the big questions in life—all of which contribute to individual spiritual belief systems.

Music, art, drama, writing, and other creative endeavors all offer ways for youth to tap into their own imaginations, the source of which is often their relationship to a higher power. Creative and experiential activities promote the use of the right brain (the intuitive side) in concert with the left brain (the rational side) (Ferguson, 1980). Moreover, when such activities are structured specifically to promote creative problem solving, they can provide a vision of the future, pleasure, meaningful involvement, a sense of community, standards that are individualized, a sense of freedom, and a sense of identity. This type of learning can occur only when what is learned in the creative setting is transferred to a new setting, such as to problems in the individual's neighborhood. Such transfer requires specific training in how to use a specific skill learned in one area of life in another area of life (Danish, Petispas, & Hale, 1993). The ability to transfer skills is incredibly important, given the changing nature of the world in which youth are developing. Creative activities may facilitate adaptive coping in ways that other educational activities cannot: "The present educational paradigm assumes that the only questions worth asking are those for which we already have the answers. Where, then, can one learn to live with the uncertainties of the real world?" (Ray Gottlieb, quoted in Ferguson, 1980, p. 302). Therefore, it is important that we continue to offer classes in art and music in our school systems; these are often the only places where youth are encouraged to use right-brain thinking. The implications for future violence of not promoting the use of young people's creative talents are vast, in terms of both the extrinsic and intrinsic values of spirituality.

Closing Comments

We cannot ignore the criticisms that have been leveled at religion, such as that it contributes to negative self-esteem (e.g., being born a "sinner"), that it instills a sense of spiritual superiority, and that it encourages blind, unquestioning loyalty. In addition, human history is full of examples of religious intolerance that have resulted in wars and ongoing oppression. In fact, even though the U.S. doctrine of separation of church and state was designed to prevent such intolerance, it may have contributed to a general avoidance of dialogue around these issues. In addition, the recent politicization of religion has contributed to a climate of intolerance that may make adolescent service providers even more hesitant to include a spiritual perspective on social issues. During a keynote speech in Houston, Texas, in November 1994, Marian Wright Edelman said, "We mustn't be afraid to address morality with our children. They [referring to the 'religious right'] don't own morality." In other words, although members of the "religious right" have been willing to discuss their views, this willingness does not translate into sole ownership of ethics and spirituality. The fact that both sides of ethical issues call to a higher truth is an example of an opportunity for a dialectic to occur between the two sides. Ideally, a critical mass could be brought to a higher level of understanding about such issues. Such an activity is in line with the belief of the Plains Indians of North America concerning the dualistic nature of humans. The message of the following parable about the forked branches of a tree may be applied to humans: "If One Half tries to split itself from the Other Half, the Tree will become crippled or die. . . . Rather than taking this barren way, we must tie together the paradoxes of our Twin Nature with the things of the One Universe" (Ferguson, 1980, p. 308).

We would like to close with two propositions. First, current programming designed to prevent youth violence and/or to promote social competence must allow and support a dialectic in which youth can critically examine and explore their belief systems. Inadvertently, we may have created a situation in which we shy away from any discussion of values and higher powers, communicating instead a neutrality of values and a belief that we are accountable only to our own senses of right and wrong. By avoiding dialogue in this area, we are missing out on an opportunity to move adolescents toward their true potential. Second, we must provide adolescents with opportunities to develop their personal spiritual belief systems and supportive relationships with others who have similar beliefs. Such opportunities for spiritual development must be included in both academic and applied efforts to prevent violence and promote positive outcomes in youth.

Note

1. In this chapter, we use the terms *spiritual belief system* and *religion* interchangeably.

References

Bahr, S., Hawks, R., & Wang, G. (1993). Family and religious influences on adolescent substance abuse. *Youth & Society, 24,* 443-465.

Barbarin, O. (1993). Coping and resilience: Exploring the inner lives of African American children. *Journal of Black Psychology, 19,* 478-492.

Benson, P., Donahue, M., & Erickson, J. (1989). Adolescence and religion: A review of the literature from 1970 to 1986. *Research in the Social Scientific Study of Religion, 1,* 153-181.

Benson, P., Williams, D., & Johnson, A. (1987). *The quicksilver years: The hopes and fears of early adolescence.* San Francisco: Harper & Row.

Bernard, B. (1991). *Fostering resiliency in kids: Protective factors in the family, school, and community.* Portland, OR: Northwest Regional Educational Laboratory.

Blumenkrantz, D., & Gavazzi, S. (1993). Guiding transitional events for children and adolescents through a modern day rite of passage. *Journal of Primary Prevention, 13,* 199-212.

Botvin, G., & Tortu, S. (1988). Preventing adolescent substance abuse through life skills training. In R. H. Price, E. L. Cowen, R. P. Lorion, & J. Ramos-McKay

(Eds.), *14 ounces of prevention: A casebook for practitioners* (pp. 98-110). Washington, DC: American Psychological Association.

Bronfenbrenner, U. (1974). Developmental research, public policy, and the ecology of childhood. *Child Development, 45,* 1-5.

Caplan, N., Choy, M., & Whitmore, J. (1992, February). Indochinese refugee families and academic achievement. *Scientific American,* pp. 36-41.

Coles, R. (1990). *The spiritual life of children.* Boston: Houghton Mifflin.

Cox, G. (1986). *The ways of peace.* New York: Paulist Press.

Crockett, L., & Petersen, A. (1993). Adolescent development: Health risks and opportunities for health promotion. In S. Millstein, A. Petersen, & E. Nightingale (Eds.), *Promoting the health of adolescents* (pp. 13-37). New York: Oxford University Press.

Danish, S., Mash, M., Howard, C., Curl, S., Meyer, A., Owens, S., & Kendall, K. (1992). *Going for the Goal leader manual.* Richmond, VA: Virginia Commonwealth University, Life Skills Center.

Danish, S., Petispas, A., & Hale, B. (1990). Sport as a context for developing competence. In T. P. Gullotta, G. R. Adams, & R. Montemayor (Eds.), *Developing social competency in adolescence* (pp. 169-194). Newbury Park, CA: Sage.

Danish, S., Petispas, A., & Hale, B. (1993). Life development intervention for athletes: Life skills through sports. *Counseling Psychologist, 21,* 352-385.

Dugan, T., & Coles, R. (Eds.). (1989). *The child in our times.* New York: Brunner/Mazel.

Durant, W. (1961). *The story of philosophy.* New York: Washington Square.

Erikson, E. (1968). *Identity: Youth and crisis.* New York: W. W. Norton.

Ferguson, M. (1980). *The Aquarian conspiracy.* Los Angeles: J. P. Tarcher.

Flay, B., Koepke, D., Thomson, S., Santi, S., Best, J., & Brown, K. (1989). Six-year follow-up of the first Waterloo school smoking prevention trial. *American Journal of Public Health, 79,* 1371-1376.

Ford, M., & Nichols, C. (1991). Using goal assessments to identify motivational patterns and facilitate behavioral regulation and achievement. *Advances in Motivation and Achievement, 7,* 51-84.

Friedlander, B. (1994). Community violence, children's development, and mass media: In pursuit of new insights, new goals, and new strategies. *Psychiatry, 56,* 66-81.

Haan, N. (1989). Coping with moral conflict as resiliency. In T. Dugan & R. Coles (Eds.), *The child in our times* (pp. 23-44). New York: Brunner/Mazel.

Harder, C. (1990). *The winner's seminar: A leadership experience for youth.* Cedar Rapids, IA: Carole Harder & Company.

Hawkins, J. (1990). *Communities that care: A community training system.* Seattle, WA: DRP.

Hawkins, J., Lishner, D., Jenson, J., & Catalano, R. (1987). Delinquents and drugs: What the evidence suggests about prevention and treatment programming. In B. Brown & A. Mills (Eds.), *Youth at high risk for substance abuse* (NIDA Publication No. ADM 87-1537). Washington, DC: Government Printing Office.

Hill, J. (1983). Early adolescence: A framework. *Journal of Early Adolescence, 3,* 1-21.

Jessor, R., & Jessor, S. (1977). *Problem behavior and psychosocial development: A longitudinal study of youth.* New York: Academic Press.

Johnson, C., Pentz, M., Weber, J., Dwyer, J., Baer, N., MacKinnon, D., & Hansen, W. (1990). Relative effectiveness of comprehensive community programming for drug abuse prevention with high-risk and low-risk adolescents. *Journal of Consulting and Clinical Psychology, 58,* 447-456.

Keating, D. (1990). Adolescent thinking. In S. Feldman & G. Elliot (Eds.), *At the threshold: The developing adolescent* (pp. 54-89). Cambridge, MA: Harvard University Press.

Kohlberg, L. (1976). Moral stages and moralization: The cognitive-development approach. In T. Lickona (Ed.), *Moral development and behavior.* New York: Holt, Rinehart & Winston.

Langer, E. (1987). *Mindfulness.* Reading, MA: Addison Wesley.

Meyer, A. (1994). Minimization of substance use: What can be said at this point? In T. P. Gullotta, G. R. Adams, & R. Montemayor (Eds.), *Substance misuse in adolescence* (pp. 201-232). Thousand Oaks, CA: Sage.

Perry, C., & Jessor, R. (1985). The concept of health promotion and the prevention of drug abuse. *Health Education Quarterly, 12,* 169-184.

Petersen, A., & Ebata, A. (1986, March). *Effects of normative and non-normative changes on early adolescent development.* Paper presented at the biennial meeting of the Society for Research on Adolescence, Madison, WI.

Rubin, R., Billingsley, A., & Caldwell, C. (1994). The role of the black church in working with black adolescents. *Adolescence, 29,* 251-266.

Taibbi, R. (1991). The uninitiated. *Family Therapy Networker, 14*(4), 30-35.

Task Force on Education of Young Adolescents. (1989). *Turning points: Preparing American youth for the 21st century.* New York: Carnegie Corporation.

Thomas, D., & Carver, C. (1990). Religion and adolescent social competence. In T. P. Gullotta, G. R. Adams, & R. Montemayor (Eds.), *Developing social competency in adolescence* (pp. 195-219). Newbury Park, CA: Sage.

Williams, D. (1989). Religion in adolescence: Dying, dormant, or developing? *Source, 5*(4), 1-3.

• CHAPTER 7 •

Understanding the Media's Influence on the Development of Antisocial and Prosocial Behavior

STEVEN J. DANISH

THOMAS R. DONOHUE

In this chapter, we will discuss the role the media play in contributing to incidents of viewer violence and antisocial acts as well as their contribution to the development of prosocial behavior and life skills. Traditionally, the media are viewed as teachers of violence, and there have been numerous calls for a ban on violence on television and in the movies. Interestingly enough, such a ban in the reporting of everyday community and neighborhood violence by television has not been lobbied for nearly as vigorously. Moreover, the almost relentless focus on the banning of violence allows media executives to ignore or overlook the decrease in the number of hours per week that the media, especially the three major television networks, allocate to prosocial and educational programming for children. The decrease in such positive programming has gone from more than 11 hours per week in 1980 to less than 2 hours per week in 1990 (U.S. Senate, Subcommittee on Telecommunications and Finance, 1994).

AUTHORS' NOTE: We would like to thank Carole Danish, Aleta Meyer, Natalie Smith, and Everett Worthington for their helpful suggestions; Tom Gullotta for providing us the freedom to pursue a different path in preparing this chapter; and Valerie Nellen for her valuable comments.

133

We have chosen to look at both the positive and the negative influences of the media because we believe the media constitute educational tools whose value has heretofore been overshadowed. The fact that the average adolescent has watched 16,000 hours of television by age 14 (Murray, 1980) underscores the urgent need to examine television's influence.

We begin the chapter with a discussion of how the concept of health-compromising and health-enhancing behaviors (Perry & Jessor, 1985) relates to life-span development. We specifically consider the concept of life skills (Danish, 1994; Danish, Nellen, & Owens, in press) and how these skills are critical to healthy development. Second, we present a historical perspective of the relationship between societal violence (aggression) and the media. Within this discussion we examine some of the research models and methods used in studying this relationship as well as some of the results of such studies. Third, we explore the prosocial impact of the media and provide several concrete examples of how the media can teach prosocial behavior and life skills. Fourth, and finally, we present a model of the media as a resource and discuss the role that parents and teachers can and should play in using this resource productively.

Developing a Framework for Studying the Effects of the Media

Our society has become increasingly focused on preventing problems before they occur rather than treating them after they arise. Although such an approach is commendable, one consequence is the development of prevention programs that have a "Just say no" orientation, such as DARE. Recent research suggests that this type of negative focus in programs tends to limit their effectiveness (Keefe, 1994). Although it is important for youth to know what not to do, focusing only on the negative does not allow them to reach their full potential. To be successful in life it is not enough to know what to avoid; one must also know how to succeed. Perhaps William Raspberry, writer for the *Washington Post,* has said it best: "Too many young people—including some with the potential to elevate themselves, to rescue their families or to change the world—allow themselves to be dragged down by the curse of low expectations."[1]

Table 7.1 Behavioral and Personality Attributes

	Health-Compromising Behaviors	Health-Enhancing Behaviors
Behavioral attributes	smoking fighting	regular exercise goal setting
Personality attributes	hopelessness low self-esteem	optimism high self-esteem

Distinguishing Prevention From Promotion

Not only is there an important distinction between prevention and treatment, there is an equally important difference between the prevention of problem behaviors, such as violence, and the promotion or enhancement of positive behaviors, such as involvement in community activities. For example, Perry and Jessor (1985) describe prevention as efforts aimed at *conserving* health, whereas promotion is aimed at *enhancing* health. They identify four domains of health: physical, psychological, social, and personal. Within each of these domains, individuals may engage in either *health-compromising behaviors,* behaviors that threaten well-being, or *health-enhancing behaviors,* behaviors that promote well-being. Perry and Jessor's strategy for health promotion is to create environments that teach and encourage health-enhancing behaviors and personality attributes, and to weaken supports for health-compromising behaviors and personality attributes. Table 7.1 gives examples of both types of behavioral and personality attributes.

By focusing on the creation of health-enhancing behaviors, personality attributes, and environments, Perry and Jessor seek to buffer youth against the impact of what many might consider "normative" risk-taking behaviors. In other words, instead of assuming that individuals can be taught to eliminate undesirable or unhealthy behaviors completely, they acknowledge that many risk-taking behaviors are normative and suggest that it is necessary to optimize the chances that engaging in these behaviors will not place youth in any type of long-term danger (Meyer, 1994).

Inherent in the development of healthy lifestyle behaviors is the necessity of teaching youth new skills for living and providing opportunities for them to explore, develop, and practice these skills. We call these new skills *life skills* (Danish, 1994).

Understanding Life Skills

Life skills are those skills that enable us to succeed in the environments in which we live. Life skills are both behavioral (e.g., skills for effective communication with peers and adults) and cognitive (e.g., skills for effective decision making). Some of the environments in which we live are in families, schools, workplaces, neighborhoods, and communities. Most individuals must succeed in more than one environment. As a person becomes older, the number of environments in which he or she must be successful increases. For example, a young child need only succeed within the family; an adolescent must succeed within the family, at school, and in the neighborhood; an adult needs to succeed in the family, the workplace, the neighborhood, and the community. Environments will vary from individual to individual, and so the definition of what it means to succeed will differ across individuals, as well as across environments.

Individuals in the same environment are likely to be dissimilar from each other as a result of the life skills they have already mastered, their other resources, and their opportunities, real or perceived (Danish, 1994). For this reason, programs designed to teach life skills must be sensitive to developmental, environmental, and individual differences as well as the possibility that individuals of different ages, ethnic and/or racial groups, and economic status may need different life skills.

Although it is necessary to be sensitive to differences, it is also important to recognize that individuals can often effectively apply life skills learned in one environment to other environments as appropriate. Examples of life skills that are transferable include leadership skills learned in sports (e.g., being willing to assume responsibility for deciding what offensive or defensive strategy to implement) that are applicable at home, school, or the workplace (e.g., planning a school-related project) and skills learned in the home or at work (e.g., listening to, and learning from, feedback from a parent or employer) that can be used to enhance academic performance (e.g., seeking help from a teacher in an area in which one is having trouble). In sum, individuals can use transferable life skills to help them reach their goals in many different situations they encounter, now and in the future. In a later section of this chapter, we discuss how life skills can be learned through the media.

Violence and the Media: A Historical Perspective

Researchers and policymakers have been interested in media effects on human behavior since the 1930s. The concern began on a grand scale in Germany during the ascendancy of National Socialism. Among the early excesses witnessed in Nazi Germany was the deliberate manipulation of the media—radio, movies, and the press—to create a climate that vilified and blamed the Jews for Germany's societal ills. Moreover, the media have been credited with nurturing a national hubris that led to war and the destruction of Germany. During the same time in the United States, mass media were emerging as purveyors of the icons of popular culture. Radio had come into its own as a national medium, movie attendance increased exponentially each year, and magazines and pulp fiction sensationalized murders, kidnappings, and violence. Producers of media content quickly learned that violent and antisocial content titillated people and was the most popular among the genres. Shortly thereafter, societal problems such as delinquency among youth and aggressive behavior in general were somehow linked to violent media exposure. In particular, many believed that viewing gangster films and other violent movies led to juvenile delinquency among teenage boys. These concerns led the Payne Fund to underwrite the first attempts to establish a link between media violence and aggressive behavior (Charters, 1933).

The Payne Fund studies, conducted by researchers at Ohio State University, involved a series of surveys designed to illuminate the relationship between media-portrayed violence and antisocial behavior among adolescents (Charters, 1933). Taken as a whole, these studies were able to establish only moderate correlations between mediated violence and aggressive behavior in adolescents.

The violence and media issue was dropped during World War II and immediately thereafter, as researchers who studied the effects of the media turned their attention to the study of the media's ability to change attitudes through propaganda. Many concentrated on motivational research—a curious blend of analytic psychology and hidden or subliminal messages in television and magazine advertising. How consumers could achieve "self-actualization" through the consumption of goods and services was the main thrust of media effects research.

By the late 1950s, television viewing was so common that even the most casual observer could see how pervasive television was becoming in American family life. Movie attendance dropped dramatically as people shifted from being habitual moviegoers to being habitual television watchers. The average viewer was soon logging nearly 3 hours per day in front of the television set. The average television set was turned on for 7 hours a day. By the 1960s, it was estimated that the average child was spending more time in a week watching television than doing anything else but sleeping (Dominick, 1994).

It was during the 1960s that serious, well-funded research on the relationship between media-portrayed violence and antisocial behavior began. Several factors led to this increased concern regarding the role of television in shaping America's youth. First, baby boomers were becoming teenagers, and they appeared to be everywhere—especially on television. Consequently, their activities were more apparent than those of teenagers in the past; although the numbers of antisocial acts committed by adolescents in this period seemed disproportionately larger than in previous generations, the actual proportion of these acts in relation to the adolescent population remained constant. Second, network programmers' instincts were reinforced by extensive research that showed that violence sells. Not surprisingly, programs with violence as an integral part of the plots proliferated. Coincidentally, the movie industry began to take its cue from television and began to offer even more spectacular violence than could be shown on television in an attempt to revive interest in moviegoing. Third, other agents of socialization (parents, schools, churches) were changing rapidly and were exerting less influence on young people than they had during previous generations. Concomitant and perhaps related to these changes was that young people were spending more time with television and with their peers, who were also watching television, than with the traditional agents of socialization. Fourth, the media have traditionally been a convenient scapegoat when causes have been sought for real or perceived social ills. A typical reaction has been, "If we take the violence out of the media, crime will diminish significantly." In other words, it has been far easier to blame the media than to examine the root causes for problems, because the inherent complexity of social and psychological issues and problems relegates simple solutions to absurdity.

During the 1960s, various government agencies began to allocate large sums of money for the study of the relationship between media violence and antisocial behavior among children and adolescents (Murray, 1980). As the decade grew increasingly violent—with much of the violence covered in excruciating detail by television and the print media—more money was made available for the study of violence and its causes. Foundations and other philanthropic organizations also began to support the hundreds of laboratory experiments, field studies, and content analyses that were emerging. Congress and other government bodies began to hold regular, well-publicized hearings; media watchdog groups sprang to life, and moribund organizations began to use media violence as a battle cry to revive members' interest and contributions. During the past 30 years, more than two dozen major investigations and hearings have been held and hundreds of conferences organized during which thousands of scholarly papers have been presented on the topic of the role of media violence in aggressive behavior. Hundreds of millions of dollars have been spent in more than 35 years of serious and ambitious research, and we are no closer to a definitive answer than we were 20 years ago. The fact remains that we are still unable to specify which media acts or portrayals of violence will trigger which violent behaviors, and under what conditions.

Frustration has emerged as the collective emotion, as legislators, policymakers, and parents attempt to devise cogent strategies for restricting media violence and limiting its effects. Underlying the frustration is the certainty held by many that media violence is responsible in some significant way for the violence in U.S. society, and there is a sense of impotence on the part of the researchers who cannot "prove it."

Most recently, researchers have tried to use meta-analysis to attempt to connect television violence and aggression (Comstock & Paik, 1990; Hearold, 1986; Rosenthal, 1986). Meta-analysis is a method in which researchers gather the findings from numerous studies in order to see the effects of a certain phenomenon. Wilcox (1994), in summarizing the meta-analyses of media violence studies, concludes that there are four kinds of effects from television violence: "copycat" violence, the removal of inhibitions concerning aggression, desensitization toward the effects of violence, and increased or exaggerated fear of violence.

Meta-analysis has been criticized on several accounts. The primary concern with this methodology is that when researchers gather the data from previous studies, they often do not consider the quality of those studies. It is as if all the studies examined are of equal quality and value regardless of differences in their designs and measures. Like the research described above, the most recent studies using meta-analysis have not seemed to be able to "prove" the existence of a relationship between media violence and societal aggression. Perhaps Freedman (1986) states the problem most succinctly:

> Laboratory findings must be confirmed in natural settings and this has not occurred. If the field studies had produced strong and consistent effects, if the longitudinal studies had shown a cumulative effect of television viewing such that the correlations between it and aggression increased with age, or if the cross-lagged correlations with all their faults consistently showed that the correlation between early television viewing and later aggression was significantly stronger than the relationship between early television viewing and early aggression, there would be a strong argument for the causal hypothesis. (p. 377)

Because none of these relationships has been found, frustration among policymakers, parents, and researchers continues unabated.

In the next section, we examine the principal elements in the violence debate and the research that has been used to bolster strategic initiatives for limiting media violence.

Models and Methods for Studying Media Effects

Much of the lack of progress in attempting to determine media effects on behavior has been based on the assumption that effects reside in the content. Specifically, most people assume that, by definition, erotic media content is sexually arousing, humorous content is funny, depictions of personal tragedy will make people sad, and violent content will make people more aggressive. Consequently, when empirical observations fail resoundingly to confirm the research hypothesis that violent video causes aggressive behavior in subjects, readers of the research focus on design faults and statistical analyses as the reason for equivocal results and cautious conclusions.

On the other hand, some researchers have adopted an interactive model of media effects. Anderson and Meyer (1988) contend that it is inconceivable that all viewers will react to a content genre in fundamentally the same way, and that what the individual brings to the viewing experience is as important in predicting effects as the predominant theme of the content. In an interactive model, content characteristics and cognitive states are used to predict behavioral outcomes. In cognitive structure, it is generally content and maturational state that are used to predict system outcomes.

There are three sets of measures in an interactive model: a measure of exposure to a content genre, a measure of the interacting conditions or influences, and a behavioral outcome measure. For example, in an interactive model, researchers would examine a violent scene for specific acts of violence; examine the aggressive behavioral history of the subject, including his or her present cognitive state; and provide an opportunity for the individual to act aggressively. A mediating condition would be a person who is predisposed to act violently ("a bomb waiting to explode"), who has, in his or her mind, motive and means but is waiting for an opportunity. Media can provide that opportunity by portraying a specific crime in a specific set of circumstances (Anderson & Meyer, 1988).

A tragic example of this "time-bomb" phenomenon happened in the 1970s. Several male adolescents were walking down a street in a high-crime section of Boston when they encountered a young woman carrying a gas can she had borrowed to put fuel in the empty tank of her car. The young men accosted her and eventually doused her with gasoline and set her on fire. They were apprehended a short time later and, after interrogation, the investigating officers speculated that there was a link between the crime and the teenagers' viewing of a Burt Reynolds movie, *Fuzz*, in which teenagers were "disposing" of winos found sleeping in the streets by dousing them with gasoline and setting them on fire.

The police suspected that the teenagers had modeled what they had seen on television. In the police investigators' minds, the teenagers had motive—their victim was a middle-class white woman of means;

opportunity was provided by the unusual circumstances; and the mediating condition was the teenagers' intention or inclination to cause harm to a helpless person. This is what Wilcox (1994) refers to as copycat violence. Would these young men have hurt this woman had they not seen the Bert Reynolds movie? Most likely. No doubt, without exposure to the film, they would have opted for another form of torture and murder. Were they looking for a means to express their rage? The adolescents were clearly predisposed to violence. Similar environmental cues in the movie and real life simply defined the type of violence. Had the woman encountered other young men from the same neighborhood who saw the same movie, the outcome may have been far different. It is not inconceivable, for instance, that assistance could have been offered to the victim instead of death.

With this interactive model as a foundation, we propose to analyze the methods and results of violence research conducted during the past 30 years.

Experimental Methods in Violence Research

If a connection is to be made between violence in the media and violent behavior on the part of viewers, it must be based on experimental studies. Experiments are the most powerful tool because causal inferences can be drawn from the results. The suspected agent of effect can be isolated, manipulated, and compared with control group findings, with the effect demonstrated or presumed to be a direct and causal relationship.

Typically, the variables in media violence research have been (a) the different types of content—violent or nonviolent, arousing or not; (b) the state of mind of the subject—frustrated, angry, aroused, or not; (c) the independent variables of sex, education, age, level of maturity, conditions existing at the time of exposure to the content, and whether the content is viewed alone or with someone else; and (d) dependent variables such as willingness to shock or "hurt" a confederate, the level of aggressiveness exhibited during play, and paper-and-pencil evaluations of confederates. A control group is used for the purpose of providing a comparison of conditions and variables in which only the content of the viewing situation is different for the experimental and control groups.

One of the criticisms of violence research is that within the context of the experiment, social norms are reversed, so that the subjects believe they are actually helping a confederate by shocking or ostensibly "hurting" him or her (Berkowitz & Geen, 1966; Berkowitz & Rawlings, 1963). For example, in a preponderance of the media violence experiments, subjects have been first frustrated or insulted by the confederate; exposed to a violent or exciting, but nonviolent, film clip; and then asked to engage in a "learning" exercise in which they have been instructed to deliver shocks to the confederate when he or she makes a mistake in a rote memory task. Subjects have been told that by delivering shocks, they are actually helping the confederate to remember more accurately. Thus, the normal sanction against aggression has been removed and redefined as a prosocial action. The criticism that social norms have been redefined during such experiments cannot be dismissed easily if the research seeks to establish a causal link between media violence and aggressive or violent behavior. When individuals commit acts of violence, most are aware that their behavior is wrong and weigh existing social norms and possible consequences before engaging in the acts. By removing taboos against violence and redefining aggressive acts as "helping," researchers have introduced an unreality into the process.

Despite this design weakness, the preponderance of studies have demonstrated that viewing violent content prior to the "learning exercise" produces statistically significantly more shocks or aggression than does viewing exciting but nonviolent content. If there were no link between viewing violence and willingness to engage in aggression, the control group would behave as aggressively as the experimental group.

In the other major type of violence experiment, researchers have demonstrated the modeling properties television and film possess for young children. The earliest studies by Bandura, Ross, and Ross (1963a) used young children who viewed a live or filmed adult, a filmed peer, or an animated character pummeling a bobo doll to determine the conditions under which children were most likely to imitate what they saw. In the prototypical experiment, a child would be placed in a room with toys and told to play as he or she wished. The experimenter would then frustrate the child by taking the chosen toy from the child. Next, the child would be led to a viewing room, where he or she would view someone or something beating up a bobo doll in specific ways. The child would then be taken back to the playroom, where a bobo doll had been added to the previous inventory of toys. The extent to which the child imitated the behaviors he or she had seen constituted the dependent variables. Variations of the experiment included showing the model being rewarded, punished, or neither rewarded nor punished for the aggressive behavior and whether there was atrophy of the learned behavior over time. The control group's regimen contained all the elements save the model beating on bobo. Comparisons included the extent to which bobo was beaten by the experimental and control groups. The most significant finding of these experiments was that the *ability* to model the mediated aggression did not atrophy over time. In other words, once learned, a behavior became a semipermanent fixture in the child's repertoire of behaviors (Bandura, Ross, & Ross, 1963b).

A similar criticism of norm redefinition that surfaced in analyses of the heuristic value of the violence experiments can be applied to the modeling experiments as well. Critics charge that bobo dolls are designed to be kicked, hit, and knocked about. Furthermore, they contend that children understand that by hitting a bobo doll they are not really engaging in acts of aggression but are simply taking advantage of the unique properties of the toy. The question is not whether children can learn behaviors from watching TV or films (or real people in their own environments); they can, and do. The issue with regard to these experiments is how to label accurately the behaviors being studied. For example, Bandura et al. (1963b) reported no statistically significant correlation between children's displayed aggression in the experimental setting and the aggressiveness ratings of the children's preschool teachers based on actual aggressive behavior in the real-life school setting. One could then conclude that the modeled behaviors being measured were not equivalent to "aggression" or "violence."

The historic value of the modeling experiments was that they demonstrated that the media are extremely viable agents from which behaviors can and will be learned. They established a causal link between the viewing of violent television and film content and the willingness to engage in behaviors that could be defined as aggressive under conditions in which the subject had been frustrated. Those findings and conclusions were a refutation of the ancient Greek theory adopted by some violence researchers who believed that viewing mediated violence was cathartic, such that frustration and anger could be purged vicariously, thus obviating the need to act aggressively (Feshbach & Singer, 1971).

However, as noted earlier, these modeling studies failed to identify under what conditions children and others use the aggressive behaviors they have learned from the media. Although it is quite clear that behaviors can be learned vicariously, the state of mind that intersects with conditions of viewing that lead to circumstances of response cannot be specified with much predictive power.

Survey Methods in Violence Research

The use of surveys in media research began in the 1930s as a means of determining what people were listening to on the radio (Dominick, 1994). The research questions focused on the demographic characteristics of the people listening, their listening habits, and their preferences. The current principal uses of survey research are to gather information on people's consumption habits and to solicit opinions, attitudes, and beliefs about various media products and services. Surveys differ from experiments in that they try to determine the presence or absence of variables but do not manipulate that presence or absence.

There are several assumptions inherent in media survey research that deserve attention. First, it is assumed that viewers can and will accurately recall past behaviors and patterns such as what they watched last week and how much they typically watch certain programs. Second, survey research assumes that consumers are sufficiently astute to be able to analyze their preferences. For example, a question about why an individual likes the television program *Cheers* assumes that the viewer has thought about the dynamic among the characters that makes the program enjoyable. Third, survey research assumes not only that viewers understand their tastes and preferences, but that they can articulate these preferences in some closed-ended, measurable way. In other words, survey research assumes that instruments such as Likert scales or semantic differentials can be used to make fairly precise differentiations in viewers' attitudes and opinions. Fourth, and finally, survey research assumes that a sample of all viewers can be selected that is representative of the entire population. A survey serves as a "snapshot" of the conditions that exist for the sample studied at the time the survey is conducted. Like a photograph, the data collected necessarily exclude considerable information, and they are dated the moment they are produced.

The strengths of properly executed survey research are that the snapshot is generalizable to a larger population and that conclusions can be made regarding the topic—in this case, media consumption behaviors. Perhaps the major criticism of the survey methodology is that it reveals very little about *why* viewers feel as they do, *why* they behave in certain ways, and *how* their feelings came about. The cause-and-effect inferences that may be drawn from experimental research methods are nonexistent in survey research. For example, when a violent movie or television series becomes a hit, the producers are not certain what caused its popularity. It could be the stars, the clever scripts, the violence, or an interaction of all the elements. Although follow-up surveys could likely reveal the elements of the movie or show that made it work for the audience, surveys would be unlikely to uncover how the elements interacted to produce a successful vehicle.

Survey research is inherently incapable of measuring behaviors that occur as a result of a series of complex, interrelated, and underlying processes that are operative over extended periods of time. Survey research is static and cannot capture "process." Surveys repeated with the same panel of participants attempt to measure changes over time, but do not purport to tap complex underlying processes. Violent or antisocial behaviors are ordinarily the products of complex underlying processes, manifesting themselves when a host of variables come together. Identifying the underlying processes that lead to aggression is incredibly difficult; it is most certainly beyond the reach of even the most sophisticated survey research protocols.

However, survey research that has related the viewing of media violence to aggressive behavior has produced many interesting results. As we mentioned earlier, the first attempts to correlate media violence to aberrant behavior occurred during the 1930s, when movie preferences and juvenile delinquency were the focus. Since then, researchers have studied large numbers of randomly selected children and youth, specialized populations including youth offenders, specific racial and ethnic groups, and gender and geographic differences. In a large number of studies, the general research question can be paraphrased as follows: To what extent are preferences for violent media content related to aggressive acts or inclinations? To answer this question, researchers have collected large inventories of television and film viewing habits and preferences from desired populations. In addition, they have cataloged and rank ordered inventories of past aggressive behaviors (hitting or striking, kicking, fighting, even the use of weapons) according to the severity of the behaviors. The researchers have then conducted analyses of the correlations between viewing and the reported behaviors. The results of these analyses were expected to establish the degree to which the two were related.

Over the past 40 years, these correlational studies of preference for media violence and aggressive behavior have consistently revealed a moderate (.30 to .50) relationship between the two variables (Murray, 1980). Although this establishes that there is indeed a relationship between the two, it is of little use in determining causation. It may be that aggressive people develop a taste for violent media content, or that violent media content leads to aggressive behavior in viewers. Of course, another possibility is that a third and unknown variable may cause both the aggressive behavior and the preference for violent content. From a policy perspective, survey research offers very little in the way of conclusive evidence on which to base a decision regarding the regulation of media violence. Even more frustrating, most survey research is conducted after the fact; it establishes a past relationship, but offers little insight into how a person who has aggressive tendencies uses violent media content to contemplate future acts.

There have been some anecdotal data, however, that provide some insight into how media violence works. Offenders in prison have reported that they find crime dramas to be very instructive. Television writers are very imaginative and creative with regard to inventing crimes and means of escaping detection, and many inmates report paying close attention to such scripts. The extent to which offenders actually attempt to implement what they have learned from crime dramas is largely undocumented, however.

The Prosocial Impact of Visual Media

Any discussion of the negative impact of television and movies would be incomplete without an examination of their prosocial effects as well. *Sesame Street,* which recently reached its 25th birthday, was one of the first major attempts to combine the syntax of television (the unique blend of visual cues, timing, and audio repetition) with research that focused on how children watch and learn from television. Although much of the original *Sesame Street* formative research was proprietary, the originators of that research at the Children's Television Workshop have reported their findings in numerous public forums, and several publications have resulted (Ball & Bogatz, 1970, 1973; Children's Television Workshop, 1980). The underlying assumption of the program's designers was that children could learn from television. It made sense that if they could learn antisocial behavior from television, they could learn prosocial behavior just as easily. Prosocial messages were an integral part of early television and movies, as the "good guys" usually won, the "bad guys" got punished, and the prevailing moral standards of the era in which the program was produced were generally reinforced. Most of the things that viewers learned from early television and movies could be classified as "unintended effects," or lessons that the creators never intended to pass on per se, but that resulted from scripts or narratives that attempted to tell believable stories. For example, a story line about teens solving a problem with their parents also shows how the family members dress, talk, and relate to one another, and transmits dozens of other subtextual messages. These are as easily assimilated as the "who did what to whom" messages. Similarly, early live television programs for children typically had hosts and supporting casts of puppets, live characters, and animals that acted out skits. An incidental component of these shows was some lesson learned by a cast member from making mistakes or misjudging the motives of one of the other supporting players.

During the 1960s, as the baby boom began to outpace communities' ability to provide classrooms and teachers, educators turned to television to ease the strain. The prevailing wisdom was that if "good" teachers could be filmed or taped, and their "performances" used in more classrooms, the shortage of teachers could be eased or compensated for. The experiment failed miserably, in part because, although it became clear that children could learn from television, the "grey person, delivering the grey lecture in front of the grey curtain" could not hold the attention of the viewers (Dominick, 1994). Student satisfaction with this learning process was low or nonexistent.

By the end of the 1960s, research on how best to use television to teach was under way. Supported by massive grants and contributions, developmental psychologists, television producers, curriculum specialists, and social engineers all became involved in determining how best to impart knowledge and "desirable" social constructs to children through television. Researchers and producers accommodated children's short attention span, their love of repetition, their experience with the compact nature of commercials, their desire for variety, and so forth. In short, the characteristics that made television attention getting and entertaining were married to a wide range of educational and social concepts, with great success.

For example, formative and evaluative research on television's teaching capacities indicated that young children could clearly learn numbers and letters from sources as disparate as cartoon characters, people, and animals. Older children could learn spatial abstractions, concepts of less and more, analogous situations and ideas, and other higher-order intellectual concepts. Moreover, as reported by the Children's Television Workshop, social concepts such as sharing, empathy, concepts of right and wrong, deferred gratification, saving, stereotyping, and appreciation of different people, cultures, and religions were also successfully communicated and learned as well. Some critics of prosocial television series such as *Sesame Street* argued that children were being "set up" to believe that all learning was going to be entertaining, fun, and easy, but most were pleased with the results. The use of television proved to be especially valuable for "at-risk" children. Clearly, television and visual media proved to be at least as effective in communicating prosocial content as they were in communicating antisocial behaviors.

Teaching Life Skills Through the Media

Rather than teaching prosocial and life-skills content on a haphazard basis or only on educational television stations, we should be making greater efforts to offer such content as an integral part of television programming. To date, much of such programming has focused only on preschoolers, either to teach them academic skills or to introduce certain prosocial concepts. These programs, for the most part, air on public television stations. We describe below two examples of programs that focus on teaching prosocial content, especially life skills, to elementary school and middle school children.

The first of these programs is currently on the air; the second is in the planning stage.

Kids Like You and Me

This reality-based television program has benefited from both qualitative and quantitative formative research in the selection of form and content. *Kids Like You and Me* is a half-hour Saturday-morning local network program about "ordinary kids doing extraordinary things"; it takes advantage of the natural curiosity preadolescents have about becoming teenagers. Quantitative research was used to determine optimum segment lengths, topics of interest, and the kinds of role models that appeal to kids without seeming to be nerdy or out of reach because of extraordinary talent or privilege. The concepts of empathy, self-determination, perseverance, and working to fulfill dreams are featured prominently because television program research indicates that these can be taught through mediated communication. Qualitative data were gathered from focus groups and in-depth interviews with children between the ages of 7 and 12 to determine specific concerns they had about becoming teenagers and to discover the types of stories they would find entertaining.

The biggest challenge in producing *Kids Like You and Me* continues to be how to make prosocial television entertaining for the intended audience. With at least a dozen animated programs available during any given half hour on Saturday mornings, it was necessary to distinguish this program. This was done by making the individual segments intensely personal. Kids facing challenges like the ones the viewers face or will face became the key. Finally, qualitative research revealed that kids are very interested in how their peers figure out unique solutions to ordinary situations and like to watch programs about peers who are willing "to swim against the tide" by being individuals without being too different.

Going for the Goal (GOAL)

This Life Skills Center program teaches youth how to (a) dream and identify positive life goals, (b) understand the importance of focusing on the process (not the outcome) of a goal, (c) use a general problem-solving model, (d) identify health-promoting behaviors that can facilitate goal attainment, (e) identify health-compromising behaviors that can impede goal attainment, (f) seek and create social support, and (g) transfer life skills from one context to another. GOAL consists of 10 one-hour skill-based workshops. Each session includes a brief skit featuring Goal Seeker, Goal Buster, Goal Keeper, and Goal Shooter—characters who dramatize the skills to be learned. The program is taught by high school students to middle/junior high school students both in school and after school. Currently, it is being taught in 25 cities (Danish, 1994).

We are in the planning stages of developing an interactive animated program for television based on the GOAL skits and other program material. One possibility is that we will create a series of animated educational interstitials (i.e., short pieces that air during the program periods between the ends of cartoons and the beginnings of commercials). These interstitials would have prosocial messages and would be directed at young people 10 to 14 years of age. Three or four interstitials, each approximately 2 minutes in length, would be developed per workshop, so that as many as 40 vignettes might be developed for use. A second possibility is that we may create a year-long network-based half-hour program using the GOAL materials and teaching more of the program through this animated format. The format of the animated programming would be interactive. In other words, during the skits, when the characters are faced with critical decisions requiring life skills, viewers will be confronted with multiple choices that have different outcomes at each decision point. By making the program interactive, we would give viewers the chance to select options and see the consequences of particular choices.

Taken as a whole, life skills can be taught in a number of ways, using a number of media and interpersonal formats. The key is to understand how to communicate with children and youth without pandering or talking down to them—they are quick to pick up on both. Those of us who work with children and youth must develop excellent listening skills, because they are aware of and can articulate their concerns, dreams, and tastes.

The Media as a Resource:
A Guide for Parents and Teachers

The dilemma for social scientists is to determine how to maximize the prosocial impact of television and minimize the antisocial impact without abrogating the First Amendment. There will always be television shows and movies to which some parents will object. The answer, it seems, lies not in the content but in how we teach people to use television and movies.

Television as a Managed Resource

Parents can be taught to view television as a resource that needs to be *managed* as they manage the other resources in their lives. If they adopt such a perspective, they can minimize the potential negative results of their children's spending too much time with television. For example, it is generally recognized that children should not have all the candy or sweets they wish, and that they should not stay up as late as they want. Generally, candy and staying up later than usual are rewards children may receive for meeting familial responsibilities and school obligations, such as homework. Television watching can be managed in the same manner. Children should be made to understand that their television viewing must be rationed, and that they must choose which programs they will view from a list of programs their parents deem acceptable. They then will come to understand that television viewing is not an activity without limits or something that one engages in when one is too lazy to find something else to do.

The process of working through the establishment of priorities and the articulation of program preferences as a family has the added benefit of teaching children decision-making skills and values that most families work hard to establish. Moreover, discussion about appropriate television programs makes children think about the issues of gratuitous sex and violence, concepts of right and wrong, and what constitutes viable entertainment. As such, it helps children form their own value systems within the family context. Deciding which programs to keep and which ones to cut out of an unregulated viewing situation is a valuable exercise for consumers of all ages.

Making Television an Educational Experience

Not only can parents help manage their children's television viewing, they can provide them with opportunities to learn from the television they watch. The following examples are from our

Guide for Helping Parents Manage Their Children's Television Viewing, which we are currently preparing. We identify in the guide a number of projects that parents can have their children do as part of their discretionary viewing. We are developing 52 such projects, one for each week of the year. Among these projects are the following:

- Have children identify three words a day with which they are not familiar, look up these words in the dictionary, and use at least one in a sentence the next day.
- Have children identify three feelings being expressed on television and compare the differences and similarities between how they would show these feelings and how the actors show these feelings.
- Have children listen to the messages of three commercials, identify the benefits of the products as presented in the commercials, and decide whether these benefits match what the children hope to gain from the products.

Summary

There are several conclusions that can be drawn about the effects of the media on children and youth, regardless of the nature of the content:

1. Television and other media generally reinforce preexisting attitudes, behaviors, and tastes. In particular, violent media portrayals are not going to turn a "normal" child into a violent person. Conversely, a child or person predisposed to antisocial behavior is most likely to be negatively affected by violent material.
2. Studies have demonstrated that children can learn both positive and negative behaviors from visual media and that those learned behaviors persist over time. What is unknown is whether those learned behaviors will manifest themselves and what conditions may cause them to surface.
3. There is an inverse relationship between the potential effect of television and the impact of the family on children. The more impact the family has, the less television and other media have. Television is a default source for socialization of young people.
4. In most instances, prosocial and antisocial messages cancel each other out in viewers' repositories of potential actions. That is, for most people under most circumstances, media have little direct effect.

5. Most of television and other media effects are incidental and unintended effects. Plot lines whose major intent is to entertain, tell a story, or keep the viewer interested have the unintended consequences of teaching about societal mores, appropriate and inappropriate treatment of others, and which fads and trends are "in" or "out."

6. Visual media are an unparalleled source for learning about the world in which we live. They have the potential to transport viewers to places and introduce them to people previous generations have only read about.

Note

1. Copyright © 1994, Washington Post Writers Group. Reprinted with permission.

References

Anderson, J., & Meyer T. (1988). *Mediated communication: A social action perspective.* Newbury Park, CA: Sage.

Ball, S., & Bogatz, G. (1970). *The first year of Sesame Street: An evaluation.* Princeton, NJ: Educational Testing Service.

Ball, S., & Bogatz, G. (1973). *Reading with television: An evaluation of The Electric Company.* Princeton, NJ: Educational Testing Service.

Bandura, A., Ross, D., & Ross, S. A. (1963a). Imitation of film mediated aggressive models, *Journal of Abnormal and Social Psychology, 66,* 3-11.

Bandura, A., Ross, D., & Ross, S. A. (1963b). Vicarious reinforcement and imitative learning. *Journal of Abnormal and Social Psychology, 67,* 601-607.

Berkowitz, L., & Geen, R. G. (1966). Film violence and the cue properties of available targets. *Journal of Personality and Social Psychology, 3,* 525-530.

Berkowitz, L., & Rawlings, E. (1963). Effects of film violence on inhibitions against subsequent aggression. *Journal of Abnormal and Social Psychology, 27,* 217-229.

Charters, W. W. (1933). *Motion pictures and youth: A summary.* New York: Macmillan.

Children's Television Workshop. (1980). *International research notes.* New York: Author.

Comstock, G., & Paik, H. (1990). *The effects of television violence on aggressive behavior: A meta-analysis* (A preliminary report to the National Research Council for the Panel on the Understanding and Control of Violent Behavior). Syracuse, NY: Syracuse University, S. I. Newhouse School of Public Communications.

Danish, S. J. (1994). *Summary of activities and plans* (Life Skills Center Report No. 6). Richmond, VA: Virginia Commonwealth University, Life Skills Center.

Danish, S. J., Nellen, V., & Owens, S. (in press). Community-based programs for adolescents: Using sports to teach life skills. In J. Van Raalte & B. Brewer (Eds.),

A practitioner's guide to sport and exercise psychology. Washington, DC: American Psychological Association.

Dominick, J. (1994). *The dynamics of mass communication* (4th ed.). New York: McGraw-Hill.

Feshbach, S., & Singer, R. (1971). *Television and aggression.* San Francisco: Jossey-Bass.

Freedman, J. (1986). Television violence and aggression: A rejoinder. *Psychological Bulletin, 100,* 372-378.

Hearold, S. (1986). A synthesis of 1043 effects of television on social behavior. In G. Comstock (Ed.), *Public communications and behavior* (Vol. 1, pp. 65-133). New York: Academic Press.

Keefe, K. (1994). Perceptions of normative social pressure in attitudes toward alcohol use: Changes during adolescence. *Journal of Studies on Alcohol, 35,* 46-54.

Meyer, A. (1994). *The effectiveness of a peer-led positive youth development program for sixth graders.* Unpublished doctoral dissertation, Pennsylvania State University.

Murray, J. (1980). *Television and youth: 25 years of research and controversy.* Stanford, CA: Boys Town Center for the Study of Youth Development.

Perry, C. L., & Jessor, R. (1985). The concept of health promotion and the prevention of adolescent drug abuse. *Health Education Quarterly, 12,* 169-184.

Rosenthal, R. (1986). Media violence, antisocial behavior, and the social consequences of small effects. *Journal of Social Issues, 42,* 141-154.

U.S. Senate, Subcommittee on Telecommunications and Finance. (1994). *U.S. Senate joint hearings on implementation of the Television Program Improvement Act of 1990* (Commission on the Judiciary, Serial No. J-103-13). Washington, DC: Government Printing Office.

Wilcox, B. (1994). Prepared statement on behalf of the American Psychological Association. In *U.S. Senate joint hearings on implementation of the Television Program Improvement Act of 1990* (Commission on the Judiciary, Serial No. J-103-13). Washington, DC: Government Printing Office.

• CHAPTER 8 •

Violence Among Youth:
Origins and a Framework for Prevention

STEPHEN E. GARDNER
HANK RESNIK

In most public opinion polls today, crime is the number-one issue. Closely associated with people's concern about crime is a prevailing fear about one of the main components of crime: violence. How serious is the problem? Recent reports about crime indicate that many forms of criminal behavior have actually declined in recent years (U.S. Bureau of the Census, 1993). Violence, however—particularly the kind of random, senseless violence we are seeing among youth at ever-younger ages—has been rising dramatically for the past decade.

The severity and widespread nature of violence were reflected in a 1994 conference held in San Francisco. Convened by the governor of California and other state leaders, the conference was organized to find solutions to the problems of California's troubled schools. Yet, as one newspaper report described it, the so-called Education Summit might have been more appropriately termed a "Violence Summit." No one in attendance could separate the challenge of improving education in the state from the challenge of reducing school violence.

AUTHORS' NOTE: The opinions expressed herein are those of the authors and do not necessarily represent the views of the Department of Health and Human Services or any of its components.

Guest speaker Marian Wright Edelman of the Children's Defense Fund told those in attendance at the conference that "the crisis of children having children has been eclipsed by children killing children." Edelman noted that 25 American children, the equivalent of an entire classroom, are killed by guns every 2 days (quoted in "Schools Summit," 1994).

Perhaps the most revealing point in this story is that increasingly the notion of violence tends to be equated with violence among youth. Widespread concern about youth violence offers a new opportunity to focus the attention of the public and policymakers on the need for strategies that address interrelated issues such as alcohol and other drug use, school failure, poverty, and lack of support for youth in families and communities. All of these are different aspects of the problem of youth violence or are closely related to it in a complex web of social disintegration. The violence problem, in short, often translates to a youth problem—and, by implication, a problem among those who are most concerned with the well-being of young people, such as family members, schools, and youth-focused community leaders.

Although there is still much to learn, one thing seems clear: Youth violence, like young people's alcohol and other drug use, is not a problem that will just go away. Like alcohol and other drug use among youth, which took a disturbing upward turn in 1994 after many years of small declines (National Institute on Drug Abuse, 1994), youth violence is becoming deeply ingrained in our society.

Violence Defined

People talk constantly about the problem of violence, but to what exactly are they referring? When we worry about growing violence, are we all concerned about the same problem, or is violence a multitude of problems? The Center for Substance Abuse Prevention (CSAP) was established to address the use and abuse of alcohol, tobacco, and other drugs and related problems. In recent years, however, CSAP has recognized the interrelationship of these problems with the problem of violence and has created several violence-related initiatives. In doing so, CSAP has sought, through program initiatives and dialogues both within CSAP and with the prevention and human services community, to define violence clearly in the context of the center's mission.

CSAP defines violence as any act that causes psychological, emotional, or physical harm to individuals and/or communities, or that causes damage to property. The CSAP position recognizes that violence is a public health, social, and economic issue affecting people of all races, ethnicities, and socioeconomic classes. Substance abuse and violence are inextricably intertwined. Closely associated with violence are the trade in illicit substances, racism, misogyny, and homophobia. Different forms of violence include homicide, assault (including rape and sexual assault), spouse abuse and battering, child physical and sexual abuse, child neglect, suicide, and vandalism and other forms of property destruction.

According to this definition, violence is not one isolated problem restricted to one type of community or one segment of the population; it is multidimensional and pervasive. As anyone working in the arena of health and human services knows, public concern about social problems can be fickle. One year drug abuse is at the top of the list; the next year it may be the economy. Yet deeply rooted social and health problems such as drug abuse and violence defy quick fixes; they are interconnected, complex, and extremely difficult to deal with and prevent.

What are most needed in addressing the violence crisis are well-planned, comprehensive, long-term solutions based on sound theory, research, and practice. An important emphasis of CSAP's approach is that, to be effective, prevention efforts and organizing should target children and youth, beginning in the preschool years and continuing into young adulthood. Young people between the ages of 3 and 18 constitute the target population for CSAP's High-Risk Youth Demonstration Grant Program and a variety of related initiatives discussed later in this chapter.

The Nature of Youth Violence: An Overview

What aspects of youth violence should be the focus of prevention efforts? Youth violence has many different faces, depending on factors such as the setting, the region, and the young person's age and racial/ethnic group. Although many issues related to youth violence are not well researched, and the research that does exist can be murky or self-contradictory, some data are salient and worthy of attention. Clearly, demographics and gender play all-important roles. We know, for example, that the homicide rates among young African American, Native American, and Hispanic males are at least four times higher than that for white males (Centers for Disease Control, 1986).

African American males are at particularly high risk, mainly because African American youth are more likely than whites to be poor, and poverty is closely associated with high rates of violence. An African American youth is approximately nine times more likely to be murdered than a young white male (Centers for Disease Control, 1986). Less widely recognized is the fact that homicide is also the most common cause of death for young African American females. The probability of a young African American female dying by homicide is four times that of a non-African American female. Nevertheless, male teenagers still have a significantly higher (about two to one) chance of becoming victims of violence than do female teens (American Psychological Association, 1994). Also, metropolitan areas show consistently higher rates of violent offenses than do nonmetropolitan areas; central cities have considerably higher rates (two to three times higher) than nonmetropolitan areas (Maguire, Pastore, & Flanagan, 1993).

Perhaps of greatest concern is the fact that serious violence is a factor in children's lives at increasingly younger ages. In a study of first and second graders in Washington, D.C., 45% said they had witnessed muggings, 31% had witnessed shootings, and 39% had seen dead bodies (American Psychological Association, 1994). Some 36% of all assaults and 40% of all robberies reported by individuals 12 to 19 years of age occur within their schools. According to the Children's Defense Fund (1991), 135,000 children take guns to school every day. Moreover, teenagers are victimized by people they know or are acquainted with and are most often victimized during the day (Bastian & Taylor, 1991). This explains, in part, the growing trend of self-perpetuating cycles of youth violence. Many youth bearing guns and other weapons today say they do so in order to protect themselves from other young people.

Unfortunately, these facts and the high rates of violence among youth are a peculiarly American phenomenon. A 1991 study found that the United States had homicide rates among youth that were eight times higher than the rates in other industrialized countries.

The sharpest increases in youth homicides in recent years have been among young people 15 to 19 years old (National Center for Injury Prevention and Control, 1993).

Violence and Substance Abuse: The Linkages

Some linkages between violence and the use of alcohol and other drugs are well established. For example, more than 50% of homicides and assaults involve assailants who are under the influence of alcohol. In homicide cases, equal numbers of offenders and victims had been drinking. Among spousal batterers, researchers have found a 60% to 70% rate of alcohol abuse and a 13% to 20% rate of other drug abuse. More than half of the convicted inmates in one study reported being under the influence of alcohol and other drugs when they committed the offenses for which they were imprisoned (Collins & Schlenger, 1988).

The relationships between substance abuse and violence are neither simple nor straightforward. Links connecting alcohol, other drugs, and violence differ widely according to the types of drugs, the amounts used, and the patterns of use. Individual histories of aggressive or violent behavior are also a factor in determining whether or not alcohol and other drug use will increase those behaviors. Although alcohol use has been associated with approximately half of all violent events, for example, the same dosage of alcohol may have entirely different effects from one individual to another (Reiss & Roth, 1993).

Most researchers agree that a variety of other factors are associated with violence even when drug or alcohol abuse is involved. According to one widely accepted view, alcohol, other drugs, and violence are interrelated in three main ways: (a) through the *pharmacological* effects of some drugs that can induce violent behavior (this appears to be particularly true of alcohol, cocaine and crack, PCP, and barbiturates), (b) through *drug-related crime* motivated by the high cost of drug use (e.g., robberies to support a drug habit), and (c) through *association with drug distribution systems,* a major arena of drug-related crime (Collins, 1990b). The third of these is sometimes referred to as *systemic* violence, because it serves a variety of purposes ranging from protection of a segment of the drug market to retaliation for violations of underworld "rules."

Although various forms of violence are associated with all three types of alcohol and other drug involvement, in recent years the third type—systemic violence connected to drug dealing—has been the most frequently reported. Here, too, the picture is complex: Systemic violence related to drug dealing is itself correlated with other factors. These include socially disorganized neighborhoods and communities, traditionally high rates of interpersonal violence, and economic disadvantage (Collins, 1990a).

Alcohol, Other Drugs, Violence, and Youth

In the past, studies relating violence and drug abuse have tended to focus on adults. As concern about youth violence grows, however, we are continuing to gain new insights into the problem. To an alarming degree, the three types of combined drug and violence involvement described above apply to children and youth as well as adults. In cities with high rates of illicit drug dealing, children ranging in age from the elementary grades to young adulthood are frequent participants in violence, drug use, and the illicit drug trade.

One study of more than 600 youth in their mid-teens actively involved in drug dealing in Dade County, Florida, in the late 1980s found that all of them had extensive histories of multiple drug use, especially crack use. More than 90% had engaged in drug sales and thefts before age 12. The study found that their criminal careers "emerged more or less in tandem with their drug-using careers" (Inciardi, 1990, p. 93). Nevertheless, in comparing the Miami/Dade County area with several other major cities, the researchers concluded that it is risky to generalize about youthful drug use and violence. The higher rates of homicide in cities throughout the United States in the 1980s commonly believed to be associated with the crack cocaine epidemic, they found, "do not necessarily go hand-in-hand with higher rates of crack use and distribution" (p. 101).

Much of what we know about the combination of youth violence and drug abuse comes from research on youth gangs. However, gang involvement, often perceived as a concomitant of youthful violence and drug abuse, is not necessarily a decisive factor. The Dade County study found that youths involved in crack dealing and multiple drug use rarely participated in youth gangs. One teenager commented that "the gangs in this town are just not where it's at" (quoted in Inciardi, 1990, p. 107). In contrast, combined gang involvement, drug use, and illegal drug dealing has been found in Los Angeles, which traditionally has had heavy gang activity.

One of the most important findings from the gang-related research of recent years has been the need to avoid some common myths about youth gangs. Although there has been a dramatic increase in youth gang activity in the past decade, reaching even into relatively affluent suburbs, many preconceptions about youth gangs, violence, and drugs are not supported by empirical evidence. Researchers have observed that the nature, structure, and activities of youth gangs vary widely from place to place and from one period of time to another. As one observer of the youth gang scene has noted: "The sporadic public concern about gangs and drugs is usually so intense and moralistic that police and media actually define the phenomena, quite apart from reality. . . . What anybody 'knows' about a gang in any given year—even a gang member's knowledge—may in certain specifics be out of date the very next year" (Inciardi, 1990, p. 107).

One study of Chicano gangs in East Los Angeles concludes that although the most intense periods of gang violence and drug abuse occur during adolescence (gang members tend to "mature out" of their gangs as they reach young adulthood), youth gangs are not as tightly organized or as focused on drugs and violence as is often believed (Moore, 1990). Much presumed gang violence or crime, in fact, consists of the actions of isolated individuals who happen to be gang members.

A comprehensive review of current knowledge about youth gangs carried out by the National Institute of Justice (1993) has identified four types of gangs: (a) "social gangs," involved in few delinquent activities and little drug use (28% of the gangs studied); (b) "party gangs," extensively involved in drug use and sales (7%); (c) "serious delinquents," gangs that engage extensively in both violent and property offenses but for whom drug use and sales are relatively unimportant (37%); and (d) "gangs involved extensively in serious drug use," gangs that are at greater risk of becoming formal criminal organizations (28%).

The important point is that we cannot say with any certainty that gangs are "the problem," because, in fact, there is no single problem that can be clearly isolated and efficiently addressed. Rather, there are multiple interrelated problems, each of which has many different dimensions.

The Origins of Youth Violence and Problem Behavior: Risk Factors and Protective Factors

Against a backdrop of complex problems and variables, individual instances of youth violence continue to shock and frighten us. Several specific categories of violence have been the main focus of attention, both in conjunction with and separate from drug use. These include violence involving weapons, particularly guns; gang violence, organized gang warfare and conflict, and the increase in youth gang activity throughout the country in recent years; youth violence in schools—both against other youth and against adults; and violence directed at specific vulnerable or distinct "targets," such as females (e.g., rape and sexual exploitation) and members of particular racial/ethnic groups (e.g., hate crimes and intergroup violence).

Even a cursory review of the literature on these and related problems reveals a picture of children and youth today in which a wide range of problem behaviors, including drug use and violence, is rooted in similar problems and follows clearly observable developmental patterns. The pioneering work of researchers such as Denise Kandel and Richard Jessor on juvenile delinquency and related problem behaviors in the 1960s is being borne out by new studies of youth today. For example, numerous studies have shown that violence in the home creates a pattern and expectation among children and youth that violence is an appropriate reaction to stress and an effective way to express anger. Children who are abused at home are much more likely to become violent youth (Widom, 1989).

Family dysfunction also contributes to gang membership (Posner, 1989). The family situations of members of hard-core gangs tend to be bleak; these are young people at high risk for a variety of negative behaviors who rarely receive adequate structure, support, nurturing, or supervision in the family setting.

School failure dominates the list of risk factors for both violence and drug abuse among youth. For example, gang members tend to be those young people who are not doing well in school or who are in danger of dropping out. At the beginning, at least, many forms of negative or problem behavior are an alternative to success in school. The peer group is another key factor in both drug use and violent behavior—both of which tend to be highly peer focused, particularly in the beginning. Often drug use and violence are ways of gaining acceptance among peers (Posner, 1989).

Community social and economic disintegration also play an important role. Young people tend to gravitate toward drug use, violence, or a combination of the two in the absence of clear goals, positive role models, and hope for the future (Posner, 1989).

In the substance abuse field, the *risk factors* described above are well known to prevention professionals and advocates. They are balanced by *protective factors* that include (a) positive bonding to family and school; (b) skills for resisting negative behavior and succeeding at home, at school, and in the community, and positive rewards and recognition for those skills and behaviors; (c) positive alternatives to negative or problem behavior (e.g., youth recreation programs); (d) close relationships with peers involved in positive and constructive pursuits; and (e) communities in which norms and expectations for the behavior of young people are clearly defined, widely accepted, and effectively communicated and supported.

The concept of risk factors and protective factors is now common parlance in the field of substance abuse prevention. More and more prevention programs throughout the country, including many funded by CSAP, have among their goals the reduction of risk factors for alcohol, tobacco, and other drug use and the increase or enhancement of protective factors (Center for Substance Abuse Prevention, 1994). Increasingly, youth-oriented substance abuse prevention programs are focusing on the development of *resilience* among youth, or the ability to resist stresses and influences that often lead to negative, unhealthy, and self-destructive behavior.

Although there are many common risk and protective factors for youth violence and alcohol, tobacco, and other drug use, some important differences should be noted. Violence and abuse in the home, for example, are more predictive of youth violence than is parental drug abuse, which is a strong predictor of youth drug use. Nevertheless, the two often occur in combination (American Psychological Association, 1994).

The Culture of Violence

Increasingly, an important discussion regarding risk factors for youthful drug use and those for youth violence revolves around the issue of young people's personal values and beliefs. Here the distinctions are more clear-cut than they are for some other types of risk factors. Evidence abounds that alcohol, tobacco, and other drug use is potentially detrimental to personal health. Most young people are aware of the hazards of cigarette smoking, excessive alcohol drinking, and the use of a variety of illicit substances such as cocaine and crack. Even when young people receive mixed messages because of powerful media promotion of cigarettes and alcohol, if they choose to use alcohol and other drugs, they are generally making a conscious choice between healthy behaviors and high-risk behaviors.

In fact, the very population about which there is the greatest concern today with regard to youth violence, young African Americans, has made the most progress recently with regard to alcohol and other drug use. According to the annual survey of youth drug use sponsored by the National Institute on Drug Abuse, African American teenagers are less likely to use illegal substances than are white or Hispanic teenagers ("Good News on Drugs," 1994). The message about the harmful effects of drug use is getting through to young African Americans, often because they have witnessed those harmful effects personally in their own homes and communities.

On the other hand, there is no clear consensus in our society that violence is always wrong or negative. The U.S. Constitution guarantees our right to bear arms and thus to protect ourselves. Our traditional esteem for rugged individualism glorifies the macho hero who stands up for himself and fights. Around the world, Americans are (or used to be) highly respected because, in contrast to people from other cultures, we value actions more than words. Add to this the fact that, as one expert on youth delinquency has noted, "the hallmark of the delinquent subculture is the explicit and wholesale repudiation of middle-class standards and the adoption of their very antithesis" (Conly, 1993, p. 19), and the result is a profound ambivalence about violence among many youth at a time in their lives when risk taking and a sense of invulnerability are both healthy and normal.

Ambivalence about violence extends to our society in general. We deplore guns in the hands of children, but we applaud when those guns are wielded by cowboys, lawmen, or middle-class citizens defending themselves against criminal intruders. Perhaps our ambivalence about violence is diminishing somewhat, however, amid growing concern about the culture of violence, which for most youth in the United States is inescapable.

A 1994 incident in Oakland, California, underscores the point. When a high school social studies teacher took a group of inner-city youth to see the film *Schindler's List,* the students began to whoop and cheer as they observed scenes of shockingly brutal human carnage—Nazis slaughtering Jews in a Polish ghetto and a Nazi commander using Jewish prisoners for target practice in a concentration camp. Finally, at the request of horrified and indignant patrons, the theater manager stopped the film and insisted that the students leave the theater.

Subsequent interviews and news reports focused on the possible anti-Semitism or pro-Nazi sentiments of the high school students. More to the point, however (and perhaps far less newsworthy), was their inability to empathize with the human suffering being portrayed. This incident reinforces the notion that young people today are hardened to violence because of their constant exposure to it through the media. Given such an attitude, the violence in *Schindler's List* becomes simply a new variation on a familiar theme.

Closely related to this is the growing awareness, often documented by anecdotal evidence and interviews with young perpetrators of violence, that these young people regard violence and participate in it with no sense of a moral dimension, no remorse, and no compassion for their victims. Although few people would challenge that statement, writer Nathan McCall, in his book *Makes Me Wanna Holler* (1994), leaves no doubt of its veracity. McCall grew up in a middle-class African American community in the Norfolk, Virginia, area, became deeply involved in crime and violence, shot and nearly murdered another young black male, and was finally sent to prison for his role in burglarizing a local restaurant. Many years later, after having been paroled from prison, he returned to school, became a news reporter, and landed a job with the *Washington Post.*

McCall's book gives us a glimpse of the culture of youth violence not just from the inside but through eyes and words that leave no doubt about the role of empathy, morality, and compassion in the life of a violence-prone teenager. He describes robbing strangers at gunpoint:

Sticking up gave me a rush that I never got from [breaking and entering]. There was an almost magical transformation in my relationship with the rest of the world when I drew that gun on folks. I always marveled at how the toughest cats whimpered and begged for their lives when I stuck the barrel into their faces. Adults who ordinarily would have commanded my respect were forced to follow my orders like obedient kids. (p. 97)

Here is his reaction after actually shooting another person for the first time, a rival youth who had been taunting him and who nearly died from the wound:

In that moment, I felt like God. I felt so good and powerful that I wanted to do it again. I felt like I could pull that trigger, and keep on pulling it until I emptied the gun. (p. 115)

Not only are young people often unaware of and insensitive to the consequences of violence; our culture is so saturated with depictions of violence that they often perceive it as normal. One of the most important conclusions of Prothrow-Stith's groundbreaking book about youth violence, *Deadly Consequences* (1991), is that violence is a *learned behavior.* Prothrow-Stith writes:

Like many psychologists I believe that the family and social environment can teach children to use violence to solve problems. The basic set of ideas that describe how this learning takes place is called social learning theory. . . . According to social learning theory, children learn how to behave aggressively by watching others use violence to their advantage and then imitating what they have seen. This process is called "modeling." (p. 45)

Along with many others today who are clamoring for stricter controls on televised violence, Prothrow-Stith singles out television as the main purveyor to youth of violent images. She acknowledges, however, that television also provides images of positive behavior and that positive social learning can also occur when children watch television (witness *Sesame Street* and *Mister Rogers' Neighborhood*). Nevertheless, she concludes:

Some children are more vulnerable than others to television's violence-promoting message. Boys and men who are poor, who are urban, and who have witnessed or been victimized by violence in their families are more at risk for the dangerous lessons television teaches. . . . Boys like this may never get to see an adult man restrain his own anger or control his own violent impulses. They may never experience nonviolent discipline. They may never have the chance to see an adult man, or a woman, resolve disputes effectively and assertively, using nonviolent strategies. Boys living in these circumstances are the ones most susceptible to television's message that heroes use violence to serve their purposes. (pp. 46-47)

George Gerbner, a professor at the Annenberg School for Communication at the University of Pennsylvania, has worked closely with CSAP in investigating the portrayal of violence and drug use and abuse on television. Through the Annenberg School's Cultural Indicators project, Gerbner and his colleagues analyzed a sample of 2,198 dramatic (fictional) television programs, including 29,110 characters, that were aired on the three major networks between 1973 and 1993. One of the major premises of the study was that "rarely, if ever, does a person encounter as many social types and relationships as often and in as compelling and revealing ways as on television. The moral and behavioral lessons that cultivate health-related behaviors are embedded in that context" (Gerbner, 1994, pp. 1-2).

Gerbner concluded that more than 6 out of 10 programs feature violence and more than half of all major characters are involved in violence. He found that although women, youth, and ethnic minorities are underrepresented on television, they have more than their share of negative characterizations as villains, failures, addicts, and victims. Furthermore, Saturday-morning children's programs "magnify and amplify the patterns of prime time" (p. 3). According to Gerbner's "Violence Index," rates of violence on Saturday-morning children's programs have been consistently higher than those in prime time. Unlike prime-time programs, these children's programs have shown no recent declines in violence.

Gerbner's work has led to the formation of the Cultural Environment Movement (CEM), a nonprofit organization currently spearheading a national network of individuals and organizations that advocates a new approach to health promotion, violence reduction, and substance abuse prevention. Based on the premise that depictions of violence and substance abuse are "integral parts of the new cultural environment pervading every community and every home," CEM seeks to promote public participation in "cultural decision making, with a view toward changing current representations of violence, substance abuse, and other aspects of physical and social well-being" (Gerbner, 1994, p. 56ff.).

What we know about youth violence, as seen in this relatively brief summary, is disturbing and challenging. Unfortunately, the statistics about increasing youth violence and daily reports in the news media help to perpetuate some common myths and stereotypes that will make it even more difficult to break the cycle. Efforts such as the Cultural Environment Movement are an encouraging sign that a better-informed public is beginning to counteract some of the most damaging yet pervasive trends in our culture.

Toward a Framework for Prevention

It has been said that the connection between alcohol and other psychoactive drugs and violence "turns out to be not an example of straightforward causation, but a network of interacting processes and feedback loops" (Reiss & Roth, 1993, p. 35). In the preceding discussion, we have examined some of those interacting processes and feedback loops. Clearly, there is a great deal more to be studied and learned. Nevertheless, we are at a point in exploring the prevention of both alcohol and other drug use and violence where we can begin to draw some conclusions and make some recommendations, particularly with regard to potentially effective approaches targeting children and youth. Although there are important distinctions between what will work in preventing alcohol and other drug use and what will work in violence prevention, there are more commonalities than differences. Exploring these commonalities, some of which are discussed below, may be the best path for prevention professionals, youth advocates, and policymakers to pursue for both the short and long term.

A focus on risk factors and protective factors. Reducing risk factors and strengthening protective factors to help individuals become more resistant to alcohol and other drug use has been one of the strongest themes of prevention programs and coalitions of the last decade. Many of the antecedents of youth violence—for example, family disorganization, early school failure, and negative peer influences—are either very similar to or the same as those for substance use and abuse. Focusing positive youth development efforts on these common risk and protective factors can help to prepare young people to deal with a variety of negative influences. Furthermore, we should not underestimate the importance of reducing risk factors and strengthening protective factors in all the different aspects of a child's life: individual development, the family, the school, and the community. Each has its own unique set of risk and protective factors and appropriate, proven, successful prevention strategies.

The importance of social learning. Social learning theory—the idea that children learn behavior by observing and imitating those around them—has provided considerable momentum to the field of alcohol, tobacco, and other drug abuse prevention. It appears to have equal validity for violence prevention. Reinforcing positive social behavior, providing positive adult role modeling, and actually teaching children skills such as how to resist negative peer pressure and how to resolve conflicts peacefully are among the most promising approaches for preventing both alcohol and other drug use and violence. The CSAP-funded Child Development Project, based in Oakland, California, and now being implemented in several school districts in other states, is one noteworthy example of a comprehensive school- and family-based approach to teaching positive social skills to children in the elementary grades that has a strong record of demonstrated success. Many programs across the United States are using similar approaches to actual instruction and role modeling that emphasize caring and concern for others and positive ways of dealing with anger and conflict.

The role of parents and families. Whatever the type of family background a child experiences, the crucial preschool years and the nature of parental support, guidance, and instruction can and will make an enormous difference in that child's ability to grow up healthy, strong, resilient, and able to resist negative influences. Many prevention programs and strategies focus on strengthening families and helping parents to establish clear guidelines and expectations for behavior.

Youth empowerment. Both violence and drug use are often reactions to feelings of hopelessness and powerlessness. They are self-destructive and inappropriate coping mechanisms that provide a temporary feeling of power and control. Increasingly, prevention programs targeting both violence and drug use recognize that *real* empowerment of youth, especially adolescents, is critically important. Young people need to be given careful preparation for the development of skills related to personal and social responsibility. Strategies for youth empowerment vary widely. They range from cooperative learning groups and school-based project learning to school and community service programs that give young people clear decision-making roles.

Addressing the culture of violence. If we wait for Hollywood and Washington to reverse the culture of violence that is clearly having such a negative impact on our youth, the result will only be frustration. In the continuing debate over regulation of television and other media images of violence, gun control, and related national policies, powerful and conflicting interests are at work. Changing the culture of violence requires meaningful activity at the community and grassroots levels. Local initiatives such as community policing, youth-oriented recreational programs, and the involvement of family members and neighbors, street by street and block by block—these are the kinds of actions that will begin to turn the tide.

Violence prevention and alcohol and other drug abuse prevention have much in common, and it will be important to continue to draw on these commonalities. However, an effective framework for prevention also needs to include the distinct differences and unique strategies that may be needed to address alcohol and other drug abuse and violence. For example, perhaps even more than with alcohol and other drug abuse prevention, support for parents and other family members when children are in the earliest developmental stages is critically important in preventing violence. Family-oriented programs that offer prenatal care for expectant mothers, teach parenting skills, and offer health, social, and educational services to parents in need are a crucial first step in violence prevention.

The social context of violence is also a critically important factor. Prevention programs need to focus on communities where young people are at highest risk. In contrast to substance abuse prevention programs, which often address the general population, violence prevention efforts and activities must be concentrated where the problem and its antecedent factors are most pronounced.

Violence is often an indirect expression of frustration and rage. At its most extreme, it is an act of desperation, a decision (whether conscious or not) to reject values and norms that promote the common good. Thus, to reduce youth violence, we must make serious efforts to provide young people with meaningful goals and roles in society and a sense that the future will offer them rewards for rejecting violence. People refrain from violence and "buy into" the dominant social order when they have something important to lose if they do otherwise. When they have nothing to lose, too often violence seems acceptable.

Implications for Policy—and CSAP's Role

Increasingly, a major premise of the youth-oriented prevention initiatives of the Center for Substance Abuse Prevention is that effective prevention efforts must take a comprehensive approach, reaching all the areas of young people's lives: the individual, the family, the school, the peer group, the community, and the broader social and policy environment. CSAP is currently exploring a variety of initiatives that link violence prevention and substance abuse prevention. These range from research and data collection to demonstration grant programs. All are based on a set of premises derived from research and the experience of CSAP's existing substance abuse prevention initiatives; all are community focused and involve evaluation and feedback mechanisms for developing, modifying, and implementing programs in a changing environment.

The current CSAP initiatives assume that many of the risk factors for substance abuse are the same as those for violent behavior; that is, youth who have a high probability of becoming involved with alcohol and other drugs frequently have a high probability of becoming perpetrators or victims of violence. They also assume that young people who have been victims of or witnesses to violence, or who live in highly violent environments, are more likely to become involved with both substance abuse and violence than those who have not been exposed to these influences. And they assume that being under the influence of alcohol and other drugs can be a major precipitating factor in violent behavior.

On the broader level of creating and sustaining a dialogue on the linkages between violence prevention and substance abuse prevention, CSAP is currently exploring a Community Early Warning Network for violence prevention related to alcohol and other drugs (AOD). The basic concept of the network is to create community focal points for planning and allocating resources to prevent AOD-related violence. Frequently, reports on patterns and trends of violence are difficult to apply to both policy and prevention programs. It can take 2 years or more for reliable data on violence to be published, and neighborhood-level information rarely reaches levels that influence planning and resource allocation. The network, still in its formative stages as of this writing, could collect up-to-date key indicators to determine new and emerging patterns of AOD-related violence as well as promising prevention strategies. It could create communication linkages at the local, state, and federal levels for information sharing. Four cities (Boston, Cleveland, Los Angeles, and Miami) are currently piloting and refining the network concept.

Another resource for information sharing and planning supported by CSAP is PREVline. This electronic bulletin board is available at no cost either through direct-dial modem connection or through the Internet, and all material is in the public domain (access PREVline via Telnet, ncadi@health.org, or call, toll-free, 800-729-6686). Containing more than 1,000 downloadable files related to AOD prevention, PREVline has recently introduced a forum on AOD-related violence prevention.

Since its inception, CSAP has provided support to hundreds of communities across the country through its demonstration grant programs. Today many of these local prevention initiatives, originally established to focus on different aspects of alcohol and other drug abuse prevention, are broadening their scope to include AOD-related violence. Noteworthy among these grant programs are the High-Risk Youth Demonstration Grant Program, which has awarded more than 330 grants over a 7-year period, and the Community Partnership Demonstration Grant Program, which currently supports a national network of 252 lead community agencies responsible for coordinating the prevention efforts of thousands of organizational partners. Both of these initiatives have recently introduced special grants and projects focusing specifically on AOD-related youth and community violence.

CSAP has also funded 147 demonstration grants under its Pregnant and Postpartum Women and Their Infants initiative. A collaboration with the Maternal and Child Health Bureau of the Health Resources and Services Administration, the initiative had as its ultimate goal improving the health of women at risk for alcohol and other drug use during pregnancy by improving the availability and quality of services such as prenatal care, drug treatment, and prevention education. Here, too, violence prevention was an important element of a comprehensive approach and a continuum of care.

To support these programmatic initiatives, CSAP has established the Violence Prevention Leadership Support Program, which is designed to provide communities with immediate and appropriate responses to violence-related crises, timely and accurate information to help prevent violence before it erupts, and strong partnerships that can identify and address the causes of violence. Through a series of regional meetings, special forums, community AOD-related violence prevention workshops, and other events, the initiative encourages rapid and intensive sharing of information, knowledge, ideas, and resources. It also contributes to the dissemination of research and the formation of meaningful social policy concerning AOD-related violence in local communities. Special programs and events associated with this initiative have included (a) development and dissemination of a series of annotated bibliographies, reports, curricula, and other materials on AOD-related violence prevention programs and services, and the relationships between alcohol, other drugs, and violence; (b) training for community teams focusing on strategies to prevent and counteract AOD-related violence against women; and (c) training for new CSAP grantees emphasizing strategies for improving violence-related community services, selecting violence indicators and appropriate measurement tools, choosing violence curricula, and refining project services to emphasize violence prevention.

All of these efforts represent an awareness on the part of CSAP's leaders that violence and substance abuse are different manifestations of interrelated, deeply rooted social and health problems. Effective solutions to those problems will come only through comprehensive approaches that build on what we know and explore new strategies to enhance the effectiveness of prevention.

References

American Psychological Association. (1994). *Violence and youth: Psychology's response* (Summary report of the American Psychological Association Commission on Violence and Youth, Vol. 1). Washington, DC: Author.

Bastian, L. D., & Taylor, B. M. (1991). *School crime: A national crime victimization survey report* (Bureau of Justice Statistics Publication No. NCH-131645). Washington, DC: Government Printing Office.

Center for Substance Abuse Prevention. (1994). [Grant announcement for AOD-related violence High-Risk Youth Demonstration Program initiative]. Rockville, MD: Author.

Centers for Disease Control. (1986). *Homicide surveillance: High risk racial and ethnic groups—blacks and Hispanics, 1970 to 1983.* Washington, DC: Government Printing Office.

Children's Defense Fund. (1991). *The state of America's children.* Washington, DC: Author.

Collins, J. (1990a). *Federal drug data for national policy.* Washington, DC: Government Printing Office.

Collins, J. (1990b). Summary thoughts about drugs and violence. In M. De La Rosa, E. Y. Lambert, & B. Gropper (Eds.), *Drugs and violence: Causes, correlates, and consequences* (NIDA Research Monograph No. 103). Washington, DC: Government Printing Office.

Collins, J., & Schlenger, W. (1988). Acute and chronic effects of alcohol use on violence. *Journal of Studies on Alcohol, 49,* 516-530.

Conly, C. H. (1993). *Street gangs: Current knowledge and strategies.* Washington, DC: U.S. Department of Justice, Office of Justice Programs, National Institute of Justice.

Gerbner, G. (1994). *Violence and drugs on television: The cultural environment approach to prevention.* Philadelphia: Annenberg School for Communication.

Good news on drugs from the inner city. (1994, February 14). *Newsweek,* p. 28.

Inciardi, J. A. (1990). The crack-violence connection within a population of hardcore adolescent offenders. In M. De La Rosa, E. Y. Lambert, & B. Gropper (Eds.), *Drugs and violence: Causes, correlates, and consequences* (NIDA Research Monograph No. 103). Washington, DC: Government Printing Office.

Maguire, K., Pastore, A. L., & Flanagan, T. J. (Eds.). (1993). *Sourcebook of criminal justice statistics 1992.* Washington, DC: Government Printing Office.

McCall, N. (1994). *Makes me wanna holler: A young black man in America.* New York: Random House.

Moore, J. (1990). Gangs, drugs, and violence. In M. De La Rosa, E. Y. Lambert, & B. Gropper (Eds.), *Drugs and violence: Causes, correlates, and consequences* (NIDA Research Monograph 103). Washington, DC: Government Printing Office.

National Center for Injury Prevention and Control. (1993). [Unpublished homicide trend data]. Atlanta, GA: Centers for Disease Control and Prevention.

National Institute of Justice. (1993). *Street gangs: Current knowledge and strategies.* Washington, DC: Government Printing Office.

National Institute on Drug Abuse. (1994, December 12). *HHS releases high school drug abuse and DAWN surveys* [Press release]. Washington, DC: Author.

Posner, M. (1989). Assaultive injuries. In National Committee for Injury Prevention and Control (Ed.), *Injury prevention: Meeting the challenge.* New York: Oxford University Press.

Prothrow-Stith, D. (1991). *Deadly consequences: How violence is destroying our teenage population and a plan to begin solving the problem.* New York: Harper-Collins.

Reiss, A. J., Jr., & Roth, J. A. (Eds.). (1993). *Understanding and preventing violence.* Washington, DC: National Academy Press.

Schools summit focuses on violence. (1994, February 16). *San Francisco Chronicle,* p. 1.

U.S. Bureau of the Census. (1993). Crimes and crime rates, by type: 1982 to 1991. In *Statistical abstract of the United States: 1993.* Washington, DC: Government Printing Office.

Widom, C. S. (1989, April 14). The cycle of violence. *Science, 244,* 160-166.

CHAPTER 9

Education and Training in Violence Prevention: A Public Health Model

GARRY LAPIDUS

MARY BRADDOCK

Violence has reached epidemic proportions in American society and has emerged as the major public health problem at the end of the 20th century (Institute of Medicine, 1985). Each year, more than 2 million Americans are victims of violent injury (U.S. Department of Health and Human Services, 1990).

Yet despite the enormous health, financial, and emotional burden that violence represents, a comprehensive, integrated strategy for violence prevention is only now beginning to emerge. Although, historically, issues of violence have been addressed within the field of law enforcement, social services, and mental health, it now appears that classic public health strategies might constitute a significant contribution to this effort. Public health emphasizes a multidisciplinary approach and employs a variety of methods to achieve primary prevention, secondary prevention, and intervention. The public health approach analyzes the interaction of host, agent, and environmental factors to identify potentially modifiable risk factors for violence. Prevention efforts may then be designed using educational, environmental, or regulatory strategies.

Although this model was originally designed to combat infectious diseases (the major public health threat at the beginning of the century), it has been employed successfully in the battle against other, modern health scourges, such as heart disease, lung cancer, and motor vehicle fatalities. In the past few years, public health experts have also been using this approach to address the myriad health problems caused by violence. In 1991, more than 800 public health experts from the public and private sectors—including federal, state, and local health agencies; federal Departments of Justice, Labor, and Transportation; academic institutions of public health, medicine, psychology, and social work; and various advocacy organizations—produced the report *Injury Control in the 1990s: A National Plan for Action,* which was published by the Centers for Disease Control in 1993.

The authors of this report note that a critical component in any injury or violence prevention effort, whether national, state, or local, is the presence of trained professionals in a wide variety of disciplines. Our purposes in this chapter are to examine the need for professional education and training in violence prevention, to emphasize the collaborative nature that is essential to such education and training, and to highlight one training effort based on strong public health principles that encourages the collaboration among disciplines critical to all successful violence prevention activities.

The Need for Trained Professionals

For more than two decades, public health and other professionals have noted the need for increased academic training in injury and violence prevention (Dana, Gallagher, & Vince, 1990). As an appreciation of the enormous impact of injuries related to violence has grown, so has awareness of the lack of trained professionals to meet the needs for prevention in this area. The 1990 health objectives for the United States detailed 19 injury-related health objectives; only two of these related to intentional injuries—one to homicide and one to suicide (U.S. Department of Health and Human Services, 1980). In contrast, the year 2000 health objectives for the United States include 40 objectives related to injury prevention, of which 18 concern violence (U.S. Department of Health and Human Services, 1990). Furthermore, the Third National Injury Control Conference recommended enhanced professional training for both practitioners and researchers at all levels (prevention, acute care, and rehabilitation) in both unintentional and violence-related injury prevention as a necessary prerequisite of the achievement of all other injury-related year 2000 objectives (Centers for Disease Control, 1992). The conference report states: "Lack of faculty expertise, support, and training materials has undermined scientific training in injury control and its incorporation into many relevant academic areas. These barriers must be addressed and injury control incorporated into allied health fields" (Centers for Disease Control, 1993, p. 31).

During the 1980s, a number of landmark publications in the field of injury control recognized the dearth of professional education and training opportunities in injury and violence prevention. The National Academy of Sciences report *Injury in America* (Institute of Medicine, 1985) identified a lack of trained scholars, health professionals, and other professionals in injury control as a major barrier to understanding and preventing injuries. The report highlighted the need for adequate funding of injury-related research, but noted that "without funds for scholarships and faculty support . . . training cannot grow to meet the need" (Institute of Medicine, 1985, pp. 147-148).

The National Committee for Injury Prevention and Control, in its 1989 publication *Injury Prevention: Meeting the Challenge,* also targeted professional education and training in its key recommendations for injury prevention. Yet a 1989 survey of school of public health and graduate programs in community health regarding injury control curricula noted that although more schools were offering courses and lectures in injury control than had been previously documented, "the leading causes of injury, such as motor vehicle crashes, homicides, and suicides, are not a focus of existing courses" (Dana et al., 1990, p. 8). A recent survey of schools of public health and graduate programs in community health regarding violence prevention found that only 9 of 23 responding schools had specialty areas of study focusing on violence (Markwardt & Rowitz, 1993). Furthermore, once students of public health graduate and enter the workplace, they find few opportunities, other than state and national conferences, for continuing professional education in injury and violence prevention (Miara, 1990).

Contributing to the gaps in professional education and training in injury and violence prevention is the multidisciplinary nature of the field. As noted in *Injury Control in the 1990s,* "Injury control includes many disciplines and sciences, such as health care, epidemiology, engineering, ergonomics, biomechanics, education, architecture, public policy, law, the behavioral sciences, the social sciences, and health communications" (Centers for Disease Control, 1993, p. 45). In addition to these recognized academic disciplines, the field of violence prevention also increasingly involves representatives of local communities, volunteer service organizations, recreational associations, clubs, religious organizations, neighborhood associations, businesses, and the media (National Center for Injury Prevention and Control, 1993). Yet, as noted in the proceedings of the Third National Injury Control Conference, "at present, few persons—either in health agencies or in high-risk communities—have both adequate experience and training to mount a comprehensive violence prevention program. This lack of trained personnel is the natural consequence of our current fragmented approach to violence prevention. Unfortunately, it also represents one of the most formidable barriers to any contemplated broad-scale violence prevention effort" (Centers for Disease Control, 1992, p. 184). This problem is so acute that even funded violence prevention initiatives often have great difficulty filling project positions with qualified people (A. Dana, Children's Safety Network, Education Development Center, Newton, Massachusetts, personal communication, October 20, 1993).

The U.S. Public Health Service's *Healthy People 2000: National Health Promotion and Disease Prevention Objectives* addresses the broad network of professionals potentially able to participate in violence prevention research and practice. The report recommends that curricular material on the identification and prevention of violent behavior be included in all schools preparing students for future careers in primary health care, education, law enforcement, juvenile justice, social work, mental health, child development and child care, elder care, religious ministry, and recreation (U.S. Department of Health and Human Services, 1990). Nevertheless, most health and many other professionals continue to study and train in relative isolation from one another, unaware of the contributions other disciplines may offer to the injury and violence prevention effort. This problem is further exacerbated by the tendency of health and other clinically oriented professionals to fail to respond to instruction or materials that are not patient oriented or clinically relevant. Professional isolation narrows individuals' vision of what is possible and inhibits the formation of the collaborative relationships necessary for the understanding and prevention of violent behavior.

The emerging consensus that violence, with its enormous physical and emotional toll, is a public health problem might encourage the bridging of gaps between professionals from a variety of fields that currently interact sporadically, if at all. During the Third National Injury Control Conference, it was noted that the

> most important new perspective that the field of public health brings to the issue of violence is a focus, from the very outset, on the outcome of interest—in this case, reducing the morbidity and mortality due to violence—rather than on any particular method or discipline for achieving that outcome. By focusing first on the outcome, public health practitioners are free to consider preventive actions across whatever disciplines and domains that might reasonably be expected to contribute to the effort. (Centers for Disease Control, 1992, p. 170)

Although most of the literature on education and training in violence prevention describes professional audiences (public health, medicine, nursing, mental health, behavioral and social science, social work, education, criminal justice and law), there are many other individuals who are necessary partners in violence prevention and who, therefore, are also in need of targeted education and training. Community leaders, both elected and nonelected, community activists, government and social service agency staff, religious leaders, parents, and youth are all potential beneficiaries of enhanced training opportunities. Although there has never been a consistent, well-recognized effort to include them in graduate-level training programs in injury and violence prevention, their participation is critical to the success of any violence prevention effort in the community. As is noted in *Injury Control in the 1990s*:

> Another unique aspect of injury control is the wide range of disciplines required for success. An intervention begins with knowledge gained from surveillance and research to determine the how, who, and why of an act that injures. The people at this stage of injury control are researchers in biomechanics, epidemiology, medicine, education, and social and behavioral science. These same people along with manufacturers, activists, and law enforcement personnel

design and test ways to prevent or reduce the impact of injury. Once an intervention reaches its ultimate destination—individuals in the community—the partners in prevention become very diverse: parents, teachers, police officers, fire fighters, doctors, nurses, bartenders, designated drivers, and the list goes on and on. (Centers for Disease Control, 1993, p. 47)

The diversity of target audiences for training efforts in violence prevention requires that equally diverse and creative methods be employed in designing and implementing training and education programs. Physician education has been a particular focus in recent medical literature. In its position statement, the American Academy of Pediatrics (AAP) recommends numerous areas for enhanced physician education and training (see Spivak & Harvey, 1994). Increasing pediatricians' knowledge about the epidemiology, risk factors, and sequelae of family, peer, and community violence, as well as training them in appropriate diagnosis, management, and referral of individual victims and perpetrators of violence, are targets included in the 1994 AAP report, "The Role of the Pediatrician in Violence Prevention" (Spivak & Harvey, 1994). Developing and disseminating training materials, including in-office and emergency department protocols, supporting research efforts in numerous violence-related areas, developing and conducting continuing educational seminars and workshops, and enhancing the interactions between pediatricians and community-based service providers and advocates are also part of the AAP's comprehensive strategy for effectively promoting childhood violence prevention.

Other medical specialties have also begun to reevaluate the role of the physician in recognizing, treating, and preventing injuries resulting from violence. A 1989 survey of family practice residency programs found that the vast majority of training programs did not include the issue of violence (Centers for Disease Control, 1991). Similarly, a survey of U.S. and Canadian medical schools during 1987-1988 revealed very little medical school instruction regarding adult domestic violence (Centers for Disease Control, 1989). During the past 3 years, the American College of Obstetricians and Gynecologists (ACOG) has developed a multifaceted approach to increasing member physicians' knowledge and skills in the area of domestic violence. Increasing curricular content in medical schools and residency training, including domestic violence materials on oral and written board exams, improving educational materials for practicing physicians, and working to increase public awareness about spouse abuse are all steps that the ACOG is taking (Randall, 1992).

In addition to medical school and residency training programs, schools of public health, social work, criminal justice, law, psychology, and education are also beginning to include violence prevention instructional material (Markwardt & Rowitz, 1993). *Injury Control in the 1990s* reports on the development during the Second World Conference on Injury Control of a national plan for increasing professional education and training in injury and violence prevention across a wide spectrum of disciplines. The following strategies are recommended:

- Develop and implement a national injury and violence prevention training plan.
- Work with government agencies that fund related training for professionals (e.g., police) to require that such training include a violence prevention component.
- Support coordinated research and training within relevant federal agencies to integrate violence prevention research and training with other priority issues, such as alcohol and drug abuse prevention.
- Train staffs of state and local health departments and faculties at medical, nursing, public health, and related professional schools as injury and violence prevention professionals.
- Require injury and violence prevention training of program staff as a component of state capacity-building grants.
- Designate and fund a resource center that would collect and disseminate violence prevention curricula, learning materials, and aids.
- Create incentives for faculty and students, such as scholarships and fellowships.
- Support the development of model curricula, instructor training manuals, and learning materials, and disseminate them nationally.
- Encourage and support the recognition of violent injuries and violence prevention education in the core curriculum of medical schools. Develop and implement teaching modules to assist primary caregivers in identifying and appropriately referring victims of violence and others at high risk of injury due to violence.

What are some of the barriers to the achievement of these recommendations? Why have we not accomplished more thus far?

It may be helpful to consider for a moment the history of injury control as a science, and to trace its first documented success story: motor vehicle injury prevention.

For many years, motor vehicle-related injuries and deaths were the sole purview of traffic engineers and scientists. Injuries were regarded as accidents, largely random and unavoidable, with blame usually assigned to driver error. In the 1960s, Haddon, Suchman, and Klein (1964) constructed a phase-factor matrix for understanding the etiology and prevention of motor vehicle injury. Building on the epidemiological triangle of host, agent, and environment, Haddon et al. developed a framework for motor vehicle collision causation that included human, vehicle, and environmental factors and interactions in time (see also Haddon, 1980). This prevention framework freed injury prevention scientists and practitioners from limiting their focus to blaming the victim ("The accident was caused by a bad driver") and providing acute medical care for the injured ("scoop and run").

What emerged were numerous strategies that proved to be effective in reducing motor vehicle injuries. These included reduction of drinking and driving; the use of child car seats and passive restraint systems, including seat belts and air bags; and the automotive industry's design and manufacture of antilock brakes, energy-absorbing steering assemblies, improved door locks, rounded front ends, tapered dashboards, and reinforced doors and tops. Improvements in roadway design, particularly on the federal interstate system, also have been credited with saving lives (National Committee for Injury Prevention and Control, 1989). These improvements included traffic signs, better illumination, guardrail upgrades, obstacle removal, and crash cushions. Smart vehicle technology, such as sensor alarms to detect vehicles in front and back, promise future reductions in traffic injury and death. It would be fair to say that most of these interventions, which have saved many lives and will continue to do so, would not have been possible if it were not for the work of a variety of professionals trained in the scientific principles of injury control developed by Haddon and his colleagues 30 years ago.

A similar analogy applies in the area of interpersonal violence. Many people today, including the general public and the scientific community, still believe that violence is not preventable, and that it is related to the perpetration of felonies. To date, our society has largely relied on the criminal justice system to respond to this problem. However, building more prisons and providing more law enforcement will do very little to reduce some of the kinds of violence occurring in the United States today. The typical violent episode that ends in injury or death occurs between acquaintances who have argued while under the influence of alcohol or other drugs, with combatants using handguns. Another common scenario resulting in violent behavior occurs between spouses or domestic partners interacting within a complex web of fear and control. As with motor vehicle injuries, a narrow or simplistic explanation for intentional injury causation or prevention will not suffice. Indeed, injuries due to violence are marked by their intentionality, by the interchange of roles between victims and perpetrators, and by a complex web of social risk factors—including poverty, racism, and unemployment—that may contribute to violent behavior. Experts in injury prevention are just beginning to address the characteristics that differentiate unintentional from intentional or violent injuries. Some researchers believe that violence prevention strategies may be more dependent on changing human behavior than on modifying the environment—traditionally the most effective unintentional injury prevention strategy (Prothrow-Stith, Spivak, & Hausman, 1988). Because of these complexities and the lack of a single successful strategy for violence prevention, the importance of a multidisciplinary approach to reducing violence, utilizing the expertise of diversely trained professionals, is paramount.

The first step in increasing the number of qualified violence prevention professionals lies in educating students. Among the field's most pressing needs are ways to attract and retain good students. The growing recognition of violence as a major health problem has stimulated student interest in the field, but there are few federal funds available for training at the predoctoral and postdoctoral levels. In addition, because injuries related to violence unduly burden women and members of minority groups, prevention strategy development and implementation must be sensitive to the special needs and circumstances of high-risk communities. It is crucial to recruit female students and students of color into the violence prevention field.

A persistent challenge in the field of violence prevention has been lack of consistent funding support for research, education, training, program development, implementation, and evaluation. The scope of these needs is so large that no single funding source will be able to meet all of them. Nevertheless, a clear leadership role for funding in the field of violence prevention rests with the federal government, specifically with the National Center for Injury Control at the Centers for Disease Control. National and local private resources can also be tapped to fill in gaps in funding and can be especially useful in funding pilot programs.

Innovative approaches also exist that can expand financial resources for violence prevention. For example, training efforts might be enhanced by linking professionals from state health departments and other federally funded violence prevention programs with experts in schools of public health, medicine, social work, law, and nursing. This same type of collaboration could also facilitate improved research opportunities for scholars in academic settings.

A further barrier to fulfilling the recommendations contained within the national plan for action is the lack of readily identifiable, easily accessible source materials for those interested in preparing students, health professionals, and other professionals for work in violence prevention. The need for training materials is complex because of the differing perspectives brought to the field by learners from various professional disciplines.

In the next section, we highlight one approach to violence prevention education and training that was designed to meet the needs of professionals in the field. This training effort, a workshop sponsored by the Connecticut Childhood Injury Prevention Center in 1994, is noteworthy for its emphasis on educating individuals in solid principles of injury prevention as well as for its focus on the collaboration among disciplines that is critical to the success of any violence prevention action. This type of educational experience is uniquely suited to increasing the understanding of a particular problem (e.g., injuries due to violence) among workers in public and private agencies and to facilitating opportunities for networking and collaboration.

An Example of Violence Prevention Education and Training

Background

In response to a request from the Connecticut Department of Public Health and Addiction Services, the Connecticut Childhood

Injury Prevention Center (a collaboration among Hartford Hospital, the University of Connecticut Health Center, Newington Children's Hospital, and the American Academy of Pediatrics—Connecticut Chapter) developed a full-day workshop titled "Organizing a Community-Based Violence Prevention Program."

The workshop was targeted at public health professionals at the local level as well as at community agency staff. The purpose of the workshop was to provide participants with (a) an overview and understanding of youth interpersonal violence in Connecticut, (b) a conceptual model through which to understand the etiology and control strategies, (c) knowledge of state-of-the-art violence prevention strategies, and (d) the skills to plan, implement, and evaluate a community-based violence prevention program.

Initially, two workshops accommodating 30 participants each were scheduled for May 1994. The geographic locations of the workshops were varied to encourage registration in different parts of the state. A small registration fee of $10 was collected to help assure workshop attendance and to defray costs. A third workshop was scheduled for June 1994 when interest in the first two workshops exceeded capacity. Each workshop participant received a packet of materials on the day of the workshop that included an address list of preregistrants, a resource bibliography, and a summary of conflict resolution curricula.

Workshop Description

The workshop was organized into two major parts. The morning session included information on the epidemiology of youth interpersonal violence and activities to prevent youth violence, which included a discussion of strategies, target groups, and settings. The second half of the morning session focused on building a community-based violence prevention program and included topics such as community organization, problem identification, setting goals and objectives, identifying and addressing program barriers, locating resources, and monitoring the progress of the program. A slide presentation was used to impart the information to workshop participants, and considerable attention was given to encouraging discussion and interaction among them.

In the afternoon session, a small group exercise was conducted that was designed to introduce participants to a typical situation encountered by those working to address youth violence in an urban setting. Participants were given background information on a hypothetical urban center (description of city, demographics, level of employment, incidence of youth violence). In the exercise, they were assigned to assume the roles of groups representing six stakeholders; the schools, parents, business/government/health, community agencies, media, and youth. The participants were instructed to develop plans to implement and evaluate a youth violence prevention initiative. In addition, they were asked to describe how they would organize the community, their process and outcome objectives, and barriers and how they would address them. Finally, participants were asked to fill out a questionnaire at the end of each workshop to aid in program evaluation and assessment of future training needs.

Workshop Experience and Evaluation

Of the individuals who preregistered, 84% (79 of 94) attended the workshops. Of those, 65% (51 of 79) completed the final questionnaire. Of these, half (51%) were community and school outreach workers. Other occupations included public health agency managers (18%), health educators (12%), public health agency staff (10%), academicians (6%), and medical providers (4%). Most workshop participants were employed by community agencies and public schools (51%). Other types of agencies represented included local health departments (37%), state health department (6%), and academic centers (4%). More than half of the questionnaire respondents (57%) reported that they had heard about the workshop from the direct mailing. The rest learned of it from supervisors and through word of mouth.

When asked why they had enrolled for the workshop, most participants said that they wanted more information and insight about violence as a public health problem. In addition, they expressed a need to become acquainted with violence prevention strategies in order to incorporate them into their everyday work. Nearly all (94%) felt the workshop had met their expectations, and 90% reported that they found the quality of the instruction to be either excellent or good. The majority (76%) thought the time and location of the workshop were convenient, and 82% thought the class was the right size.

During the first workshop, the epidemiology of youth violence was presented in a lecture format, using slides. This process drew some criticism from participants, and in the two subsequent workshops more interactive discussion was promoted, with less reliance on slides. This portion of the workshop was critical, for it provided participants with a common frame of reference. A shared understanding of the magnitude, characteristics, and risk factors of youth violence based on national, state, and local data laid the groundwork for a productive learning experience.

An important component of the workshop dealt with program design, implementation, and evaluation. Participants were eager to learn about program design and implementation. Of particular interest was the process of identifying and addressing barriers to the implementation of community-based violence prevention programs. Information on this topic was presented in the morning session and was also part of the afternoon small group discussion.

The major barriers to successful violence prevention programs in communities, as seen by participants, included (a) problems working effectively with community agency staff, (b) difficulty maintaining a strong and viable community coalition, and (c) the challenge of securing adequate funding.

Working effectively with community agency staff. Based on the experiences of the workshop presenters and several of the participants, it was discussed that community agency workers are often told by their agency directors that they must implement violence prevention efforts, but they are not involved in decisions about how and when to do so. Furthermore, if agency staff are trained to implement a program they have not "bought into," they can be resistant and resentful. In other cases agency staff may resent the increased workload a new program represents. Resistance makes training difficult and proper program replication unlikely. All workshop participants agreed that this barrier requires significant attention. If community agency staff are to be the effective implementers of violence prevention programs, they must be involved when decisions are made about the types of programs to be employed as well as the most appropriate ways to introduce them.

Another important point that was discussed was the fact that not all agency staff are effective violence prevention advocates, and some may neither believe in nor model nonviolent conflict resolution.

Recommendations included first working with those who are both willing and able to become involved at a level required for effective program implementation. Other agency staff may then be drawn in by the enthusiasm of the innovators, who can provide support to others. Finally, gaining support from agency directors and, perhaps most important, providing a budget to support staff and activities will increase the likelihood that a program will be applied consistently.

Maintaining a strong and viable coalition. Workshop participants were able to list the common pitfalls of coalition work as falling into five major areas: group dynamics, problems with hard-to-please members, frequent turnover in representatives, poor planning by the lead agency, and changes in the issues the coalition is designed to address. Members' commitment to the coalition can be heightened if they can see that they share in its benefits (e.g., media attention, opportunities for staff training) and if they are certain that members and their organizations will receive credit for the group's successes. Coalitions, like violence prevention programs, can benefit from process and outcome evaluation. One recommendation was to survey coalition members on such process measures as increases in skills and commitment, formation of new working relationships among member agencies, and satisfaction with coalition activities and products. Another suggestion was to measure the community coalition's achievement of its formally stated outcome objectives.

Securing adequate funding. Workshop participants agreed that for almost all violence prevention programs, stable, long-term funding is nonexistent. Many foundations, especially local ones, do not offer funding in amounts large enough to support an entire program. This translates into an inability to hire needed staff, to operate program activities of significant scale or duration, and to provide continuity of services. Underfunded evaluations are unable to follow youth over time in order to determine whether or not an intervention really does make a difference.

Participants acknowledged that although there are no easy answers, the long-term solution to insufficient funding is to gain ongoing and long-term financial support. To this end, violence prevention programs must continue to seek stable monies from several funding streams and to institutionalize the violence prevention staff within participating community organizations.

Workshop participants also highlighted the important benefits to violence prevention programs of in-kind support. For example, the development and implementation of violence prevention public awareness campaigns are often supported with significant in-kind contributions from local public relations companies and local television and radio stations. In addition, many communities are able to obtain significant program evaluation expertise from local universities, where faculty and students often provide the computer hardware and software and the additional data management and statistical consultation required to complete evaluations.

Final comments from the workshop evaluation included the recognition of the importance of including the basic principles of effective community-based health promotion programs as part of the workshop. An important aspect that was mentioned by several participants was the fact that each community must assess its own needs and adapt the framework for community action to its own characteristics.

Conclusions Drawn From the Workshop

There is a great need and interest among public health practitioners and community agency staff for more training in violence prevention and program management. We believe these workshops were a beginning step in this process. Possibly because of a lack of formal training opportunities and the short time they have been in the field, staff in public health and community service agencies are especially enthusiastic about receiving violence prevention training. Although interested in a number of specific strategies to reduce violence, most participants were most interested in building their skills in conflict resolution. They acknowledged this as an important aspect of the workshop, and there was much less eagerness to learn about program design, implementation, and evaluation.

It is encouraging that the workshop participants were very enthusiastic that the workshops brought together professionals from different disciplines and cultural backgrounds to address violence prevention. The networking and information exchange that occurred during the workshops was viewed by the faculty as a crucial element in developing a base of experienced violence prevention practitioners.

Finally, to make training attractive to the largest number of people possible, plans for future workshops need to take into

account the financial and travel constraints of potential participants—a low-cost, one-day training program, including lunch, in
selected sites around the state is the most feasible and preferred
format.

Conclusion

Despite the terrible costs to individuals, families, communities,
and society as a whole, prevention of the epidemic of violence in
the United States has been hampered thus far by a lack of trained
violence prevention professionals in a wide variety of academic
disciplines. Recent national recommendations call for federal leadership in violence prevention—specifically, for increased funding
for research, training, and education. The content and the format
of the educational opportunities that need to be developed and
implemented will vary depending on the professional backgrounds
and experiences of those being trained. However, any strategy to
improve professional education and training in the field of violence
prevention must also include collaboration among professionals as
well as commitment to form partnerships with nontraditional disciplines. Finally, a successful strategy for enhancing violence prevention education and training must seek to include members of
the communities most at risk for experiencing the devastating
consequences of violence in their lives.

References

Centers for Disease Control. (1989). Education about adult domestic violence in
    U.S. and Canadian medical schools, 1987-88. *Morbidity and Mortality Weekly
    Report, 38*(2), 17-19.
Centers for Disease Control. (1991). Violence education in family practice residency
    programs: U.S., 1989. *Morbidity and Mortality Weekly Report, 40*, 428-430.
Centers for Disease Control. (1992). *Position papers from the Third National Injury
    Control Conference: Setting the national agenda for injury control in the 1990s.*
    Atlanta, GA: Author.
Centers for Disease Control. (1993). *Injury control in the 1990s: A national plan
    for action.* Atlanta, GA: Author.
Dana, A. J., Gallagher, S. S., & Vince, C. J. (1990). *Survey of injury prevention
    curricula in schools of public health.* Paper presented at the annual meeting of
    the American Public Health Association, New York.

Haddon, W. (1980). Options for the prevention of motor vehicle crash injury. *Israeli Journal of Medicine, 16,* 45-68.

Haddon, W., Suchman E. A., & Klein, D. (1964). *Accident research: Methods and approaches.* New York: Harper & Row.

Institute of Medicine. (1985). *Injury in America: A continuing public health problem.* Washington, DC: National Academy Press.

Markwardt, R., & Rowitz, L. (1993). *Public health educational response to violence: A draft report.* Chicago: Center for Public Health Practice/University of Illinois, School of Public Health, Illinois Public Health Leadership Institute.

Miara, C. (1990). *National survey of the training needs of health department and traffic safety injury control professionals.* Paper presented at the annual meeting of the American Public Health Association, New York.

National Center for Injury Prevention and Control. (1993). *The prevention of youth violence: A framework for community action.* Atlanta, GA: Centers for Disease Control and Prevention.

National Committee for Injury Prevention and Control. (1989). *Injury prevention: Meeting the challenge.* New York: Oxford University Press.

Prothrow-Stith, D., Spivak, H., & Hausman, H. (1988). *Violence: The public health approach.* Unpublished manuscript, Harvard School of Public Health.

Randall T. (1992). ACOG renews domestic violence campaign, calls for changes in medical school curricula. *Journal of the American Medical Association, 267*(80), 151-154.

Spivak, H., & Harvey, B. (Eds.). (1994). The role of the pediatrician in violence prevention [Special issue]. *Pediatrics, 94*(4) (Suppl.).

U.S. Department of Health and Human Services, Public Health Service. (1980). *Promoting health, preventing disease: Objectives for the nation.* Washington, DC: Government Printing Office.

U.S. Department of Health and Human Services, Public Health Service. (1990). *Healthy people 2000: National health promotion and disease prevention objectives* (DHHS Publication No. PHS 91-50212). Washington, DC: Government Printing Office.

CHAPTER 10

A Public Health Approach to Violence Prevention: The Los Angeles Coalition

BILLIE P. WEISS

Most U.S. citizens take pride in espousing a social contract that respects the rights of individuals, promotes equality, and values the sanctity of life. These citizens also pride themselves on being peace-loving people. Compare these peaceful images with images that glorify the nation's violent past and make modern-day heroes out of those who behave violently, the images that teach our children that the West was won—justifiably—by violence. Many in this nation believe that it is their right to be armed with any weapon of their choosing. Our society has produced images that glorify the violence of Jesse James, George Custer, and Bonnie and Clyde, and has helped to create film characters like Rambo and Dirty Harry. These images have contributed in part to the present situation, in which more people are killed in the United States by violent acts than in any other industrialized country in the world, and the majority of these homicides are committed with firearms. This situation has led former Surgeon General C. Everett Koop (1991) to conclude that "the professions of medicine, nursing, and the health-related social services must come forward and recognize violence as their issue and one that profoundly affects the public health" (p. vi).

In this chapter, I examine the impact of violence on communities, particularly Los Angeles, California. I present a case study of the Violence Prevention Coalition of Greater Los Angeles to illustrate the importance of collaborative efforts to reduce and prevent violence in our communities.

Violence in the United States

Each year, more than 50,000 people die in the United States as the result of violent acts (Rosenberg & Mercy, 1991). Of this number, approximately 20,000 persons die from homicide and a greater number (30,000+) from suicide (Baker, O'Neill, Ginsburg, & Li, 1992; Rosenberg & Mercy, 1991). Homicide is the fourth leading cause of death for children between the ages of 1 and 14, and it ranks second for youth between the ages of 15 to 24 (Baker et al., 1992). Among African Americans 15 to 34 years of age, it is the leading cause of death (Baker et al., 1992). In contrast, among white youth in this age group, the leading cause of death is motor vehicle accidents (National Center for Health Statistics, 1994). Furthermore, homicide is the leading cause of injury death for all infants less than 1 year of age (Waller, 1985). It is estimated that firearms are responsible for 60% to 80% of the homicides in the United States.

Homicide rates are highest in urban areas, a fact that often leads to the erroneous assumption that most violence is the result of random street killings. On the contrary, the majority of homicides, with estimates ranging from 40% to 60%, occur between people who know each other (Rosenberg & Mercy, 1991; Weiss, 1994). As to location, Fingerhut and Kleinman (1990) compared homicide rates for 1988 for central cities with other population centers. These authors found that 72% of black male teenage homicides occurred in metropolitan core counties, compared with only 6% in nonmetropolitan areas.

Other factors, such as alcohol and other drugs, are believed to be contributing factors in escalating anger into homicide (Reiss & Roth, 1993). The role of firearms, particularly handguns, in these deaths is significant. Increasing homicide rates parallel the increasing availability of firearms, including handguns (Wintemute, 1994). Rates of homicide are higher in underserved, impoverished communities (Weiss, 1993). Although race or ethnic background is often identified as a risk factor for victimization, this may actually matter less than either social class or poverty. For example, one study that examined injury rates by race, ethnicity, and poverty found that when the racial and ethnic groups were held constant, the same communities remained at risk for violence, suggesting that poverty may play an important role (Chang, Weiss, & Yuan, 1992).

Although rates of homicide are greater in urban areas, it is not clear whether the discrepancy between urban and rural areas is the same for nonfatal violent injuries, because fatal outcomes are systematically reported, whereas nonfatal outcomes are not. Biased reporting and the lack of case ascertainment may greatly underestimate the magnitude of the problem. It is clear, however, that available data point to higher rates of self-inflicted violence than interpersonal violence in rural settings. Further investigation is needed to document the variance in rates of violent injury between urban and rural settings.

Firearm Violence in the United States

On an average day in the United States, one child dies from an unintentional shooting. Accidental shootings are the third leading cause of death for 10- to 29-year-olds and the fifth leading cause of death for children from 1 to 15 years of age. Some 50% of all unintentional child shootings occur in the victims' homes, and an additional 40% occur in the homes of friends or relatives (Smith & Larman, 1988; Wintemute, Teret, Kraus, Wright, & Bradfield, 1987). In many parts of the United States, suicide rates exceed homicide rates. In 1991, 48% of the total 38,317 firearms-related deaths nationwide were classified as suicides; that proportion was again found in 1992 (Fingerhut, 1994). However, in many urban areas, such as Los Angeles, deaths caused by interpersonal violence exceed those caused by self-inflicted wounds. The common element in both of these types of violence is the availability of firearms: In the case of suicide, a gun can escalate ideation into fatal reality; in the case of homicide, a gun can escalate an argument into a fatal outcome.

Los Angeles Gang Violence

Youth street gangs are not a new phenomenon. A review of the history of gangs shows that in 19th-century London adolescent street gangs terrorized city residents. Prior to the U.S. Civil War, it was reported that New York City had approximately 30,000 street gang members. At other times, Philadelphia and Chicago were proclaimed to be gang capitals. Currently, this dubious distinction is believed to belong to Los Angeles (Office of the Los Angeles County District Attorney, 1992).

In Los Angeles, it is estimated that there are currently more than 100,000 gang members, who belong to more than 1,000 gangs (W. McBride, L.A. County Sheriffs Department, Youth Services Bureau, Street Gang Detail, personal communication, 1993). In many respects, youth gang behavior parallels the typical behavior of adolescents (e.g., peer association, peer acceptance, and independence). It is not these behaviors, in my opinion, that are the problem; rather, the violent and criminal behavior of gang members is what makes them a menace to society.

Despite the illegal activities associated with gangs, it has been my experience that L.A. youth join gangs for many reasons having nothing to do with such activities. It is true that gang members commit more types of crime and commit crimes more often than nongang youth, but many gang members are not involved in crime. Many are not involved in drug trafficking, and many are not organized into drug distribution rings. Most L.A. gangs are loose-knit, with several members who fill leadership roles, depending on their ages and situations. Membership fluctuates, and gang members have varying degrees of commitment to their gangs. In Los Angeles, gang cohesiveness is highest when a gang is challenged by other groups or outsiders (Office of the Los Angeles County District Attorney, 1992).

Drive-by shootings and other gun-related activities carried out by gang members have increased as guns on the streets have proliferated (Office of the Los Angeles County District Attorney, 1992). Gang-related homicides in Los Angeles in 1992 were four times higher than the comparable figures for 1978. However, the annual totals of gang-related homicides decreased in 1981, 1982, 1984, and 1993 (W. McBride, personal communication, 1993). Preliminary data for 1994 indicate a slight increase once again.

The Los Angeles Police Department (LAPD) defines a gang as a group of three or more persons who have a common identifying sign or symbol and whose members engage in criminal activity (B. Jackson, LAPD, Operations Bureau, Gang Information Section, personal communication, February 1992). It defines gang-related crimes as those in which at least one identified active or associate gang member is the criminal, the victim, or both. Reported gang-related crimes have included assault with a deadly weapon, attempted murder, shooting at an inhabited dwelling, and homicide. Several researchers have attempted to test the reliability of reporting methods (e.g., Maxson & Klein, 1990; Meehan & O'Carroll, 1992), and some have affirmed that the LAPD gang-related homicide classification has been consistent between cases, between investigators, and between stations and over time (Klein, Gordon, & Maxson, 1986; Maxson, Gordon, & Klein, 1985; Maxson & Klein, 1990). Data on gang-related homicides in Los Angeles from 1989 to 1991 show that 92% of all victims were male. Although Hispanics constituted 40% of the L.A. population and blacks 13%, 95% of the victims were either Hispanic or black; 86% of the victims were between the ages of 15 and 34 years of age; 58% were killed by other gang members and 42% were not gang members (Gustafson, Weiss, & Jackson, 1992). For the same period, approximately 66% of all homicides in Los Angeles were firearm related, whereas 88% of gang homicides were firearm related (Los Angeles County Department of Health Services, 1992). A handgun was the weapon of choice for 84% of these gang-related homicides.

The Public Health Approach to Prevention

The reduction of violent injuries requires a comprehensive public health approach. This approach is built on a three-tiered model of primary, secondary, and tertiary prevention. Applying this perspective to violence, primary prevention would seek to reduce the incidence of *new* cases of violence, or first-time violent behavior. Secondary prevention would *intervene early* in the sequence of violent acts to arrest violent behavior. Tertiary prevention would happen *after* a violent act has occurred to restore as much functioning as possible to the individual or community. According to a public health model, violent behavior is assumed to follow a pattern similar to the patterns of other public health epidemics. That is, its occurrence can be measured and monitored, and groups at risk can be identified. If these assumptions are correct, then the adverse outcomes associated with violent behavior can be predicted and prevented.

Of the three tiers of prevention in the model, primary prevention holds the greatest promise for programs aimed at preventing violence, even though primary prevention requires a long-term commitment.

It also requires a comprehensive effort from all segments of the community, beginning with the individual and involving education, community action, social support, and competency building.

Community Coalition Building for Prevention

Among the many local and regional public health efforts currently addressing the epidemic of violence, the Los Angeles County response is one example of a comprehensive effort that is in keeping with the public health model in that it draws on a broad base of community support. The Los Angeles Violence Prevention Coalition was formed by the Los Angeles County Department of Health Services in 1991 and consists of more than 400 members with expertise in particular categories of violence or violence prevention. Coalition members include representatives from the community as well as from business, medicine, public health, law enforcement, community-based organizations, the academic community, secondary schools, the religious community, and the California State Department of Health Services.

The coalition was formed based on the belief that the level of violence and resulting injuries then found in Los Angeles were unacceptable. The coalition is based on a multidisciplinary approach that uses the specific talents and skills of its various members' disciplines. The coalition calls attention to the problem of violence, promotes and implements prevention and intervention programs, and evaluates program effectiveness. In addition, the coalition provides a forum for influencing public policy regarding violence prevention in Los Angeles.

The Los Angeles Violence Prevention Coalition has adopted three goals with specific objectives to address over the next 4 years:

1. To reduce the availability and accessibility of firearms
2. To change community norms so that violence is not acceptable
3. To create and promote alternatives to violence

Goal 1

The coalition's first goal is to reduce the availability and accessibility of firearms in Los Angeles. In order to achieve this goal, the coalition is working on developing a baseline estimate of the number of federally licensed firearm dealers in Los Angeles County. Estimating the number of firearm dealers is complicated and time-consuming; therefore, this objective is ongoing and long-term. The Violence Prevention Coalition, along with the Los Angeles County Department of Health Services, has purchased a data tape from the U.S. Bureau of Alcohol, Tobacco and Firearms that lists federal licensees with L.A. addresses, either for license or retail outlets. A federal licensee is not required to maintain a permanent business address to obtain a license. Thus, many individuals maintain federal licenses in order to purchase firearms for their own use, and many legitimate retail dealers are licensed in a single location but maintain branch stores throughout the county. Also, holding a federal firearm dealer license allows the license holder to sell firearms from a car or other mobile facility, which makes it more difficult to determine the exact number of dealers operating in a particular jurisdiction. Even though efforts toward this objective do not directly affect illegal gun sales, they do begin the process of identifying the original sources of many guns.

The second objective related to firearms reduction is to meet with local law enforcement agencies and other local groups to develop strategies for reducing the access and availability of firearms in the Greater Los Angeles region. For example, California, like many other states, has enacted a law that gives the state the right of preemption regarding local laws that limit or control the sale of firearms and ammunition. One strategy under consideration involves working toward overturning the state preemption law, thus allowing jurisdictions to pass their own laws concerning the sale and licensing of firearms. If the state preemption law were overthrown, local jurisdictions would be able to pass legislation more stringent than current state law, not less. In other words, local ordinances would have to be at least as stringent as current state law.

The third objective for the reduction of firearms-related violence is to develop and implement a policy designed to reduce the availability and accessibility of firearms through a coordinated public health campaign. Initial success has already been achieved in this area, as evidenced by the 1995 decision of the city of Los Angeles to pass a local ordinance requiring firearms dealers within the city to obtain business licenses. In addition, in order to operate within the city, gun dealerships must purchase liability insurance in the amount of $1 million.

Goal 2

The coalition's second goal is to change community norms to reflect support for nonviolent behavior. In trying to change the norms of the larger community, it is important for local communities and neighborhoods to develop their own coalitions and networks that reflect their own areas' demographic makeup. The Violence Prevention Coalition, for example, is ethnically and racially representative of the Los Angeles County population and includes youth. The coalition has served as a model for the formation of smaller local coalitions in the cities of Inglewood and Pasadena and in L.A. neighborhoods such as Pico/Union and Blythe/Delano. The Los Angeles Violence Prevention Coalition also provides technical assistance to other coalitions, community agencies, and citizen groups, which may involve helping community-based organizations develop program evaluations to determine program effectiveness or providing pro bono assistance to grassroots organizations that are trying to identify funding resources and learn about grant writing.

The most crucial objective related to changing community norms in Los Angeles has been to involve the media and entertainment community, which is intimately involved in the lives of the area's citizens. Mediascope, one of the Violence Prevention Coalition members, is an organization dedicated to addressing the ways in which violence is portrayed in the entertainment industry. This organization has joined the Media Committee of the coalition, the entertainment community, and representatives of the print and news media in a cooperative effort to promote nonviolent entertainment and to encourage the presentation of nonviolent solutions to societal problems in the media. Mediascope holds educational seminars for the entertainment media, and frequently works with producers, studio heads, the Writers Guild, the Directors Guild, the Academy of Motion Picture Arts and Sciences, and the American Film Institute.

Goal 3

The final goal of the Los Angeles Violence Prevention Coalition is to create and promote alternatives to violence. In order to achieve this goal, the first objective of the coalition is to promote education and training in conflict resolution and dispute mediation in the L.A. school system. Efforts are under way to require the teaching staffs within the 85 school districts of Los Angeles County to receive training to improve their skills in the area of conflict resolution. Furthermore, parents of infants born in Los Angeles will receive information on childhood development, alternative methods of expressing anger, and nonviolent child discipline. The Los Angeles County Health Department distributes information through the "Public Health Letter," a newsletter sent to more than 24,000 health care providers in Los Angeles County and other media venues.

The Violence Prevention Coalition believes that the local business community is an important partner in promoting alternatives to violence. In partnership with the area United Way, the coalition has established a joint business task force to review violence prevention policies, activities, and strategies in the workplace and wider community. Businesses are being encouraged to adopt local schools, to develop personnel policies regarding workplace violence, and to offer employees and supervisors training in conflict resolution and alternative methods for dealing with anger.

Evaluation. An integral part of the public health approach includes evaluating program effectiveness and disseminating findings. The Epidemiology Committee of the coalition has been charged with developing a method to promote the systematic evaluation of violence prevention programs and activities. The committee is also engaged in initiating a strategy for disseminating the results of these evaluations, including the methodologies, samples, and reliability and validity of the data produced by the projects that have been undertaken.

Community organization and systems prevention. As part of the primary prevention model, the coalition is working toward modifying or removing institutional barriers and building community resources. These activities include tracking and sponsoring legislation, investigating the media's role in violence, and advocating a balanced approach to violence and alternatives to violence in the entertainment and news media. The coalition also identifies curricula used in schools, studies the effects of violence in the schools, establishes a comprehensive educational campaign about the effect of violence on the community, documents community resources and programs, and facilitates networking and the opportunity to share information among community-based organizations.

Funding. The coalition operates with in-kind support from the Los Angeles County Department of Health and seeks funding through grants and contributions. The coalition functions as a nonprofit organization under the auspices of Public Health Foundation Enterprises, a nonprofit corporation that administers and manages grant-funded programs.

Organization. The coalition meets quarterly and generally features a speaker or educational program on specific topics related to prevention, evaluation, and intervention. The majority of the work of the coalition occurs within committees formed along lines of solutions to violence rather than categories of violence. Those committees are the Business Task Force, the Community Mobilization Committee, the Education Committee, the Epidemiology Committee, the Health Care Intervention Committee, the Media Committee, and the Policy and Planning Committee. The committees meet monthly and are chaired by coalition members.

Conclusion

We will not solve the problem of violence in our communities by putting 100,000 more police officers on the streets, by constructing more prison cells, by extending the death penalty to more crimes, or by executing more rapidly those convicted of capital offenses. Solutions to the problem of community violence will be found in the reestablishment of a sense of community ownership of the streets and neighborhoods, such that every resident exercises a positive governing influence, and in rebuilding decayed neighborhoods. Solutions to the problem of community violence will be found through the work done by community groups like the Los Angeles Violence Prevention Coalition.

References

Baker, S. P., O'Neill, B., Ginsburg, M. J., & Li, G. (1992). *The injury fact book* (2nd ed.). New York: Oxford University Press.

Chang A., Weiss, B., & Yuan, C. (1992). *Fatal childhood injury: Risk factors.* Unpublished manuscript.

Fingerhut, L. (1994). [Unpublished data from the National Vital Statistics System]. Centers for Disease Control and Prevention, National Center for Health Statistics.

Fingerhut, L., & Kleinman, A. (1990). *Firearm and non-firearm homicide among teenagers: Metropolitan status, United States 1979-1988.* Atlanta, GA: Centers for Disease Control, National Center for Health Statistics, Division of Analysis.

Gustafson, L., Weiss, B., & Jackson, B. (1992, November). *Gang related homicides and assaults in Los Angeles.* Paper presented at the annual meeting of the American Public Health Association, Washington, DC.

Klein, M. W., Gordon, M. A., & Maxson, C. L. (1986). The impact of police investigation on police-reported rates of gang and nongang homicides. *Criminology, 24,* 489-512.

Koop, C. E. (1991). Foreword. In M. L. Rosenberg & M. A. Fenley (Eds.), *Violence in America: A public health approach* (pp. v-vi). New York: Oxford University Press.

Los Angeles County Department of Health Services, Injury and Violence Prevention Program. (1992). *Injury mortality: A baseline report, 1980-1989.* Los Angeles: Author.

Maxson, C. L., Gordon, M. A., & Klein, M. W. (1985). Differences between gang and nongang homicides. *Criminology, 23,* 209-222.

Maxson, C. L., & Klein, M. W. (1990). Street gang violence: Twice as great, or half as great? In C. R. Huff (Ed.), *Gangs in America.* Newbury Park, CA: Sage.

Meehan, P. J., & O'Carroll, P. W. (1992). Gangs, drugs, and homicide in Los Angeles. *American Journal of Diseases of Children, 146,* 683-687.

National Center for Health Statistics. (1994). *Health, United States 1993.* Hyattsville, MD: U.S. Public Health Service.

Office of the Los Angeles County District Attorney. (1992). *Gangs, crime, and violence in Los Angeles County: Findings and proposals from the District Attorney's Office.* Los Angeles: Author.

Reiss, A. J., Jr., & Roth, J. A. (Eds.). (1993). *Understanding and preventing violence.* Washington, DC: National Academy Press.

Rosenberg, M. L., & Mercy, J. (1991). Violence is a public health problem. In M. L. Rosenberg & M. A. Fenley (Eds.), *Violence in America: A public health approach.* New York: Oxford University Press.

Smith, D., & Larman, B. (1988). *Child's play: A study of unintended handgun shoots of children.* Washington, DC: Center to Prevent Handgun Violence.

Waller, J. A. (1985). *Injury control: A guide to the causes and prevention of trauma.* Lexington, MA: Lexington Books.

Weiss, B. P. (1993). [Data from vital records of Los Angeles County, Data Collection and Analysis Unit]. Los Angeles: County of Los Angeles, Department of Health Services, Injury and Violence Prevention Program.

Weiss, B. P. (1994, October). *Understanding violence as a public health issue.* Paper presented at a special session of the American Public Health Association, Washington, DC.

Wintemute, G. J. (1994). *Ring of fire: The handgun makers of Southern California.* Sacramento: University of California, Davis, Violence Prevention Program.

Wintemute, G. J., Teret, S. P., Kraus, J. F., Wright, M. A., & Bradfield, G. (1987). When children shoot children. *Journal of the American Medical Association, 257,* 3107-3109.

• CHAPTER 11 •

A Schoolwide Approach
to Violence Prevention

KATHLEEN R. BELAND

As more and more children are experiencing conflict at home, substance abuse within the family, less access to their parents, and television as their primary source of entertainment and values, they consequently are displaying impulsive, aggressive, and often violent behavior at home, at school, and in the larger community. Between 1970 and 1992, arrests for violent crime by children under 18 jumped 91% (Federal Bureau of Investigation, 1993). By adolescence, the trend becomes deadly. Homicide is the second leading cause of death for 15- to 34-year-olds (Centers for Disease Control, personal communication, 1993). In the majority of these cases, the assailants are friends or acquaintances of the victims.

In schools, teachers find themselves spending increasing amounts of time attending to students' disruptive and angry outbursts, interpersonal conflicts, and off-task behavior, or worse. Every day, approximately 100,000 children are assaulted at school, 5,000 teachers are threatened with physical assault, and 200 are actually attacked (Geiger, 1993). Although teachers are expected to concentrate on teaching academics, they are finding that student behavior often prevents them from doing so; eventually, it drives many of them from the teaching profession.

To address this problem, a growing number of violence prevention programs have been implemented in schools across the country in recent years. These programs vary in research base, content, method of delivery, length, and effectiveness. My goal in this chapter is to present promising directions in violence prevention programming and to state the case, as well as to offer guidelines, for schoolwide implementation of prevention strategies. In so doing, I draw on my own experiences in developing, piloting, and evaluating a violence prevention program designed for schoolwide implementation (Beland, 1988, 1989, 1990, 1991).

Understanding the Need

In attempting to address youth violence, it is important for educators first to have an awareness of which children are in need of prevention programming. Virtually all children are affected by impulsive and aggressive behavior, whether they are perpetrators of this behavior, victims of it, or witnesses to it. Approximately 20% to 30% of children experience general behavioral problems early in their school careers (Achenbach & Edelbrock, 1981), and these problems often have lasting or cumulative effects due to such psychosocial factors as reputational bias and self-fulfilling prophecy (Coie & Dodge, 1983; Horn & Packard, 1985). In addition, virtually every classroom has students who are labeled "high risk." These children are characterized by excessively aggressive and impulsive behavior that is a burden to all members of their classrooms and a major cause of peer rejection (Coie, Dodge, & Kupersmidt, 1990).

Although the problem of youth violence is most visible in adolescence (Wentsel, 1993), aggression and antisocial behavior can be reliably predicted from early childhood behavior (Loeber, 1991; Patterson, Reid, & Dishion, 1992), which emerges as early as 3 years of age (Chamberlain & Nader, 1971: Westman, Rich, & Bermann, 1967). The early indicators of this high-risk pattern include:

a tendency to become involved in poking, pushing, and other annoying social behavior;

a tendency to rush into things;

negative and defiant behavior; and

self-centered verbal responsiveness to others, exemplified by interrupting others, blurting out thoughts, and talk that is irrelevant to the
ongoing conversation. (Spivack & Cianci, 1987)

Bullies fall into this high-risk category. They perceive every bump
or slight as an act of aggression that requires retaliation; they often
believe that others are out to get them. It is estimated that 15% of
schoolchildren are involved in bully-victim problems, and that 1 in 10
students is regularly harassed or attacked by bullies (Olweus, 1984).

What is in store down the road for these high-risk children if their
impulsive and aggressive behavior remains unchecked? Research
shows that many are headed for a lifetime of failure, exacting a
great toll on society. Young people in this group are particularly at
risk for underachieving in school or dropping out, as well as for
performing below their potential throughout their careers. As parents, they are often physically and/or sexually abusive, and one in
four is imprisoned for adult crimes by age 30 (Eron, Huesmann,
Duow, Romanoff, & Yarmel, 1987).

Although aggressive children have been the subject of numerous
studies, the plight of children neglected by their peers (an estimated
10% to 20% of school children) has gained the attention of researchers and educators only relatively recently (Coie et al., 1990).
Socially neglected children usually go unnoticed by their peers but
may fall victim to bullying and suffer such ill effects as low self-confidence, underachievement in school, and withdrawal. In some
cases, extended persecution has ended in suicide or violent retaliation on the part of victims. By the time they reach high school,
approximately 25% of students fear victimization by their peers
(National Association of Secondary School Principals, 1987).

Because educators can reach large numbers of children at an early
age and over an extended period of time, school-based violence
prevention programs have enormous potential. Because all children
are affected at some level, the classroom has emerged as an ideal
location for implementing violence prevention strategies.

Understanding the Problem

Before they select and implement a violence prevention program,
it is critical that educators understand why children act impulsively

and aggressively, as well as how children learn prosocial behavior. Children with minor behavior problems, as well as high-risk children, fail to act prosocially because they have one or more of the following deficits:

- They do not know what appropriate behavior is, because of a *lack of modeling* of alternative ways of resolving conflict.
- They have the knowledge but *lack the practice* because of inadequate reinforcement.
- They have *emotional responses,* such as anger, fear, or anxiety, that inhibit the performance of desirable behavior (Cox & Gunn, 1980).
- They have *inappropriate beliefs* and attributions regarding aggression (Dodge & Frame, 1982; Perry, Perry, & Rasmussen, 1986).
- They have *developmental delays* due to physiological problems, sometimes caused by the mother's substance abuse during pregnancy (Rutter, 1982) or early exposure to violence.

Children from dysfunctional homes, as well as homes that lack adult supervision, often fail to learn problem-solving skills that will help them achieve more socially acceptable solutions to everyday problems. Parents may fail to model these skills or fail to recognize and reinforce appropriate behavior when it does occur. All too often, it is inappropriate behavior that is modeled or that gets attention. To a child needy for any recognition, negative attention is often better than no attention at all (Patterson, 1975).

High-risk children are frequently victims of violence themselves (Dodge, Bates, & Pettit, 1990). They may be abused at home or may witness parental abuse of a spouse or their siblings, and may often shut down their empathic response as a means of psychological survival. These children learn that violence is an acceptable way to interact with others, and it may be the only means they have learned to attain a goal. Thus, violence tends to be an intergenerational problem, with children imitating the deficient social skills of their parents.

Parents of aggressive children sometimes fail to nurture or show interest in their offspring. There may have been a lack of bonding between mother and child from birth or an interruption during the bonding process (Bell & Ainsworth, 1972). Parents may be authoritarian, controlling, untrusting, and rejecting. They may fail to provide adequate supervision, and their discipline may be arbitrary, punitive, and extreme.

Violent television programs reinforce the message that violence is acceptable and that it is okay to dominate others. Research shows that children who view violent programs act more aggressively with their peers than children who do not (Bandura, 1973; Huesmann & Eron, 1986; Lefkowitz, Eron, Walder, & Huesmann, 1977).

Increasing numbers of children are being put at risk from the moment of conception. Substance-abusing pregnant women significantly increase the chances that their children will be born with related neurological and physical problems. Such children have significantly shorter attention spans and greater aggressive tendencies than their more normal peers. Consumption of crack cocaine has caused an epidemic of these special-needs children in recent years (Reese-Potter, 1992).

Aggressive children have often missed a key developmental step or have been delayed in their reasoning processes. Verbal mediation, or thinking out loud to guide oneself in problem solving, is thought to be important for the great shift in thinking that occurs between the ages of 5 and 7. Before this shift, children tend to respond to events superficially and in an associative fashion, often acting on the first ideas that pop into their heads. When children begin to substitute logic and reasoning for association, they become able to inhibit or regulate their behavior; that is, they stop and think before they act (Kohlberg, Yaeger, & Hjertholm, 1968; Luria, 1961; Vygotsky, 1962; White, 1965). If children fail to develop these reasoning skills—the tools of independent thinking—they will feel increasingly handicapped, both socially and academically (Achenbach, 1971).

Children learn to act prosocially in some of the same ways they learn to act antisocially: through *modeling, practice,* and *reinforcement.* Rather than witnessing and repeating negative behavior, prosocial children witness and repeat positive behavior. Reinforcement, in the form of both praise and natural rewards (resolving the problem), further ensures skill acquisition.

Prosocial children also have emotional responses—pride, happiness, security, feeling loved—that further encourage appropriate behavior. High self-esteem is not a skill, but a consequence that appears to be the result of deep acceptance by primary caregivers and/or a level of social competence that allows a child to affect her or his environment positively.

Many teachers feel they cannot fill the voids in children's lives created by their experiences at home, yet studies have shown that high-risk children who have survived and flourished in adverse conditions and against all odds have had strong connections with one or more significant adults outside of their families (Goleman, 1987). Often these stabilizing forces have been teachers. In addition to providing a foundation of love and acceptance, teachers can help children develop and use the skills that are the building blocks of social competence, resulting in indirect increases in their self-esteem.

Teaching Methodologies

With a better understanding of the problem, it becomes apparent what types of programming and teaching methodologies offer the most hope for reducing impulsive and aggressive behavior in children. Social learning theory suggests that prosocial behaviors are best taught in the ways children naturally learn them—through *observing a role model, practicing the behavior,* and *receiving feedback and reinforcement* (Bandura, 1973). Teacher modeling forms the basis for student skill acquisition. Research on modeling has shown it to be an effective means of promoting the learning of prosocial skills (Canale, 1977; Grusec, Kuczynski, Rushton, & Simutis, 1978; Rogers-Warren & Baer, 1976; Toner, Moore, & Ashley, 1978). Modeling not only demonstrates how to perform prosocial behaviors, it allows teachers to share their human side, shows that role playing can be fun, and acknowledges that mistakes are an acceptable part of the learning process.

Without student practice of a skill, the positive effects of modeling are short-lived. Student role play is an effective way to structure practice of prosocial skills and change student behavior (Spivack & Shure, 1974; Staub, 1974). During role plays, teachers coach the students by providing cues and suggestions. After role plays, teachers, as well as other students, provide feedback and reinforcement.

Being capable of performing prosocial behaviors, however, does not guarantee that children will use them in real-life situations. Children need first to *choose* to perform the behaviors, and this will not happen unless they feel the behaviors will meet their goals and be in their best interest. This is why it is important for violence prevention programs to challenge the belief structures of at-risk children through critical analysis of short- and long-term consequences of violent and aggressive behaviors and by enlisting the support of children in exerting positive peer pressure. An understanding of cultural norms and socioeconomic realities is critical for teachers in leading these discussions. Because it did not address this dynamic, the "Just say no" substance abuse prevention campaign, which sought to change behavior through simple exhortations, was doomed to failure.

Teaching methods must also be developmentally appropriate for children. Many conflict resolution programs apply methods and strategies initially developed for adult populations, with little or no adaptation for children. It is important that curricula present age-appropriate vocabulary and steps that are few and easy to remember. Grade-level content should be sequenced, with skills introduced at lower grades reinforced and expanded on in subsequent years. This building-block effect holds the most hope for student acquisition and internalization of prosocial skills.

Violence Prevention Strategies

Knowing what prosocial behaviors should be taught is as important as knowing how to impart them to students. Research suggests that the early indicators of violent adolescent and adult behavior translate into specific skill deficits: lack of empathy, impulse control, problem-solving skills, and anger management (Feshbach & Feshbach, 1969; Kendall & Braswell, 1985; Novaco, 1979; Spivack & Cianci, 1987). The following review of existing programs for children that focus on teaching skills in these deficit areas demonstrates that these directions in prevention show effectiveness and promise.

Empathy

Empathy appears to be a significant factor in the control of aggressive behavior (Feshbach & Feshbach, 1969; Feshbach & Roe, 1968). Because empathic people tend to understand others' points of view, they are less likely to misunderstand and become angry about others' behaviors. Empathic people also tend to inhibit their own aggressive behavior because observation of pain and distress in others elicits their distress responses.

Evidence suggests that preschool children as well as elementary and middle school students can learn empathy skills (Beland, 1988, 1989, 1990, 1991; Feshbach, 1984; Saltz & Johnson, 1974). The empathy "skill set" includes the abilities to (a) identify how another person is feeling, (b) take the perspective of the other person, and (c) experience what the other is feeling and show empathic behavior toward that individual. The first step alone, recognizing how another person might be feeling, is a critical skill for impulsive children and a significant deterrent to aggressive behavior. By learning to encode relevant social cues and "read the scene," these children can effectively slow down their reaction time and, thus, prevent conflicts from arising in the first place.

In piloting the Second Step program (Beland, 1988, 1989, 1990, 1991), a curriculum designed to reduce aggressive behavior for prekindergarten to eighth graders, I have found that many educators initially underestimate the importance of empathy to problem solving and anger management. Classrooms that are marked by recurrent angry flare-ups and conflicts prompt some teachers to reach first for more cognitive-based strategies. The anger reduction techniques that appear later in the curriculum are usually what enticed these educators to adopt the curriculum in the first place. Failure to establish a foundation of empathy skills, however, may rob students of the attainment of higher levels of moral reasoning in which the goals of problem solving encompass not only what is agreeable, but also what is right, fair, and in the best interests of long-term relationships. Focusing on empathy is well worth the investment of time and energy up front.

Impulse Control

Impulse control has been taught effectively to children in therapeutic as well as classroom environments (Beland, 1988, 1989, 1990, 1991; Camp & Bash, 1981; Goldstein, 1981; Meichenbaum, 1977; Spivack & Shure, 1974). Two strategies have shown promise when used with groups of impulsive and aggressive youngsters: interpersonal cognitive problem solving (Spivack & Shure, 1974) and behavioral social skills training (Michelson, 1987). For the purposes of this chapter, I refer to these strategies as *problem solving* and *behavioral skills training*. The former systematically teaches reasoning steps applied to social situations. The latter teaches target behaviors, such as "apologizing" or "joining in" an activity, that have a broad application to a variety of social situations.

In the Second Step program, the steps for problem solving are presented in the form of questions children can ask and answer of themselves. This helps to promote verbal mediation, or thinking out loud, as well as impulse control. The steps are designed to be used as an internal process to prevent problems from arising, as well as an external process for solving existing conflicts with peers or siblings. The ask-and-answer technique has a significant advantage over techniques suggested in conflict resolution programs that solely focus on *inter*personal problem solving and ignore *intra*personal problem solving and its relation to impulse control and the origins of conflict. The think-out-loud technique also aids teachers in modeling reasoning skills in everyday situations. Reasoning, essentially a covert process for adults, is made overt for the instruction of children. Repeated exposure to the strategy in natural settings helps children to acquire this skill.

Programs that utilize the problem-solving approach generally have four to six steps that focus on (a) identifying the problem, (b) brainstorming solutions, (c) evaluating solutions and predicting consequences, (d) selecting a solution or making a plan, and (e) evaluating the outcome. These strategies are most effective when they are developmentally worded for the target audience. For young children (ages 4-8), the strategy also needs to reflect different learning styles. Songs, movement, and visual presentations such as puppets and "thinking clouds" held over the head help to reinforce the problem-solving strategy in Second Step.

I have found that one of the most challenging techniques for teachers to adopt is the use of nonjudgmental responses when facilitating problem solving with students. For students to internalize the problem-solving strategy, it is important that they have free rein when brainstorming solutions; this requires that the teacher, as well as other students, refrain from critiquing responses during this phase. This requires holding back on positive reinforcement as well as negative comments. "That's one idea, what is another?" is an example of an appropriate nonjudgmental response. After the solutions have been generated, the students can then be guided to discover the most appropriate solution. This is not a "value-free" process; a well-developed problem-solving strategy should provide the criteria needed for prosocial solutions to rise to the top.

Behavioral skills are the how-tos for carrying out chosen solutions. If a child chooses to *offer a trade* as a solution for getting to
play with a peer's toy, then the child may need two or three simple
steps to follow, as well as some coaching, to pull it off effectively.
Skill steps are best generated by students rather than provided by
the teacher. Based on personal style, individual children will vary
in the steps they choose for any given solution. Like problem
solving, behavioral skills are best learned by observing a model,
practicing the behavior, and receiving feedback and reinforcement.

I have found that the interface between problem solving and
behavioral skills is the most difficult and critical for teachers to
understand and impart to students. Both strategies are designed to
come *from the students*; it is the students, not the teacher, who
generate and critique solutions, and then choose one. And it is the
students who devise a plan for carrying out a chosen solution. This
student-centered approach is critical to the students' internalization
of the skills. Teacher guidance is important, but teachers must take
care not to spoon-feed solutions or behavioral steps to the students.

Anger Management

Anger management, like empathy training, is an increasingly
popular strategy for use with aggressive adults, and it can be taught
effectively to children and adolescents as well (Beland, 1988, 1989,
1990, 1991; Novaco, 1975; Trotter & Humphrey, 1988). Anger
management strategies usually include the recognition of anger cues
and triggers, the use of positive self-statements and calming-down
techniques to prevent the onset of angry feelings, and reflection on
anger-provoking incidents.

As with the problem-solving strategy, anger management techniques should be developmentally geared to the audience. Songs
are especially useful for helping young children remember the
techniques. For angry adolescents, resorting to aggression may be
a means of regaining control when feeling threatened by others. In
these cases, it is helpful to reframe the question of control by
suggesting that someone who acts impulsively when angry is instead
being controlled by others, by being induced to fight. A cognitive
restructuring that emphasizes self-control may motivate such youth
to use anger management techniques (Frey, 1993).

A combination of empathy training, impulse control, and anger management, rather than one approach in isolation, shows the most promise for violence prevention. Empathy provides the basis for problem solving. Often conflict resolution or peer mediation programs focus solely on the cognitive side of problem solving, and, in so doing, fail to get beyond the "I'll scratch your back if you'll scratch mine" form of bartering. When empathy skills are promoted, children begin to care more about doing what is right or fair, attending to how the other person might be feeling or thinking (as well as themselves), and preserving and stabilizing the relationship. Teaching empathy helps to create bonds within the classroom that foster negotiation and reduce conflicts in general.

Problem solving and behavioral skills training complement anger management skills. The problem-solving approach guides children in resolving interpersonal problems after they have effectively reduced their anger. Behavioral skills training also combines well with anger management when the focus is on skills to use with specific types of provocations, such as pushing, grabbing, and teasing.

Transfer of Training

If prevention curricula are implemented in isolated lessons, without any effort to transfer the skills to real situations, the benefits are largely lost. The most common approach to prevention has been to "train and hope" that students use the skills, but there is growing recognition in the field that educators need to take a more proactive role. Facilitating *transfer of training* is a key role of the teacher and a skill in which most teachers need some training and support. To start, teachers can adapt role plays to the environments and realities of their student population. They can also model use of the skills as situations arise, as with the think-out-loud technique.

In addition, teachers can adopt an overt strategy that structures transfer of training. Teachers can help students target upcoming times and situations in which they might use the skills, and they can also plan some activities that call for certain skills. During these activities, teachers can coach students in their use of the skills by cuing and prompting. Finally, teachers as well as peers can provide reinforcement when students successfully use the skills. It is especially important for novice teachers to plan for transfer of training in their daily curriculum, rather than just haphazardly waiting for situations to arise. Any violence prevention program should offer guidance in this area.

Schoolwide Implementation

Because developing student ability to transfer skills to real-life situations is a major goal of any violence prevention effort, it is important to plan for schoolwide implementation of prevention programming. *Schoolwide implementation* means that students receive instruction from their core teacher at every grade level and that the school support staff (other teachers, administrators, counselors, coaches, and so on) actively reinforce student and staff use of the skills. This approach maximizes the probability that students will learn prosocial skills and concepts because they receive review and reinforcement throughout their entire school experience. This approach also recognizes that behavioral change *takes time*.

It is highly recommended that classroom teachers be the primary presenters of prevention programs, with school counselors or social workers playing a key supporting role. There are several advantages to this plan. At the elementary school level, teachers can better facilitate transfer of training throughout the day. In middle school or junior high, core teachers who have the most consistent contact with students are the optimal choice. By presenting the curriculum, teachers clearly establish themselves as support people to whom the students can easily turn at any time. Teacher presentation also ensures that *all* students receive the lessons and thus helps to set new norms for behavior in the classroom and elsewhere on the school grounds.

School counselors or social workers can provide important program support by facilitating implementation. This might entail planning for training, organizing discussion groups for teachers, modeling lessons, observing lesson presentations, giving feedback, and providing follow-up for high-risk students through pull-out groups. These students can spend more time role playing and discussing how to apply the strategies to their personal conflicts. Pull-out groups, however, should not become the sole means of presenting a program in a school. When *all* students learn and use the strategies, prosocial behavior can become the norm, and high-risk children will not feel isolated or labeled.

Getting Buy-In

Planning for schoolwide implementation presents a special challenge to those leading prevention efforts. Without the support of the entire school staff, especially teachers who will present the program to students, implementation can easily become stymied. Therefore, securing buy-in from the staff is a critical first step and a sometimes arduous task, especially when programs are initiated at the district level.

It is best to identify key school staff members who share a commitment to addressing the problem of youth violence. This team can help create an awareness of the need for violence prevention programming by discussing with other staff members the particular problems the school is facing. What antisocial behaviors are staff members seeing in students? How are these behaviors affecting students' ability to learn and teachers' ability to teach?

Once the school staff have reached an agreement to address the problem, the team may take on new members to complete the next task: researching available prevention programs. Prior to previewing program materials, the team should establish selection criteria that address several key areas. What is the research base on which the program is built? What teaching methodologies are used? What concepts and skills are taught, and have they shown to be effective with children in controlled studies? How are children guided to transfer skills to real-life situations? Are the materials developmentally appropriate at each grade level? Are the materials user-friendly to the teacher and engaging to students? What is the background of the program developer(s)? How was the program pilot tested, and what were the results?

After reviewing programs and selecting one to propose for adoption, the team should provide an overview presentation to the rest of the staff and allow them time to look over the program and ask questions. At this stage, it is critical that the team make the staff aware of the level of commitment the program requires. The commitment may entail not only time spent on lesson preparations and presentations but also possibly changing present teacher behaviors. In addition, prevention programs are most successful when the concepts are integrated into other subject areas and reinforced throughout the week—both of which represent additional time investments. Staff who would not directly present lessons need to develop a clear understanding of their role in reinforcing prevention strategies. Staff meeting and in-service time is also needed for training and ongoing support of the curriculum. These commitments of time and attention come easier if an initial enthusiasm is created when the decision is made to address the problem.

A common concern of teachers is whether prevention programming will further cut into already tight schedules and compromise the teaching of academics. Violence prevention programming as outlined in this chapter will eventually free up *more time* in the schedule. As student conflicts and off-task behaviors are reduced, teachers and students will be better able to pursue academic objectives. In addition, skills such as problem solving can be applied to academic subjects as well. For some teachers, buy-in may not happen until they see "proof." Contacting local schools and districts that have implemented the chosen program may help to convince them.

If staff buy-in is not fully achieved, a next-best step is to have several interested teachers pilot the program in the school and report back to the staff on their experiences. The piloting teachers should meet periodically to discuss progress, compare notes, and provide mutual support.

Creating a Support Team

If the entire staff makes a preliminary decision to implement the chosen program, other aspects of implementation can then be addressed. At this point, the team may again add or subtract members to create a support team. The purpose of the support team is to provide leadership and coordination in the planning, purchasing, training, ongoing implementation, and evaluation of the program. Several members of the support team should have flexibility in their work schedules so that they can go into classrooms to offer support. Support team members might include the school counselor and/or social worker, the principal or vice principal, the nurse, and two or three committed classroom teachers. In elementary schools, it is beneficial to include at least one classroom teacher from the primary and one from the intermediate grades, as it is critical for those who are actually teaching the program to be represented. At the middle school or junior high level, each grade level should be represented on the support team.

The first task of the support team is to decide on and coordinate the purchase of program materials, dates and types of staff training, timing of classroom implementation, and parent involvement. As lawmakers and citizens in general are becoming increasingly aware of and concerned about youth violence, funding options for prevention programming are opening up at the federal, state, and local levels. At the federal level, funds are available through the Crime Prevention Act, the Safe and Drug-Free Schools program, and Learning for Living. Individual states offer some support, and local businesses and service organizations, such as the Rotary, Kiwanis, and Lions Clubs, often underwrite the purchase of prevention materials. At the school level, PTA support is another option for financing prevention programming.

When funding is tight, staff training is often cut or compromised, although it is critical to the successful implementation of any prevention program. To help offset the cost of training, many prevention programs have trainer training models that allow a school to select an individual staff member or members to be trained who then in turn deliver training to the whole staff.

When planning for training, the support team should address not only the needs of teachers, but the needs of classified staff as well. Virtually all adults in a school come into contact with the children, and it is often the classified staff members—secretaries, cafeteria workers, custodians, playground supervisors—who have the most opportunity to interact with children on an informal basis. Because conflicts often arise outside the classroom, in more social and less structured situations, it makes good sense to provide these staff with program strategies as well as practice in how to help students transfer the skills to real-life situations.

Another critical element in successful schoolwide implementation of a prevention program is ongoing support for all staff persons who interact with children and, in particular, those classroom teachers who are teaching the lessons to students. This support can help ensure that the curriculum is being taught (and taught correctly) and that staff members continue to feel motivated and encouraged. For some teachers, program strategies that place greater emphasis on affective experiences than on cognitive information, and that teach thinking skills over didactic presentations, constitute a dramatic departure from teaching methodologies that have been in place for years. After exposure to psychoeducational programs, many educators speak of a new awareness of their own interpersonal skill deficiencies. Behavioral change during the first year of program implementation often takes place on the part of the teachers as they work to internalize the new strategies. Providing ongoing support helps to ensure that students have the maximum possibility of incorporating these skills into their daily lives because they are receiving the lessons, concepts, and skills in a consistent, cohesive manner throughout their tenure at the school.

The support team plays a significant role in providing this ongoing support. Team members can visit classrooms to observe or coteach lessons, and provide technical assistance and specific feedback. Team members can also provide classroom teachers with release time so that they can observe others who are implementing the program. The support team can also lead discussions at staff meetings to share ideas and success stories and to deal with any issues and concerns that surface. During subsequent years and/or as new teachers come on staff, the team can provide "booster" training sessions. To facilitate schoolwide commitment, the team can coordinate activities such as assemblies, school climate projects, and, most important, parent involvement.

Schools that have adopted the Second Step program and the schoolwide approach testify to the impact of staff members' all speaking the same language. Students encounter the same approach whether they are talking with the classroom teacher, the principal, or the school nurse. Teachers feel empowered and supported by other staff, and the locus of control for student behavior shifts from the administration back to the classroom (as indicated by fewer students sent to the office), where it is eventually internalized by the students.

Parent Involvement

Behavior changes at school rarely generalize to the home unless parents and guardians help to reinforce the skills (Briener & Forehand, 1981; Ramsey, Patterson, & Walker, 1990; Simon & Johnston, 1987). This is why any prevention program should include materials and strategies that address families. Research indicates that many families want to be more involved with their children's school lives but lack the confidence or specific knowledge they need to take on a more involved role (Canter & Canter, 1991; McLaughlin & Shields, 1987).

How best to reach parents is key. Many schools present information through one-time meetings and/or a series of parent training sessions. Parent training programs have proven to be effective in improving parenting strategies and children's behavior (Gard & Berry, 1986; Gray, 1986; Graziano & Diament, 1992). Meetings and sessions should be led by a staff member, such as the school counselor, who is committed to and very involved with the program in the classroom. Efforts should be made to ensure safe passage to the meeting or group session, to create a nonthreatening environment, and to provide child care during the meeting.

Parenting presentations or materials should not suggest that one way will work for all families; rather, it is the facilitator's role to modify information in a way that meets the particular school's families' needs and values and builds on the parents' strengths. Sensitivity to participant characteristics and family background is critical. Research shows that parents from the lowest income levels can benefit from parent training sessions, but, to be effective, presentations need to minimize lecture and written materials and increase modeling, role playing, and coaching (Knapp & Deluty, 1989).

Even when presentations are well planned and sensitive to different cultures and socioeconomic levels, the majority of parents and guardians still may not attend. Written send-home materials also tend to be ineffective with hard-to-reach families. These are the families that may stand to benefit the most from prevention programs. Some families may be reached through mandatory classes in which the parents choose between training and expulsion of their children from school. Less coercive methods include holding sessions in the neighborhood at a community center or one of the parents' homes. For parents who themselves had negative experiences in school, the use of alternative sites may increase their comfort level.

To meet the needs of a broad array of parents, the Committee for Children has developed a pilot take-home video designed to provide information and skill training to support the Second Step program presented in the classroom (Ramsey, 1995). Research suggests that videos viewed in the privacy of the home are effective in training parents to impart social skills to their children (Webster-

Stratton, Kolpacoff, & Hollinsworth, 1989). The pilot video also forms the basis for six parenting sessions for those who desire more information and interaction with other parents. It is hoped that the current study will provide information on the type of logistical planning and support that makes such an approach successful.

Evaluating a Prevention Program

When prevention programs are implemented schoolwide, it is prudent to monitor progress and measure results. This task can be undertaken by the support team, depending on the type of evaluation used. The first evaluation question should center on use of the program. Are teachers implementing the program, and are they doing so in a timely and sequential fashion? If not, what are some of the roadblocks to presenting the program, and how can they be addressed? Teacher, student, and parent opinions can be obtained through questionnaires. Teachers should also have the opportunity to share their views and experiences verbally with each other, using a focus group format. It also is helpful to obtain some verbal feedback from students. Student skills acquisition can be measured by paper-and-pencil tests and interviews. Some prevention programs provide forms for these purposes.

When evaluating programs, it is important to keep in mind that behavioral change takes time. During the first year of program implementation there may be more change in the teachers' behavior than in the students'. Violence prevention strategies that focus on discussion, role plays, and student use of problem-solving skills may run against the grain of teachers who are used to providing direct instruction. Teachers may also be unfamiliar with techniques for facilitating transfer of training. As with student skills, it takes time for teachers to reach a level of confidence and competence with new teaching methodologies.

Behavioral changes in students are often evaluated through measures that count disciplinary actions in the classroom or trips to the office and recordings of antisocial and prosocial behaviors by teachers or trained observers. Teachers may also complete behavioral checklists for each student at the beginning of the year and again at the end of the year; these ratings can then be compared.

When assessing behavioral changes in students, it is important to look for benchmarks of change. These benchmarks may entail (a) student ability to perform the skills, (b) use of the skills with prompting in real situations, (c) student initiation of skill use, (d) consistency in applying the skills, and (e) success in applying the skills. The acquisition of social skills is not always a straight-line progression, depending on the particular skill and what is currently happening in the life of the individual child (Selman, 1980). Children may regress a stage or two for a while or in certain situations, or may display progress in some skills but not in others. To date, little research has been undertaken in this area. It bears more attention as the effectiveness of prevention programs is more critically measured over time.

Summary

Increasingly, schools are recognizing their unique position for helping children learn how to get along better, both in and out of school. Children spend a large percentage of their waking hours in school. For some, teachers are the only positive adult role models in their lives. Schools also offer an opportunity to reach children at an early age, when behavior is not so entrenched, and over a period of years, the time required to effect behavioral change. Given that most incidents of youth violence occur within peer groups, classrooms are the logical place for children to learn and practice interpersonal skills.

To be successful, schoolwide violence prevention programs require a concerted effort on the part of school staff. Before adopting a curriculum, educators need to understand the origins of antisocial and prosocial behavior, which teaching methodologies and skills have proven to affect behavior, and which programs offer the most promise. In the initial stages of implementing a program, attainment of teacher buy-in and provision of training and ongoing support are critical to success. Nonteaching staff and parents and guardians also need training and support in reinforcing violence prevention skills. Evaluation of the program should be carefully designed and conducted over time. By following these guidelines for implementation, educators can help ensure that the risk of violence is reduced for our children.

References

Achenbach, T. M. (1971). The children's associative responding test: A two-year follow-up. *Developmental Psychology, 5,* 477-483.

Achenbach, T. M., & Edelbrock, C. S. (1981). Behavioral problems and competencies reported by parents of normal and disturbed children aged four through sixteen. *Monographs of the Society for Research in Child Development, 46*(1, Serial No. 188)

Bandura, A. (1973). *Aggression: A social learning analysis.* Englewood Cliffs, NJ: Prentice Hall.

Beland, K. R. (1988). *Second Step: A violence-prevention curriculum: Grades 1-3.* Seattle, WA: Committee for Children.

Beland, K. R. (1989). *Second Step: A violence-prevention curriculum: Grades 4-5.* Seattle, WA: Committee for Children.

Beland, K. R. (1990). *Second Step: A violence-prevention curriculum: Grades 6-8.* Seattle, WA: Committee for Children.

Beland, K. R. (1991). *Second Step: A violence-prevention curriculum: Preschool-kindergarten.* Seattle, WA: Committee for Children.

Bell, S. M., & Ainsworth, M. D. S. (1972). Infant crying and maternal responsiveness. *Child Development, 43,* 1171-1190.

Briener, J., & Forehand, R. (1981). An assessment of the effects of parent training on clinic-referred children's school behavior. *Behavioral Assessment, 3,* 31-42.

Camp, B. W., & Bash, M. S. (1981). *Think aloud: Increasing social and cognitive skills—a problem-solving program for children (primary level).* Champaign, IL: Research Press.

Canale, J. R. (1977). The effects of modeling and length of ownership on sharing behavior of children. *Social Behavior and Personality, 5,* 187-191.

Canter, L., & Canter, M. (1991). *Parents on your side: A comprehensive parent involvement program for teachers.* Santa Monica, CA: Lee Canter & Associates.

Chamberlain, R. W., & Nader, P. R. (1971). Relationship between nursery school behavior patterns and later school functioning. *American Journal of Orthopsychiatry, 41,* 597-601.

Coie, J. D., & Dodge, K. A. (1983). Continuities and changes in children's social status: A five-year longitudinal study. *Merrill-Palmer Quarterly, 29,* 261-570.

Coie, J. D., Dodge, K. A., & Kupersmidt, J. B. (1990). Peer group behavior and social status. In S. R. Asher & J. D. Coie (Eds.), *Peer rejection in childhood* (pp. 17-59). New York: Cambridge University Press.

Cox, R. D., & Gunn, W. B. (1980). Interpersonal skills in the schools: Assessment and curriculum development. In D. P. Rathjen & J. P. Foreyt (Eds.), *Social competence: Interventions for children and adults.* New York: Pergamon.

Dodge, K. A., Bates, J. E., & Pettit, G. S. (1990). Mechanisms in the cycle of violence. *Science, 250,* 1678-1683.

Dodge, K. A., & Frame, C. L. (1982). Social cognitive biases and deficits in aggressive boys. *Child Development, 53,* 629-635.

Eron, L. D., Huesmann, R. L., Duow, E., Romanoff, R., & Yarmel, P. W. (1987). Aggression and its correlates over 22 years. In *Childhood aggression and violence.* New York: Plenum.

Federal Bureau of Investigation. (1993). *Uniform crime reports.* Washington, DC: Government Printing Office.

Feshbach, N. D. (1984). Empathy, empathy training, and the regulation of aggression in elementary school children. In R. W. Kaplan, V. J. Konecni, & R. W. Novaco (Eds.), *Aggression in youth and children.* Boston: Martinus Nijhoff.

Feshbach, N. D., & Feshbach, S. (1969). The relationship between empathy and aggression in two age groups. *Developmental Psychology, 1,* 102-107.

Feshbach, N. D., & Roe, K. (1968). Empathy in six- and seven-year-olds. *Child Development, 39,* 133-145.

Frey, K. (1993, Spring). Harnessing student motivation: Second Step in grades 6-8. *Prevention Update* (newsletter of the Committee for Children, Seattle, WA), pp. 1-2, 5.

Gard, G. C., & Berry, K. K. (1986). Oppositional children: Taming tyrants. *Journal of Clinical Child Psychology, 15,* 148-158.

Geiger, K. (1993, January 14). *Violence in the schools.* Statement presented at a news conference given by the president of the National Education Association, Washington, DC.

Goldstein, A. P. (1981). *Psychological skill-streaming.* New York: Pergamon.

Goleman, D. (1987, October 13). Thriving despite hardship: Key childhood traits identified. *New York Times,* pp. 19, 22.

Gray, E. (1986). *Research findings on three model parenting support and education programs* (Working Paper No. 829). Chicago: National Committee for Prevention of Child Abuse.

Graziano, A. M., & Diament, D. M. (1992). Parent behavioral training: An examination of the paradigm. *Behavior Modification, 16,* 3-38.

Grusec, J. E., Kuczynski, L., Rushton, J. P., & Simutis, Z. M. (1978). Modeling, direct instruction and attributions: Effects on altruism. *Developmental Psychology, 14,* 51-57.

Horn, W. F., & Packard, T. (1985). Early identification of learning problems: A meta-analysis. *Journal of Educational Psychology, 77,* 597-607.

Huesmann, L. R., & Eron, L. D. (1986). *Television and the aggressive child: A cross-national comparison.* Hillsdale, NJ: Lawrence Erlbaum.

Kendall, P. C., & Braswell, L. (1985). *Cognitive-behavioral therapy for impulsive children.* New York: Guilford.

Knapp, P. A., & Deluty, R. H. (1989). Relative effectiveness of two behavioral training programs. *Journal of Clinical Child Psychology, 18,* 314-322.

Kohlberg, L., Yaeger, J., & Hjertholm, E. (1968). Private speech: Four studies and a review of theories. *Child Development, 39,* 691-735.

Lefkowitz, M. M., Eron, L. D., Walder, L. O., & Huesmann, L. R. (1977). *Growing up to be violent: A longitudinal study of the development of aggression.* New York: Pergamon.

Loeber, R. (1991). Antisocial behavior: More enduring than changeable? *Annals of the American Academy of Child and Adolescent Psychiatry, 30,* 393-397.

Luria, A. (1961). *The role of speech in the regulation of normal and abnormal behaviors.* New York: Liberight.

McLaughlin, M., & Shields, P. (1987, October). Involving low income parents in the schools: A role for policy? *Phi Delta Kappan.*

Meichenbaum, D. (1977). *Cognitive-behavior modification: An integrative approach.* New York: Plenum.

Michelson, L. (1987). Cognitive-behavioral strategies in the prevention and treatment of antisocial disorders in children and adolescents. In J. D. Burchard & S. N. Burchard (Eds.), *Prevention of delinquent behavior* (pp. 275-310). Newbury Park, CA: Sage.

National Association of Secondary School Principals. (1987). [Data on bullying and victimization]. In J. R. Gruen (Ed.), *School bullying and victimization* (NSSC Resource Paper). Malibu, CA: Pepperdine University, National School Safety Center.

Novaco, R. W. (1975). *Anger control: The development and evaluation of an experimental treatment.* Lexington, MA: D. C. Heath.

Novaco, R. W. (1979). The cognitive regulation of anger and stress. In P. C. Kendall & S. P. Hallon (Eds.), *Cognitive-behavioral interventions.* Orlando, FL: Academic Press.

Olweus, D. (1984). Aggressors and their victims: Bullying at school. In N. Frude & H. Gault (Eds.), *Disruptive behavior in schools.* New York: John Wiley.

Patterson, G. R. (1975). *Families: Applications of social learning to family life.* Champaign, IL: Research Press.

Patterson, G. R., Reid, J. B., & Dishion, T. J. (1992). *Antisocial boys.* Eugene, OR: Castilla.

Perry, D. G., Perry, L. C., & Rasmussen, P. (1986). Cognitive social learning mediators of aggression. *Child Development, 45,* 55-62.

Ramsey, E. (1995). *A family guide to Second Step: Promoting caring and understanding in children.* Seattle, WA: Committee for Children.

Ramsey, E., Patterson, G. R., & Walker, H. M. (1990). Generalization of the antisocial trait from home to school settings. *Journal of Applied Developmental Psychology, 11,* 209-223.

Reese-Potter, C. A. (1992). The effects of maternal cocaine abuse on children: Educational implications. In R. C. Morris (Ed.), *Solving the problems of youth at-risk.* Lancaster, PA: Technomic.

Rogers-Warren, A., & Baer, D. M. (1976). Correspondence between saying and doing: Teaching children to share and praise. *Journal of Applied Behavior Analysis, 9,* 335-354.

Rutter, M. (1982). Prevention of children's psychosocial disorders: Myth and substance. *Pediatrics, 70,* 883-894.

Saltz, E., & Johnson, J. (1974). Training for thematic fantasy play in culturally disadvantaged children: Preliminary results. *Journal of Educational Psychology, 66,* 623-630.

Selman, R. L. (1980). *The growth of interpersonal understanding.* New York: Academic Press.

Simon, D. J., & Johnston, J. C. (1987). Working with families: The missing link in behavior disorder interventions. In R. B. Rutherford, C. M. Nelson, & S. R. Forness (Eds.), *Severe behavior disorders of children and youth* (pp. 447-460). New York: John Wiley.

Spivack, G., & Cianci, N. (1987). High-risk early behavior pattern and later delinquency. In J. D. Burchard & S. N. Burchard (Eds.), *Prevention of delinquent behavior* (pp. 44-74). Newbury Park, CA: Sage.

Spivack, G., & Shure, M. B. (1974). *Social adjustment of young children: A cognitive approach to solving real-life problems*. San Francisco: Jossey-Bass.

Staub, E. (1974). The use of role-playing and induction in children's learning of helping and sharing behavior. *Child Development, 42*, 805-816.

Toner, I. J., Moore, L. P., & Ashley, P. K. (1978). The effect of serving as a model of self-control on subsequent resistance to deviation in children. *Journal of Experimental Psychology, 26*(1), 85-91.

Trotter, J. C., & Humphrey, F. A. (1988). *Feelings, body changes and stress*. Atlanta, GA: Wholistic Stress Control Institute.

Vygotsky, L. S. (1962). *Thought and language*. New York: John Wiley.

Webster-Stratton, C., Kolpacoff, M., & Hollinsworth, T. (1989). The long-term effectiveness and clinical significance of three cost-effective training programs for families with conduct-problem children. *Journal of Consulting and Clinical Psychology, 57*, 550-553.

Wentsel, K. R. (1993). *Social competence in early adolescence: A multiple goals perspective*. New Orleans: SRCD.

Westman, J. C., Rich, D. L., & Bermann, E. (1967). Relationship between nursery school behavior and later school adjustment. *American Journal of Orthopsychiatry, 37*, 725-731.

White, S. H. (1965). Evidence for a hierarchical arrangement of learning processes. In L. O. Lipsitt & C. C. Spiker (Eds.), *Advances in child development and behavior* (Vol. 2). New York: Academic Press.

• CHAPTER 12 •

An Ecological Model for Early Childhood Violence Prevention

LYNN ANDREWS

JEFFREY TRAWICK-SMITH

Sheila is a bright, outgoing 5-year-old who has made friends in kindergarten and can read at a first-grade level. That she is so confident and competent is surprising, given the challenges of her young life. Sheila lives in a squalid, three-room public housing unit with her mother and father, who are both alcoholics. Also living in her home are her two sisters and a half brother who is also her nephew (Sheila's father has had a child by her older sister; social service providers have been struggling for months to sort out the complexities of this family relationship). Sheila has been largely on her own since she was 2 years old. She wanders her tough city neighborhood at all hours. She has witnessed drug deals, shoot-outs, and racially motivated assaults. She has had a real education in life on the streets at an age when most of her peers are just learning to ride a bike or to tie their shoes.

Because her parents are rarely up early enough to get her ready for school, Sheila dresses and gets breakfast on her own. Her kindergarten teacher must pick her up to make certain she gets to class. In spite of the conditions of her life, Sheila has managed exceptionally well. She has excelled in kindergarten, is well liked by peers, and always has a smile on her face. "Sheila will make it," her kindergarten teacher reports. "You just know it. There's something within her, something that will allow her to succeed."

233

Bobby is another story. His family is also dysfunctional. His mother is an alcoholic. His father, who is at home only sporadically, is physically abusive. Bobby displays unpredictably aggressive behavior at school. He will be engaged in positive activities, then suddenly lash out. His peers stay away from him. His kindergarten teacher remembers an instance when Bobby did nothing but walk past another child who was sitting at a table and the other child ducked instinctively and covered her head.

Some days, Bobby comes to school listless and out of touch. He has been prescribed Ritalin for hyperactivity; a social service team working with Bobby's family suspects that Bobby's mother often overmedicates him.

Bobby's kindergarten teacher tells a revealing story: Once, she took her whole class to the circus. Bobby's father, whom Bobby talked about incessantly and clearly cared about, showed up at the circus with Bobby's younger brother. Sitting only a few rows in front of the kindergarteners, Bobby's father laughed and joked with the younger brother but ignored Bobby completely. On the bus ride home, Bobby, who virtually never showed emotion, cried.

Bobby was in trouble with the law by the time he was in the third grade and was incarcerated in a juvenile detention center by middle school.

These stories illustrate two critical concepts regarding positive social development. The case of Bobby shows that at a very early age, behaviors, attitudes, and conditions of personal history can be identified that, for some youngsters, predict ongoing aggressive and antisocial patterns of social interaction later in life. Sheila's case demonstrates that even in the harshest of environmental circumstances, some children flourish. The critical question to be addressed in this chapter is, How can we use what we know about Sheila and Bobby to address the growing problem of violence in our society?

A child's early years present opportunities for positive development, but they also present risks. The stories of these two children taken together suggest that although much attention has been focused on addressing the alarming rise in adolescent violence, there is good reason to extend the scope of intervention to early childhood.

Our purpose in this chapter is to review the factors in early life that put children like Bobby at risk of becoming violent and the factors that protect children like Sheila from becoming so. We describe interventions that address these risk and protective factors, and focus especially on an ecological model of early childhood intervention that we are currently testing.

Why Early Intervention?

Several longitudinal studies have shown that children as young as age 6 who are rated as aggressive or antisocial by parents, teachers, or peers continue to exhibit these characteristics into adulthood (Eron & Huesmann, 1984; Farrington, 1991; Olweus, 1991). In fact, aggressive behavior in childhood is the single best predictor of aggression in later life (Eron, Huesmann, & Zelli, 1991). These patterns of behavior appear to be stable over time and across social domains.

Early age of onset is an obvious argument for focusing violence prevention efforts on young children. Limited success in changing the behavior of aggressive adolescents has led some researchers to suggest that intervention should begin much sooner (Eron, 1988; Forgatch, 1988). Early childhood presents a critical window of opportunity for ameliorating risk factors for violent behavior and promoting protective factors that help make children resilient to stresses that contribute to violence. Patterson, Capaldi, and Bank (1991), developers of the "early starter model," posit that children who begin to engage in aggressive antisocial behavior at ages 4 to 9 are at greatest risk for becoming chronic, serious offenders in adulthood. Young children are vulnerable to both negative and positive environmental influences related to aggression. At this age, key social-cognitive constructs and responses are being formulated that will guide their interactions in more or less successful directions.

The etiology of violent behavior and theoretical models for the prevention of youth violence are discussed elsewhere in this volume. We agree with the authors of previous chapters that violence has multiple, interactive determinants at the individual, family, peer group, community, and societal levels. To be effective, any prevention effort must employ multiple strategies at these various levels. Some factors, such as history of abuse, seem to put individuals at risk; other factors, such as male socialization, seem to put whole populations at risk. Later in this chapter we describe an ecological

model for the prevention of violence in preschool children living
in high-risk communities. This model assumes that risk factors and
protective factors interact, reinforcing and canceling each other out
depending on how individuals construct meaning—that is, what
they learn—from their experiences. It further assumes that violence
is an acquired behavior determined through life experience. Its
beginnings may be traced to relationships with peers, adults, and
environmental influences in the earliest years of life. The approach
focuses on reducing or mitigating the effects of risk factors and
strengthening protective factors that are most immediate and amenable to intervention for this target population.

The model we propose does not distinguish among different forms
of violence—such as child abuse, sexual assault, drive-by shootings,
spousal abuse, or school violence. Nor does it distinguish between
proactive and reactive aggression (Dodge, 1991). The state of our
knowledge about risk and protective factors related to specific forms
of violence is not sufficiently advanced to indicate highly focused
interventions. Furthermore, we believe that there are many underlying
factors in common across types of violence and that a broadly focused
primary prevention approach will be most effective.

Levels of Risk and Protection

In an ecological model for violence prevention, interventions
should address risk and protective factors at the individual, family,
peer group, community, and societal levels.

The Individual Level

Certain interpersonal and cognitive characteristics are related to
violent behavior. Qualities such as low IQ, impulsivity, attention
deficit, high risk taking, and low empathy, for example, have been
found to be risk factors (Farrington, 1989; Reiss & Roth, 1993).
Other qualities appear to contribute to children's healthy adaptation to even the most stressful situations. These include problem-
solving skills (Shure & Spivack, 1988), self-control (Anthony &
Cohler, 1987; Garmezy, 1981), and a positive balance between
autonomy and the ability to ask for help (Werner, 1990). The ability
to read accurately and engage successfully in social situations is also

predictive of positive development (Cowen & Work, 1988; Werner & Smith, 1982).

At the individual level, prevention goals would be to stimulate children's cognitive development, to reduce levels of aggression and impulsivity, and to enhance a constellation of skills related to social competence.

The Family Level

In early childhood, family interventions are potentially the most powerful. Young children are dependent on family members for vital nurturance and guidance. In the early years, children have less access to other social supports or role models. Family factors associated with violent behavior include child abuse and neglect (Widom, 1992), domestic violence (Margolin, Gorin-Sibner, & Gleberman, 1988; Stark & Flitcraft, 1991), harsh and erratic punishment, poor parental supervision, high levels of family conflict (National Research Council, 1993), parental substance abuse (Farrington, 1978; McCord, McCord, & Howard, 1963), and criminal behavior of family members (West & Farrington, 1977).

We know that secure, nurturing attachments with caregivers and a predictable environment are strong protective factors (Cowen & Work, 1988; Werner, 1990). It would seem a reasonable goal to promote positive, nurturing interactions between parents and children. Specifically, parents could be encouraged to use consistent, nonpunitive disciplinary techniques. Anger management, problem-solving skills, and communication skills could be promoted. Parent training of this type has been found to be moderately effective in intervening with delinquent and acting-out children (Forehand & Long, 1991; Forgatch, 1991; Kazdin, 1985).

Dodge (1991) has hypothesized that nurturing, consistent caregiver interactions with children lead to more accurate encoding and interpretation of social cues by children. Likewise, parents who model various prosocial, noncoercive approaches to problem solving may contribute to a broader repertoire of social strategies in their children. Decreases in aggression are likely to result.

Increasing parents' social support may help to relieve stressors that can contribute to negative parent-child interactions and family conflict and disorganization. Parent support groups and supportive relationships with child care providers can promote parents' sense of self-efficacy in nurturing and protecting their children (Miller-Heyl, 1994).

The Peer Level

Children are beginning to form stable relationships with peers and to show preferences for certain playmates as early as toddlerhood (Howes, 1987). The peer environment is rich with opportunities for children to test out emerging social skills; it is the ideal context for interventions to promote cooperation, empathy, and problem solving. Because social perspective taking is so rudimentary in 3- to 5-year-olds, the kinds of peer group strategies that are effective with older children (e.g., those of the "social influence" prevention model proposed by Hawkins, Catalano, & Miller, 1992) may not be warranted in early childhood prevention efforts. Approaches that encourage peer groups to monitor or guide one another's behaviors, for instance, may not make sense at an age when children have little interest in being like everyone else.

However, child care settings may provide young children with their primary socialization experience with peers. Encouraging cooperative learning, group problem solving, and an awareness of the needs and feelings of others can begin to give young children a sense of "community," including feelings of shared support and responsibility (Levin, 1994). A sense of community has been shown to act as a protective factor for older children (Felsman, 1989; Garbarino, Dubrow, Kostelny, & Pardo, 1992). Fostering positive peer interactions and emerging friendships may help to prevent peer rejection, a risk factor for aggression, and set the stage for peer attachments, a protective factor (Anthony & Cohler, 1987; Cowen & Work, 1988; Hartup & Moore, 1990).

Just as the elementary or secondary school is a significant focal point of intervention for older children, the preschool or child care program is very influential in young children's cognitive and social-emotional development. This is particularly true for children who are in all-day child care situations. This group constitutes an increasing proportion of preschool-age children, as more than 60% of mothers of children ages 3 to 5 are now in the workforce (Children's Defense Fund, 1994). Thus, staff in child care programs assume a more significant caretaking role than in the past, with all its implications for these youth.

Zigler, Taussig, and Black (1992) conclude that a high-quality early childhood education is, in and of itself, a powerful prevention strategy. Studies demonstrate long-term positive effects that include the reduction of school failure and antisocial behavior, factors that contribute to aggression and violence (Schweinhart, Barnes, & Weikart, 1993). Working with child care staff to ensure a program of developmentally appropriate activities in an organized, predictable, safe, and nurturing environment can, therefore, be instrumental in achieving prevention goals for the children in their care.

The Community/Societal Level

Family and school environments most directly influence the development of aggression and social competence in young children. However, there are also community and societal factors that can increase risk or influence family and school interactions with children. The media constitute one such factor. There is now a considerable body of research that suggests that a high rate of exposure to media violence is a risk factor for some children in terms of aggressive behavior (Eron, 1982; Heath, Bresolin, & Rinaldi, 1989). Parents and teachers of young children report concern over the increased time children are spending in play with violent or aggressive themes that imitate the latest cadre of television superheroes (Carlsson-Paige & Levin, 1990, 1991). Of equal concern is the possibility that this exposure may either desensitize children to the effects of real violence or hypersensitize them to its prevalence (American Psychological Association, 1993). Over time, this can create a sense of complacency about violent acts that may allow violence to flourish, or it may lead to feelings of fear that contribute to opportunities for violence (e.g., when students bring weapons to school to protect themselves).

When children are watching TV, whether they are watching violent programming or not, they are not engaged in other activities that may promote social and problem-solving skills. Although it is unlikely that television has the same impact on children as direct exposure to violence in the home or in the community (Friedlander, 1994), it is such a pervasive presence in the lives of young children that it merits attention as a target for preventive intervention.

Communities with high-density housing, high rates of mobility and economic deprivation, and strong illegal markets are more likely to expose children to violence (Sampson, 1985). In addition to the immediate stresses placed on children by this exposure, these conditions create a norm of violence as a fact of life and, for some segments of the community, an acceptable means of solving problems and obtaining status and power. In such an environment, it becomes difficult to transmit prosocial values to children (Reiss & Roth, 1993). More concretely, these conditions put stresses on families that make parenting difficult; they interfere with parents' ability to meet their children's basic needs and can contribute to family-level risk factors implicated in the development of violent behavior. Risk factors in these communities reflect larger issues of social policy. As Zigler (1990) has stated:

> The problems of many families will not be solved by early intervention efforts, but only by changes in the basic features of the infrastructure of our society. No amount of counseling, early childhood curricula or home visits will take the place of jobs that provide decent incomes, affordable housing, appropriate health care, optimal family configuration, or integrated neighborhoods where children encounter positive role models. (p. xiii)

Although no single prevention program can take on all these issues, even in a single community, and there are no social policy superheroes waiting in the wings, we believe that any early childhood prevention program must include in its approach public awareness and community mobilization efforts. Strategies must be designed to effect social policies that support families; promote nonviolent, cooperative mechanisms for dispute resolution; and provide equal access to legitimate routes by which people can meet their fundamental needs. In this arena in our ecological model, the primary goal for intervention would be to provide opportunities and support for parents and child care staff to participate in the life of their community (in the broadest sense) in a meaningful way and to build their capacity to advocate effectively for these changes (Garbarino et al., 1992; Gullotta, 1987).

Early Childhood Violence Prevention Initiatives

Most of the research and program development initiatives that specifically focus on the prevention of violent or aggressive behavior in children under the age of 6 have been undertaken relatively recently. Program designs and research findings have appeared in the literature with greatest frequency over the past 5 years. Several early intervention models launched in the 1960s and 1970s had as primary goals the prevention of school failure and/or improvement of parenting and family functioning for "at-risk" children and families. These are relevant to our purposes because they also examined the long-term impacts of early childhood programs on social development and the reduction of antisocial and violent behavior.

Broad-Focus Early Childhood Education Programs

Zigler et al. (1992) have reviewed longitudinal findings from a number of programs aimed at enhancing child development. Typically, these have included various combinations of early childhood education or care, parent education and support, health care, and case management for families identified as at risk. One of the programs reviewed, the Perry Preschool Project, focused on the early education of low-income, African American 3- and 4-year-olds and their parents. Longitudinal data from the project show that at age 15, participants exhibited fewer instances of personal or property violence in school and at age 19 enjoyed greater achievement in school, higher employment rates, and fewer arrests than did control group subjects.

In another program reviewed by Zigler et al., the Syracuse University Family Development Research Program, high-risk new mothers and their young children were provided educational and social services. Ten years later, these children had fewer court referrals than those in the control group, and experimental group referrals that did occur were for less serious offenses. Similar data have been obtained from another parent-oriented program, the Houston Parent-Child Development Center, which served low-income Mexican American families and their toddlers over a 2-year period. Intervention children demonstrated fewer aggressive and acting-out behaviors for up to 8 years following participation in the program. By grades 4 to 11, however, these advantages over control group children disappeared.

The outcomes of these broadly focused early education programs suggest that supportive interventions used with families and young children can promote positive intellectual and social development and reduce risk factors. These positive effects can, in turn, reduce aggressive, antisocial behavior in children.

Focused Social Competence Interventions

More recently, early intervention programs have been developed with a more specific focus on promoting social competence and reducing aggressive behavior in children as a method of stemming later violence. One such program, Interpersonal Cognitive Problem-Solving (ICPS) (Shure, 1992, 1993; Shure & Spivack, 1982), teaches children a process for interpersonal problem solving that requires skills in understanding cause and effect, identifying feelings, listening and attending, and creating alternative solutions. Shure and Spivack (1982) have established links between these skills and a reduction in impulsivity and physical aggression in urban African American preschool and kindergarten children. Children participating in ICPS also have been rated higher than control subjects in overall adjustment, ability to get along with peers, sharing, and caring about the feelings of others.

ICPS makes use of drawings, puppets, stories, and role plays of interpersonal situations to teach social skills, relying on a "dialoguing" technique that leads children to generate their own solutions to problems. It also provides suggestions for using situations that occur naturally in the classroom as well as regular daily activities to reinforce the skills being learned. For example, lunchtime conversation is an opportunity to help children understand differences in feelings by discussing personal preferences for foods. There are classroom and parent versions of the program.

The Committee for Children has developed the Second Step preschool and kindergarten curriculum to reduce impulsive and aggressive behavior in children and to increase social competence in children from 4 to 6 years old (Beland, 1991). It incorporates problem-solving strategies similar to those taught in ICPS, with specific behavioral training in skills such as joining in, taking turns, interrupting politely, and managing anger. The classroom-based lessons rely on puppets, role plays, and photographs to encourage discussion of conflict situations and to model social skills. Activities for "transfer of training" are stressed for use during classroom routines.

Letters to parents with suggestions for follow-up are another feature of the curriculum. It is worth noting that Second Step explicitly acknowledges cultural and family differences that need to be taken into account in implementing this type of program—an issue that has not been addressed in other curricula. The formative evaluation for Second Step indicates that preschool and kindergarten children who have received the curriculum have acquired social skills knowledge (Moore & Beland, 1992).

Both ICPS and Second Step are primary prevention approaches; they do not specifically target children who are exhibiting problem behaviors or deficits. One program that is designed to work with children identified as at risk is Skill Streaming in Early Childhood (McGinnis & Goldstein, 1990), which is a behavioral approach to teaching prosocial skills to preschool and kindergarten children who are impulsive, aggressive, or withdrawn or who have other learning problems. In this program, 40 specific social skills are broken down into component behaviors that are taught through a highly prescribed process of modeling, role playing, performance feedback (social and material reinforcement and self-evaluation), and transfer training. These skills are grouped into clusters, such as school-related skills, friendship-making skills, and dealing with feelings. Children are taught primarily those skills in which they are deficient.

Another program for at-risk children is FASTTrack, which is being developed by the Conduct Problems Prevention Research Group (1992). This is an intensive and comprehensive violence prevention program that works with schools, families, and individual children who are identified as being at high risk for conduct disorders, including aggression. Children are taught in small groups, during regular classroom lessons, and in pairs that include one well-adjusted peer to resolve conflicts, manage feelings, and solve problems. They also receive academic tutoring. Parents participate in weekly groups, individual home visits, and family-focused activities.

Families participating in FASTTrack will continue in the program through middle school. Components such as adult mentoring will be added as the children grow older. After 2 years, evaluation results indicate that parents' involvement in their children's education has increased and that intervention children exhibit fewer behavior problems than control children (Dodge, 1993).

Programs that emphasize skills training, such as ICPS, Second Step, and Skill Streaming, have had some short-term success in

improving children's social behavior. However, there are no longitudinal data demonstrating reductions in violent behavior in adolescence or adulthood. The current thinking in prevention is that
approaches using multiple, sustained strategies rather than single-
focus, short-term initiatives have more significant, lasting effects
(Guerra, Tolan, & Hammond, 1992). This would predict the longer-
range success of the broadly focused early education programs
described earlier and of FASTTrack, which include strategies targeting the family, peers, the school, and, to a limited extent, the
community, as well as the individual child.

An Ecological Intervention Model

There are strengths and limitations in all the programs described
above. General early education models, such as the Perry Preschool
Project, meet global developmental needs by laying a foundation
for overall positive child development. Furthermore, they often
include family and community intervention. However, these programs may not provide specialized, focused support for children
who are at risk of becoming aggressive. Narrowly focused programs, such as ICPS, intensively address the skill deficits of children
at risk of becoming violent by reducing aggression and promoting
social competence. However, these programs may not provide for
long-term overall child and family development or address environmental influences, such as community norms.

An ecological model of violence prevention, which contains
elements of both general educational approaches and more focused
social development interventions, is proposed here. The model is
based on Bronfenbrenner's (1979, 1986) ecological systems theory
of human development, which holds that children are influenced
by four distinct and interrelated ecological systems: the microsystem, the mesosystem, the macrosystem, and the exosystem. The
microsystem includes persons and institutions in the child's immediate environment (e.g., parents or child care providers). The
mesosystem comprises the interrelationships among those in the
microsystem (e.g., relationships between parents and child care
providers). The *macrosystem* consists of societal institutions affecting children (e.g., the media, social services). The broadest of the
systems, the *exosystem,* includes the attitudes of the larger culture

(e.g., public opinions about violence). Bronfenbrenner contends that any successful intervention must not only focus on positive change in all systems but must create "supportive linkages" among them. The model proposed here addresses risk and protective factors in all ecological systems in the child's life.

This model is currently being tested in a child care center-based early childhood violence prevention program that incorporates professional education activities and support for early childhood educators and parents of 3- to 5-year-olds. The initial pilot site is the Smith-Bent Children's Center in New London, Connecticut, a family resource center providing full-day and before- and after-school care for up to 54 children. Parents must be working or in school, or must have a child with special needs. The families served are ethnically diverse, and 88% are at or below 125% of the poverty line. Supportive linkages are being established between the child care program and elementary schools, and community awareness and advocacy efforts are being promoted. The model will also be field tested in three other small, ethnically diverse, economically disadvantaged cities in Connecticut over the next 2 years.

Child Care Support and Enhancement

Professional development activities are being offered to child care staff over a 1-year period. Instruction is provided through two vehicles. One consists of video-based Distance Learning Modules facilitated by child care center directors on-site, in which participants have telephone access to the instructor. These modules focus on (a) creating a safe, caring environment that fosters a sense of security, autonomy, and community in children; (b) promoting social competence, including cooperation, helping behaviors, and friendship skills; (c) helping children resolve conflicts and reduce aggressive and impulsive behavior; (d) decreasing the negative effects of violent media and using media to enhance prosocial learning; (e) supporting children who have direct experience with family or community violence to cope with its impact; and (f) encouraging each child's positive identification with his or her family, gender, and culture. In addition to the Distance Learning Modules, child care staff are participating in special topics workshops to enhance their personal competence in anger and stress management, conflict resolution, and working with parents. Because we believe that these professionals are important role models for children, our hope is that their management of interpersonal situations will reflect the skills they are teaching the children in their care. (Examples of specific strategies recommended to address these topics are included in a later section.)

Over the 1-year period, participants will receive a total of 35 hours of course work, for which they can obtain either college credit or continuing education units. They will also receive at least 10 hours of on-site individual and classroom team consultation to support the implementation of strategies they have learned in the modules and workshops. Each site will be taught to conduct "child staffing" (Garbarino et al., 1992) meetings to assess and plan for the needs of individual children who may be experiencing difficulties or to resolve classroom issues.

Kindergarten teachers from participating public schools are invited to attend training sessions as one strategy to foster linkages between community child care programs and schools. Early childhood teachers and administrators are invited to participate in local advisory committees as another linkage strategy. Child care centers have been supplied with computers to enable them not only to enhance their curricula but to communicate with other centers. Child care programs are often isolated from each other, from other services or families in the community, and from larger community violence prevention efforts (Stremmel, Benson, & Powell, 1993). Participants are reporting that the opportunity to network with other teachers and providers is a valuable part of this experience for them. We suspect that building this sense of "community" will be one of the most powerful outcomes of this model, in that it gives participants the necessary support to work for meaningful change at the micro level, in their own teaching and relationships with children, and at the macro level, in their participation in organizations and communities.

Parent Education and Support

Following an ecological model, family intervention is a critical component of the program. A parent education and support system has been designed that allows parents to choose a setting and format for learning that best suits their individual needs and learning styles. They can select any or all of the following services:

1. A series of 10 workshops are offered on personal growth and parenting, focusing on the following topics: anger and stress management,
changing roles of men and women/sex role stereotyping, discipline,
play, conflict resolution, helping children deal with differences, and
positive use of media. Each workshop includes a meal and time for
parents to share their experiences with each other. In at least one site,
a $50 stipend is being offered to parents who complete 7 of 10
sessions.

2. Biweekly visits at home or work are offered to provide individual
support, guidance, and information on the issues listed above as well
as assistance in accessing resources to meet other family needs.

3. Parent support/family activity meetings are held monthly at which
parents may socialize with other parents and discuss whatever issues
are of interest to them in an informal setting. Parent-child activities
are included in these meetings to create opportunities for parents to
do something both enjoyable and educational with their children and
other families.

In the early piloting of the project, recruitment and maintenance
of parents' participation has been difficult. Evaluation of these
specific interventions as initial primary prevention strategies will
be an important aspect of our work.

Contextual Play Intervention

A unique aspect of this model is that it emphasizes "contextual"
strategies for teaching children rather than an add-on curriculum
that includes specific lessons in conflict resolution, friendship skills,
and so on, such as those found in ICPS and Second Step, described
earlier. A theme of this program is that children's positive social
development is best promoted within the real-life contexts of home
and classroom. In particular, caregivers and parents are taught to
facilitate social skills within children's actual play. Play has been
viewed as a particularly rich context for the development of social
competence. In naturally occurring playful activities, children regularly resolve conflicts (Rubin, 1980), persuade peers (Trawick-
Smith, 1992), and gain entry into play activities already in progress
(Cosaro, 1981). Research suggests that teachers and parents can
help children acquire these important skills when they model or
prompt social problem solving and nurture friendships (Mize,
Ladd, & Price, 1985).

A decision-making approach to play intervention is recommended, based on the work of Lev Vygotsky (1962, 1978), who has argued that adults must make judgments about how much help children need when real-life social problems arise. In some cases, children can resolve conflicts independently, and adult intervention only interferes with social development. At other times, children may need hints or prompts, and through indirect guidance adults can help them resolve their own disputes. Children lacking social competence—highly aggressive children, for example—may initially need very direct support in solving social problems. Words and actions to deal with social dilemmas might be provided (e.g., "You can't hit. When you are angry you should say in a loud voice, 'I'm angry with you!' "). From Vygotsky's perspective, the goal of social intervention is gradually to give over regulation of social problems to children—that is, to move from directive to nondirective to nonintervention strategies.

Caregivers and parents participating in the program are encouraged to use this framework to enhance key social behaviors, including general attachment, social participation, and friendship formation, and more specific interpersonal skills such as conflict resolution and peer group entry.

Attachment to Adults

As discussed previously, early attachment is crucial in human development; often, a child who is aggressive or rejected by peers has not formed a secure attachment to an adult (Hartup & Moore, 1990). Recommendations in the literature for promoting attachment include consistent, predictable classroom and home environments, and nurturing and supportive teaching and parenting (Lay-Dopyera & Dopyera, 1987). As one strategy for promoting attachment, teachers in the program are encouraged to establish small groups of consistent membership for certain activity periods during the day. These groups should include children who are friends and should be assigned to one adult, giving the children an opportunity to develop closer relationships. Parents are encouraged to set reasonable rules for their children, to help their children understand the consequences of rule breaking ahead of time, and to follow through consistently when their children break the rules they have set.

Research has suggested that children become attached to adults who respond authentically and with enthusiasm to their initiatives (Ainsworth, 1973). If teachers and parents are taught to respond regularly and with enthusiasm to children's accomplishments, verbal bids, and requests for assistance, bonds will be strengthened (Trawick-Smith, 1994). We encourage teachers and parents to use fewer directives with children and more descriptive, nonjudgmental comments and open-ended questions (e.g., "You've been working very hard with the blocks. What are you building?" rather than "You've made a very nice building with your blocks. Is it a fort?")

Social Participation

Playing alone can be valuable; solitary play can provide a peaceful respite from the active classroom or a stressful home life and has been found to be related to aspects of cognitive development (Rubin, 1982). Some children rarely interact with peers, however. In the case of rejected children, this may be because they are actively avoided by playmates (Dodge, 1983). It is futile to try to teach specific social skills to children who only play alone. Enhancing general social participation may be the most positive outcome of play intervention. Refinements to specific play skills may be secondary in importance to increases in overall peer interaction.

Using a Vygotskian framework, teachers and parents in the program are taught to promote general social participation—that is, to make decisions about how much help to give children in their social interactions and then to guide their entry into play situations as needed. It is not uncommon in peer groups for several children to begin a play theme and then exclude others who wish to join in, particularly children who are aggressive (Scarlett, 1983). To gain entry into a play group, children often will simply ask if they can play or stand and watch in hopes of being invited to join in. Aggressive and rejected children often take toys and objects away from group members or try to take control of play activities forcefully. These strategies usually are not effective (Ramsey, 1989). Instead, teachers and parents can model and suggest more effective strategies for joining a group unobtrusively, for example, by initiating a parallel or related activity (Ramsey, 1989), such as making a food delivery to a group of children playing restaurant. Pointing out the consequences of children's aggressive acts (e.g., "Look how

Sara is crying. You hurt her and she doesn't want to play with you now.") may gradually lead to an understanding of the negative social consequences of aggression (Mize & Ladd,1990).

Calling individual playmates by name is another effective way to be included in ongoing play. Children who are having difficulty being accepted in groups might also be directed initially to play situations where there is a greater likelihood of success, such as play with another single child or with a group that includes a friend.

Friendships

Most preschool children have at least one reciprocal relationship with a peer (Matheson & Wu, 1991). Those who maintain long-term friendships tend to be more competent socially (Howes, 1983, 1987). Some children lack friends; teachers and parents can help such children enter into meaningful relationships with others, an important goal for a number of reasons. A single friendship can insulate a child from some of the negative effects of being rejected or neglected by other peers (Hartup & Moore, 1990). It may be that having a friend is affirming. It shows children that they can be successful and liked, even if by only one other child.

Friendships are very useful for social skills intervention. Conflicts among friends are less heated in open-ended play and are more likely to result in compromise. Friendship interactions, therefore, may be the ideal context for teaching highly aggressive children to resolve conflicts without violence.

Our program recommends that teachers and parents observe classroom and neighborhood interactions to identify children who show signs of mutual interest or compatibility. Once potential friends have been identified, participants are encouraged to make arrangements for these children to spend time together in informal, nonthreatening settings. A teacher might bring the children together in the classroom by asking them to help with tasks or projects or by encouraging them to enter joint play activities. Activities that help children to learn about each other are also helpful. For example, group discussions or class graphs that show where children live, their pets, or favorite activities can point out common interests (Levin, 1994). With teacher guidance, parents can arrange for outside-of-school contacts with potential friends.

Conflict Resolution

As noted earlier, aggressive behavior leads to peer rejection (Dodge, 1983). Through teacher and parent intervention, aggressive children can be shown the futility of their forceful initiatives or reactions to frustration and can be taught alternatives to violence for solving social problems (Mize & Ladd, 1990). This can be done most effectively through intervention in real-life classroom or home conflicts. Very directive interventions that point out unacceptable or ineffective behaviors, reflect consequences, and offer specific alternative solutions may be most effective for aggressive children (e.g., "Adam, don't hit. That hurts Robert. Use words if you're angry. Say, 'I don't like that!' "). Research has shown that when teachers give specific verbal alternatives to young children, classroom aggression is reduced (Caldwell, 1977). Some children may need less direct assistance; in such cases, hints or prompts may guide them in solving their own problems (e.g., "Adam, hitting Robert made him angry. What else could you do to get to use the red crayon?").

One of our interventions involves teaching parents and teachers to use a three-step process for conflict resolution with children that is similar to the ICPS process. The first step involves assessing the need for intervention, including the children's readiness to work on the problem. The next step is to ask open-ended questions to help the children identify the problem, the consequences of their behavior, and possible solutions. Once the children have proposed a solution, the adults assist them in "getting started" on the solution and then check in later to see how it has worked.

To be socially competent, children must be able to vary their strategies to fit particular play situations (Trawick-Smith, 1992). This conflict resolution process can also help children to interpret social situations accurately, so that they can choose responses that fit different situations. This is particularly important for aggressive children, who tend to attribute hostile intent to the nonhostile acts of peers (Crick & Ladd, 1987). Because modeling prosocial behaviors in family or peer disputes is an effective teaching technique (Lay-Dopyera & Dopyera, 1987), teachers and parents are coached in using a similar conflict resolution process in their own disputes and in reflecting warmth and altruism in their interactions with children. In addition to demonstrating caring and concern themselves, adults can provide opportunities for children to practice helping behaviors by inviting them to call or make cards for children who are ill, for example, or by encouraging a child who has hurt another child to make reparations ("Tonya feels sad that her painting is ripped. What can you do to help her feel better?").

Media Interventions

Earlier, we mentioned the potential negative effects on young children of viewing TV violence. Many child care providers are aware of these effects, have chosen to ban toy guns and other toys associated with violent superheroes, and attempt to ban any play predicated on these themes. Although some examples of this play are clearly repetitive imitation, other examples represent children's efforts to understand and gain control over personal experiences (Garbarino et al., 1992) or to work through normal developmental issues related to "good" and "bad" or autonomy and power (Carlsson-Paige & Levin, 1990). Consistent with the overall emphasis on contextual interventions in this program, parents and child care staff are taught how to use this type of play as a learning opportunity. This involves guiding children to expand their superhero play to include prosocial themes or to evaluate the problem-solving strategies used by these figures. In addition, parents and children are introduced to videos and books that represent nonviolent problem solving and other positive themes, such as cooperation and altruism, through a lending library and a "Family Night at the Movies" activity that incorporates reading a story to children and then showing a video based on the same story or a work by the same author.

Supporting Children Exposed to Violence

Child care providers are likely to encounter children who are victims of child abuse or who have witnessed violence in their homes or communities, perhaps repeated incidents of violence. Many of these children demonstrate signs of distress, including posttraumatic stress disorder, and may never receive any treatment (Garbarino et al., 1992). To enable them to provide effective care and educational programming for these children, child care staff are trained to identify the signs of trauma and to use a team process to plan for the needs of affected children, in particular, individual-izing the general strategies already learned for creating a safe, predictable environment and for helping children to feel in control. Strengthening relationships with families and with other commu-nity service providers should also enable child care staff to help children get other needed services.

Gender and Cultural Sensitivity

Most of the research on aggression in children has been done with boys, presumably because they are disproportionately at risk for aggressive behavior problems (Fagot, 1984; Offord, Boyle, & Racine, 1991). Statistics on adult crime show that men constitute 89% of arrests for violent offenses (Federal Bureau of Investigation, 1991, Table 37). Men and adolescent boys are at higher risk than women/girls for assaulting each other, their female partners, and their children (Reiss & Roth, 1993). Interventions developed to address risk factors for aggression are based on data derived from studies with boys and men, but they have not explicitly identified maleness as a risk factor, nor have they attempted to explain the gender differences in levels of risk. In general, prevention programs have not distinguished between the needs of male children and those of female children as either perpetrators or victims. Research supports the need to do so. For example, outcomes of one primary prevention project designed to reduce aggressive behavior in first and second graders did show positive effects on aggressive behavior in boys. The same intervention had little effect on aggressive behavior in girls, which had a low rate of occurrence initially, but did decrease girls' self-destructive behavior (Hawkins, Von Cleve, & Catalano, 1991). This is consistent with gender differences found in children's responses to witnessing violent incidents in the home and the community. First- and second-grade girls have been found to show higher levels of depression and anxiety—in-ner-directed problems—whereas boys display higher levels of impul-sivity in response to violence (Martinez & Richters, 1994).

As Donna Garske discusses in Chapter 13 of this volume, sex role socialization of girls and boys is sometimes included in risk-factor models of family and sexual violence, in particular, but it is con-spicuously missing in any explicit way from most interventions based on these models. We do know that children who are raised without gender stereotypes appear to be more resilient, which, as we have discussed, is closely linked to prosocial behaviors. For girls, a home that is not overprotective and that encourages risk taking and independence while providing reliable emotional support is a protective factor (Werner, 1990). Research also suggests that for boys, a home that provides structure and supervision and encourages emotional expression is a protective factor. Conversely, as early as toddlerhood, teachers respond to aggressive behavior in boys and to dependent behavior in girls in ways that tend to perpetuate these behaviors (Fagot, 1984), increasing the likelihood of children's developing sex role stereotyped behaviors that may contribute to risk patterns for later violence.

The developers of prevention programs for economically and ethnically diverse populations must understand and appreciate differences in values, beliefs, and socialization practices. Child rearing, education, family and gender roles, and experiences with social institutions will vary among the populations being served. These differences must be considered in the design and delivery of interventions. For example, beliefs about what behaviors constitute social competence may vary across cultural groups (Laosa, 1979). Some families might value obedience in children more highly than autonomy. Children in these families must accommodate to these expectations. Preventionists must respect and accommodate the needs of children to be bicultural within our society.

We are attempting to address these issues in our training for early childhood educators and parents. The program provides 12 hours of instruction for child care staff on integrating into the curriculum antibias themes related to both gender and cultural differences. Participants are assisted in assessing the "cultural competence" of their centers to ensure that their policies and practices are sensitive and responsive to the diverse families they serve. Two parent workshops focus on gender roles, culture, and bias. The lending library for parents and children includes books and videos that reflect a broad range of cultural backgrounds and family structures. Family activities include creation of a "family scrapbook" in which children and parents record significant events, traditions, and family history.

Linkages to Elementary Schools

Success in negotiating major life transitions has significant implications for later development (Bronfenbrenner, 1979, 1986). Entering kindergarten is such a transition. Schools traditionally have recognized this event by holding orientation programs for parents, inviting parents and children to visit the schools prior to enroll-ment, and doing kindergarten screenings to prepare children for school and the school for the children. Another goal of these activities is to initiate a positive relationship between parent and school, or, from Bronfenbrenner's perspective, to strengthen sup-portive linkages within the child's mesosystem. These strategies appear to have lost some of their effectiveness with the changes in recent years in family structure and school and community demo-graphics.

Two avenues for facilitating a positive transition to kindergarten are being taken with participating families. One is to invite kinder-garten staff to the child care centers to meet incoming parents and children. The other is to develop a Parent-to-Parent program, in which Parent-Teacher Organizations distribute "welcome" packets to new families and visit or telephone new parents before the school year begins and periodically during the year.

Community Intervention

A final initiative is to integrate the activities of this early child-hood violence prevention program with other violence prevention initiatives in target communities. This is accomplished by develop-ing local advisory committees with broad-based representation. Project staff are assisting participating community groups in assess-ing needs related to violence and young children and linking child care staff and parents to local, statewide, and national advocacy and community awareness efforts. The direction and specific outcomes of this strategy will necessarily vary from community to community. Examples of activities at the local level include consciousness-raising events, community mediation training, and the organization of support groups for victims of violence. In two of the pilot commu-nities, a "nonviolent video exchange" is being planned in conjunc-tion with the "Week of the Young Child." Parents of young children will be encouraged to turn in videos that have antisocial, violent, or other content inappropriate for young children in exchange for videos with prosocial messages. At the same time, workshops and written materials will be available on the impact of television on children and on constructive use of media. Social service agencies, child care centers, schools, parents, local libraries and health departments, high school students, supermarkets, and video distributors will all be involved in this project.

The program promotes linkages with organizations at the state and national levels. Groups such as the National Association for the Education of Young Children, the National Parents Association, and the Children's Defense Fund have assigned top priority to initiatives concerning children and violence. These groups can give child care providers and parents a voice in social policy recommendations. The rationale for this component is to provide early childhood educators and parents a sense of hope for the future and faith in their individual and collective ability to have an impact on their own and their children's lives. This is perhaps the most fundamental protective factor for any social problem, and no less so, we believe, for preventing violence.

Conclusion

As problems of violence have grown in our communities, researchers, educators, and social policymakers have designed and implemented numerous interventions. Recently, these have focused most often on middle childhood or youth violence. A compelling argument can be made for earlier intervention, however. Patterns of violent behavior are established early in life; risk and protective factors may have their most potent influence in early childhood.

A small number of early intervention programs have shown promising, though often short-term, outcomes. Many of these have addressed one or several spheres of early influence—such as the family or the school—but not all. We have described in this chapter an ecological model that includes support at the individual, family, peer, and community/societal levels. In this model, educational programs for child care providers and families are integrated with community and political action initiatives. A unique focus of the model is contextual intervention, in which children's social learning is enhanced informally within authentic play contexts.

Another unique aspect of this model is its interdisciplinary nature. Although there has been a growing trend toward collaboration between educators and mental health preventionists at the middle and high school levels, transdisciplinary efforts at the early childhood level have lagged behind in recent years. As we are learning in our own project, there is much to be gained from combining expertise in child development and educational strategies at the individual level with a broader perspective of systems change. More support is needed for violence prevention initiatives that seek to integrate strategies that have been found to be effective across disciplines concerned with children, families, and communities.

References

Ainsworth, M. A. (1973). The development of infant-mother attachment. In B. Caldwell & H. Ricciuti (Eds.), *Review of child development research* (Vol. 3). Chicago: University of Chicago Press.

American Psychological Association, Commission on Violence and Youth. (1993). *Violence and youth: Psychology's response* (Vol. 1). Washington, DC: American Psychological Association.

Anthony, E., & Cohler, B. (Eds.). (1987). *The invulnerable child.* New York: Guilford.

Beland, K. R. (1991). *Second step: A violence prevention curriculum: Preschool-kindergarten.* Seattle, WA: Committee for Children.

Bronfenbrenner, U. (1979). *The ecology of human development: Experiments by nature and design.* Cambridge, MA: Harvard University Press.

Bronfenbrenner, U. (1986). Ecology of the family as a context for human development: Research perspectives. *Developmental Psychology, 22,* 723-742.

Caldwell, B. N. (1977). Aggression and hostility in young children. *Young Children, 32*(2), 4-13.

Carlsson-Paige, N., & Levin, D. (1990). *Who's calling the shots: How to respond effectively to children's fascination with war play and war toys.* Philadelphia: New Society.

Carlsson-Paige, N., & Levin, D. (1991). The subversion of healthy development and play. *Day Care and Early Education, 19*(2), 14-20.

Children's Defense Fund. (1994). *The state of America's children: Yearbook 1994.* Washington, DC: Author.

Conduct Problems Prevention Research Group. (1992). A developmental and clinical model for the prevention of conduct disorder: The FASTTrack Program. *Development and Psychopathology, 4,* 509-527.

Cosaro, W. A. (1981). Friendship in the nursery school: Social organization in a peer environment. In S. Asher & J. M. Gottman (Eds.), *The development of children's friendships.* New York: Cambridge University Press.

Cowen, E. L., & Work, W. C. (1988). Resilient children, psychological wellness and primary prevention. *American Journal of Community Psychology, 16,* 591-607.

Crick, N. R., & Ladd, G. W. (1987, April). *Children's perceptions of the consequences of aggressive behavior: Do the ends justify the means?* Paper presented at the biennial meeting of the Society for Research in Child Development, Baltimore.

Dodge, K. A. (1983). Behavioral antecedents of peer social status. *Child Development, 54*, 1386-1399.

Dodge, K. A. (1991). The structure and function of reactive and proactive aggression. In D. J. Pepler & K. H. Rubin (Eds.), *The development and treatment of childhood aggression*. Hillsdale, NJ: Lawrence Erlbaum.

Dodge, K. A. (1993). The future of research on the treatment of conduct disorder. *Development and Psychopathology, 5*, 311-319.

Eron, L. D. (1982). Parent-child interaction, television violence and aggression of children. *American Psychologist, 37*, 197-211.

Eron, L. D. (1988). *Relation of parental rejection and nurturance to child aggression.* Paper presented at Earlscourt Symposium on Childhood Aggression, Toronto.

Eron, L. D., & Huesmann, L. R. (1984). The relation of prosocial behavior to the development of aggression and psychopathology. *Aggressive Behavior, 10*, 201-212.

Eron, L. D., Huesmann, L. R., & Zelli, A. (1991). The role of parental variables in the learning of aggression. In D. J. Pepler & K. H. Rubin (Eds.), *The development and treatment of childhood aggression*. Hillsdale, NJ: Lawrence Erlbaum.

Fagot, B. I. (1984). The consequents of problem behavior in toddler children. *Journal of Abnormal Child Psychology, 12*, 385-396.

Farrington, D. P. (1978). The family backgrounds of aggressive youths. In L. Hersov, M. Berger, & D. Shaffer (Eds.), *Aggression and antisocial behavior in childhood and adolescence*. Oxford: Pergamon.

Farrington, D. P. (1989). Early predictors of adolescent aggression and adult violence. *Violence and Victims, 4*(2), 79-100.

Farrington, D. P. (1991). Childhood aggression and adult violence: Early precursors and later life outcomes. In D. J. Pepler & K. H. Rubin (Eds.), *The development and treatment of childhood aggression*. Hillsdale, NJ: Lawrence Erlbaum.

Federal Bureau of Investigation. (1991). *Uniform Crime Reports: Crime in the U.S., 1990*. Washington, DC: Government Printing Office.

Felsman, J. K. (1989). Risk and resiliency in childhood: The lives of street children. In T. F. Dugan & R. Coles (Eds.), *The child in our times: Studies in the development of resiliency*. New York: Brunner/Mazel.

Forehand, M. S., & Long, N. (1991). Prevention of aggression and other behavior problems in the early adolescent years. In D. J. Pepler & K. H. Rubin (Eds.), *The development and treatment of childhood aggression*. Hillsdale, NJ: Lawrence Erlbaum.

Forgatch, M. S. (1988). *The relation between child behavior, client resistance, and parenting practices.* Paper presented at the Earlscourt Symposium on Childhood Aggression, Toronto.

Forgatch, M. S. (1991). The clinical science vortex: A developing theory of antisocial behavior. In D. J. Pepler & K. H. Rubin (Eds.), *The development and treatment of childhood aggression*. Hillsdale, NJ: Lawrence Erlbaum.

Friedlander, B. Z. (1994). Community violence, children's development, and mass media: In pursuit of new insights, new goals, and new strategies. *Psychiatry, 56*, 66-81.

Garbarino, J., Dubrow, N., Kostelny, K., & Pardo, C. (1992). *Children in danger.* San Francisco: Jossey-Bass.

Garmezy, N. (1981). Children under stress: Perspectives on antecedents and correlates of vulnerability and resistance to psychopathology. In A. I. Rabin, J. Aronoff,

A. M. Barclay, & R. A. Zucker (Eds.), *Further exploration in personality.* New York: John Wiley.

Guerra, N., Tolan, P., & Hammond, R. (1992). *Prevention and treatment of adolescent violence.* Report to the American Psychological Association, Commission on Violence and Youth.

Gullotta, T. P. (1987). Prevention's technology. *Journal of Primary Prevention, 8*(1/2), 5-24.

Hartup, W. W., & Moore, S. G. (1990). Early peer relations: Developmental significance and prognostic implications. *Early Childhood Research Quarterly, 5,* 1-17.

Hawkins, J. D., Catalano, R. F., & Miller, J. Y. (1992). Risk and protective factors for alcohol and other drug problems in adolescence and early adulthood: Implications for substance abuse prevention. *Psychological Bulletin, 112,* 64-105.

Hawkins, J. D., Von Cleve, E., & Catalano, R. F. (1991). Reducing early childhood aggression: Results of a primary prevention program. *Journal of the American Academy of Child and Adolescent Psychiatry, 30,* 208-217.

Heath, L., Bresolin, L. B., & Rinaldi, R. C. (1989). Effects of media violence on children. *Archives of General Psychiatry, 46,* 376-379.

Howes, C. (1983). Patterns of friendship. *Child Development, 54,* 1041-1053.

Howes, C. (1987). Peer interaction of young children. *Monographs of the Society for Research in Child Development, 53*(1, Serial No. 217).

Kazdin, A. E. (1985). *Treatment of antisocial behavior in children and adolescents.* Homewood, IL: Dorsey.

Laosa, L. M. (1979). Social competence in childhood: Toward a developmental, socioculturally relativistic paradigm. In M. W. Kent & J. E. Rolf (Eds.), *Social competence in children.* Hanover, NH: University Press of New England.

Lay-Dopyera, M., & Dopyera, J. E. (1987). Strategies for teaching. In C. Seefeldt (Ed.), *The early childhood curriculum: A review of current research.* New York: Teachers College Press.

Levin, D. (1994). *Teaching young children in violent times: Building a peaceable classroom.* Cambridge, MA: Educators for Social Responsibility.

Margolin, G., Gorin-Sibner, L., & Gleberman, L. (1988). Wife battering. In V. B. Van Hasselt, R. L. Morrison, A. S. Bellack, & M. Hersen (Eds.), *Handbook of family violence.* New York: Plenum.

Martinez, P., & Richters, J. (1994). NIMH community violence project: II. Children's distress symptoms associated with violence exposure. *Psychiatry, 56,* 22-35.

Matheson, C., & Wu, F. (1991, April). *Friendship and social pretend play.* Paper presented at the biennial meeting of the Society for Research in Child Development, Seattle, WA.

McCord, J., McCord, W., & Howard, A. (1963). Family interaction as antecedent to the direction of male aggressiveness. *Journal of Abnormal and Social Psychology, 66,* 239-242.

McGinnis, E., & Goldstein, A. P. (1990). *Skill Streaming in Early Childhood: Teaching prosocial skills to the preschool and kindergarten child.* Champaign, IL: Research Press.

Miller-Heyl, J. (1994). *Evaluation, "Dare to Be You" program.* Unpublished manuscript.

Mize, J., & Ladd, G. W. (1990). A cognitive-social learning approach to social skills training with low-status preschool children. *Developmental Psychology, 26,* 388-397.

Mize, J., Ladd, G. W., & Price, J. M. (1985). Promoting positive peer relations with young children: Rationales and strategies. *Child Care Quarterly, 14,* 221-237.

Moore, B., & Beland, K. R. (1992). *Evaluation of Second Step, preschool-kindergarten, a violence-prevention curriculum kit: Summary report.* Seattle, WA: Committee for Children.

National Research Council. (1993). *Understanding child abuse and neglect.* Washington, DC: National Academy Press.

Offord, D. R., Boyle, M. H., & Racine, Y. A. (1991). The epidemiology of antisocial behavior in childhood and adolescence. In D. J. Pepler & K. H. Rubin (Eds.), *The development and treatment of childhood aggression.* Hillsdale, NJ: Lawrence Erlbaum.

Olweus, D. (1991). Bully/victim problems among schoolchildren: Basic facts and effects of a school-based intervention program. In D. J. Pepler & K. H. Rubin (Eds.), *The development and treatment of childhood aggression.* Hillsdale, NJ: Lawrence Erlbaum.

Patterson, G. R., Capaldi, D., & Bank, L. (1991). An early starter model for predicting delinquency. In D. J. Pepler & K. H. Rubin (Eds.), *The development and treatment of childhood aggression.* Hillsdale, NJ: Lawrence Erlbaum.

Ramsey, P. G. (1989, April). *Successful and unsuccessful entry attempts: An analysis of behavioral and contextual factors.* Paper presented at the biennial meeting of the Society for Research in Child Development, Kansas City.

Reiss, A. J., Jr., & Roth, J. A. (Eds.). (1993). *Understanding and preventing violence.* Washington, DC: National Academy Press.

Rubin, K. H. (1980). Fantasy play: Its role in the development of social skills and social cognition. In K. H. Rubin (Ed.), *Children's play.* San Francisco: Jossey-Bass.

Rubin, K. H. (1982). Nonsocial play in preschoolers: Necessary evil? *Child Development, 53,* 651-657.

Sampson, R. J. (1985). Neighborhood and crime: The structural determinants of personal victimization. *Journal of Research in Crime and Delinquency, 22*(1), 7-40.

Scarlett, W. G. (1983). Social isolation from agemates among nursery school children. In M. Donaldson, R. Grieve, & C. Pratt (Eds.), *Early childhood development and education.* New York: Guilford.

Schweinhart, L. J., Barnes, H. V., & Weikart, D. R. (1993). *Significant benefits: The High/Scope Perry Preschool Study through age 27.* Ypsilanti, MI: High/Scope Educational Research Foundation.

Shure, M. B. (1992). *I Can Problem Solve (ICPS): An interpersonal cognitive problem solving program (preschool).* Champaign, IL: Research Press.

Shure, M. B. (1993). I Can Problem Solve (ICPS): Interpersonal cognitive problem solving for young children. *Early Childhood Development and Care, 96,* 49-64.

Shure, M. B., & Spivack, G. (1982). Interpersonal problem solving in young children: A cognitive approach to prevention. *American Journal of Community Psychology, 10,* 341-356.

Shure, M. B., & Spivack, G. (1988). Interpersonal cognitive problem solving. In R. H. Price, E. L. Cowen, R. P. Lorion, & J. Ramos-McKay (Eds.), *14 ounces of prevention: A casebook for practitioners.* Washington, DC: American Psychological Association.

Stark, E., & Flitcraft, A. H. (1991). Spouse abuse. In M. L. Rosenberg & M. A. Fenley (Eds.), *Violence in America: A public health approach.* New York: Oxford University Press.

Stremmel, A. J., Benson, M. J., & Powell, D. R. (1993). Communication, satisfaction, and emotional exhaustion among child care staff. *Early Childhood Research Quarterly, 8,* 221-233.

Trawick-Smith, J. W. (1992). A descriptive study of persuasive preschool children: How they get others to do what they want. *Early Childhood Research Quarterly, 7,* 95-115.

Trawick-Smith, J. W. (1994). *Interactions in the classroom: Facilitating play in the early years.* Columbus, OH: Merrill.

Vygotsky, L. (1962). *Thought and language.* Cambridge: MIT Press.

Vygotsky, L. (1978). *Mind in society.* Cambridge, MA: Harvard University Press.

Werner, E. E. (1990). Protective factors and individual resilience. In S. J. Meisels & J. P. Shonkoff (Eds.), *Handbook of early childhood intervention* (pp. 97-116). Cambridge, MA: Cambridge University Press.

Werner, E. E., & Smith, R. S. (1982). *Vulnerable by invincible: A longitudinal study of resilient children and youth.* New York: McGraw-Hill.

West, D. J., & Farrington, D. P. (1977). *The delinquent way of life.* London: Heinemann.

Widom, C. S. (1992, October). The cycle of violence. *National Institute of Justice: Research in Brief,* pp. 1-6.

Zigler, E. F. (1990). Foreword. In S. J. Meisels & J. P. Shonkoff (Eds.), *Handbook of early childhood intervention.* Cambridge, MA: Cambridge University Press.

Zigler, E. F., Taussig, C., & Black, K. (1992). Early childhood intervention: A promising preventative for juvenile delinquency. *American Psychologist, 47,* 997-1006.

CHAPTER 13

Transforming the Culture: Creating Safety, Equality, and Justice for Women and Girls

DONNA GARSKE

The public discourse on violence in the United States tends to focus on random violence or violence perpetrated by strangers, missing much of the violence committed against women and girls by men known to them. Available statistics reveal alarming levels of incidence and prevalence of such violence against females. In January 1994, the U.S. Department of Justice published *Violence Against Women: National Crime Victimization Survey Report,* in which the authors report that "whereas men were more likely to be victimized by acquaintances or strangers, women were just as likely to be victimized by intimates, such as husbands or boyfriends, as they were to be victimized by acquaintances or strangers" (Los Angeles County Special Panel on Domestic Violence, 1994, p. 12). In 1992, the U.S. surgeon general ranked abuse by husbands and partners as the leading cause of injuries to women between the ages of 15 and 44. The American Medical Association reported in 1990 that 50% of all female homicide victims were killed by a husband or boyfriend (cited in Los Angeles County Special Panel on Domestic Violence, 1994).

Over the past 20 years, more than 12 million American women have survived rape; 640,000 are newly victimized each year. The National Women's Study report issued in 1992 indicated that in 78% of rape cases, the victims were assaulted by someone they had

263

seen before or knew well (cited in Buchwald, Fletcher, & Roth, 1993).

The wide range of violence against women becomes even more alarming when one considers the number of girls who experience childhood sexual abuse, which often results in severe problems later in life. Estimates vary, but a number of studies have concluded that one out of four girls will be sexually abused by age 18 (Minnesota Women's Fund, 1993). Some research suggests that the prevalence of child sexual abuse may be as great as 62% for females (Conte, 1993). In a study of 3,100 teenagers attending public schools, 35% of the young women surveyed reported having been abused, molested, beaten, or raped by male intimates (Relationship Abuse Prevention Project, 1987).

Despite the prevalence of violence committed against females by males, a gender-based analysis of violence in the United States has not been incorporated into the public discourse on violence to any significant extent; rather, women's experience of violence has been marginalized or even excluded from consideration. Discussions of family violence in general often overlook the gender-based nature of the problem: In the majority of cases, males are the perpetrators of family violence and females and children are the ones victimized. Intimate violence against women constitutes the major form of family violence. Although intimate violence is not perpetrated exclusively by men—sometimes women are violent, both in heterosexual and in lesbian relationships—this chapter focuses on male violence because males are the perpetrators of 95% to 98% of violence against women (California Office of Criminal Justice Planning, 1994). Exclusion of the gender-based analysis of violence ignores the essential fact that women are the victims of the majority of intimate violence occurring in the United States.

In order to address the problem of violence in the United States effectively, it is essential to confront this preference for gender-neutral analysis over gender-based analysis. The terms and theories used to define and analyze any problem ultimately determine the nature of the interventions and solutions developed. I will argue throughout this chapter that the current preference for a gender-neutral analysis of violence and for preventive strategies stemming from that analysis ultimately hinder attempts to address the problem. Gender-neutral analysis excludes consideration of the *root cause* of violence against women, which is the widely accepted belief that men have the right to exert superiority over women, family members, and other "subordinates" through any means, including violence (Dobash & Dobash, 1979; French, 1985; Sinclair, 1995). Violence in the family is merely a special instance of a pattern of male control over women, children, and even other men that extends from dating relationships through parenting and marriage to economic life (Stark & Flitcraft, 1991). In order to illustrate the differences between gender-neutral analysis and gender-based analysis of violence in the United States, I will examine current approaches to violence against women within the context of intimate relationships with men.

Differences in Theories and Interventions

Although earlier feminists devoted some attention to wife beating, it was not until the early 1970s that wife abuse was recognized as a serious social problem. Since that time, two main theoretical viewpoints have emerged: the family or domestic violence perspective, which tends toward a gender-neutral approach, and the violence against women perspective. Although the types of practices and interventions derived from these respective positions are not mutually exclusive, the two views present significantly different consequences for the ultimate prevention of violence.

From the family violence perspective, violence between husbands and wives is seen as a pattern of abuse occurring among family members; from this perspective, any family member has equal potential to carry out violence and/or to be victimized by violence (Gelles, 1993; Kurz, 1989). Thus, research focuses on individuals and relations within families, and the occurrence of violence is seen as resulting from factors such as psychological or mental stress or illness, substance abuse, or intergenerational tensions.

Although the family violence approach centers on individual and psychological causes, it does acknowledge the relevance of some additional factors. Some stressors affecting the family, such as unemployment, are generally viewed as risk factors for violence. The larger issues of sexism and power dynamics are also sometimes acknowledged as factors in intimate violence, but not as the basis for the abuse of women. More often, family therapists focus on "reciprocal transactions between two systems (man and woman)" rather than on the power dynamics of the relationship (Edleson & Tolman, 1992, p. 19). Intervention strategies that derive from this perspective usually consist of couples and/or family counseling to improve communication skills or reduce stress; training in self-esteem, resilience, and conflict resolution skills; and efforts to provide therapeutic support for recovery from childhood trauma and personality disorders (Gelles, 1993; Kurz, 1989).

The violence against women approach, on the other hand, focuses on the belief system prevalent in relationships between women and men, wherein the male believes he is entitled to control and coerce the female by a variety of means, including violence. This belief system is examined in terms of its operation both inside and outside the family, in the past and the present, as the key unit of analysis of men's violence against their wives/partners (Dobash & Dobash, 1979; Sinclair, 1988). The violence against women perspective connects all forms of male violence against women—such as child sexual abuse, rape, sexual harassment, workplace violence, beatings, and homicide—as related to men's efforts to control and coerce females and men's belief that such efforts are justified in maintaining their authority over women.

Intervention strategies derived from this perspective include holding the male abuser accountable for his behavior through arrest and other appropriate interventions, such as mandatory time in a men's batterer program or rape offender treatment; providing shelter and support for women victimized by violence and their children; and advocating for change in the social practices of institutions, such as the law enforcement and courts systems, in order to promote due justice for women and children victimized by violence (Adams, 1989; Dobash & Dobash, 1992; Gelles, 1993; Kurz, 1989).

Approaches to Framing and Solving Social Problems

The emphasis placed by the family violence perspective on therapeutic individual and family-based causes of and solutions to violence still dominates public perception in the United States (especially in terms of carrying out interventions and accessibility to resources and attention) (Edleson & Tolman, 1992, p. 135), even though battered women's advocacy groups across the country have worked to advance the gender-specific view for the past 20 years.

In understanding why the gender-neutral family violence perspective is usually favored over the gender-based violence against women perspective, two analytic frameworks are useful: the contemporary culture's proclivity toward therapeutic and/or mental health responses to address individual problems (discussed in this section) and political and other underlying factors that determine how and whether issues are placed on the social agenda (discussed below in the section headed "Marginalization of the Gender-Based Perspective").

Dobash and Dobash (1992) describe North American approaches to social problems as being "packed with the perceptions and language of psychiatry, psychology and the mental health movement" (p. 214). These authors suggest that this emphasis is derived from the significant rise in the number of such professionals in the United States in recent decades: Between 1968 and 1982, the number of clinical psychologists more than tripled—more than half the world's psychologists now work in the United States; the number of family therapists tripled between 1975 and 1985. Dobash and Dobash assert that this "therapeutic society" is rooted in several key beliefs and practices: an emphasis on extreme individualism versus community solutions, the belief that those who are deemed abnormal and/or delinquent should be institutionalized and thus separated from those considered normal, the emergence of specialists to assess and treat those individuals, and the spread into wider society of the idea that even relatively normal people are in need of help and intervention.

This cultural context for problem solving frames how strategies for the prevention of violence are defined. Although the family violence field has advanced from examining individual characteristics alone to including the public health model perspective of environmental influences, gender-based analysis is still lacking. Publications on the prevention of family violence, in alignment with the public health model of understanding this problem, emphasize prevention interventions that identify risk factors and then treat those who are most at risk.

The influence of the therapeutic emphasis on risk factors, along with an emphasis on blaming female victims of violence, can be seen at work in the first national funding for the *primary* prevention of violence against women and girls within intimate relationships. In the summer of 1994, the Centers for Disease Control (CDC) released a funding announcement for five national demonstration grants; the announcement included requirements for applicants to identify "at-risk" populations of women and girls to "target" for intervention. The underlying logic suggested by this focus is that women's individual pathology and environmental characteristics are the major contributing factors to females' being victimized by male violence. This rationale results in interventions that are likely to have limited impact in terms of "primary" prevention, which addresses root causes before violence starts, versus secondary or tertiary prevention, which ameliorates the effects of violence after the fact.

Stark and Flitcraft (1991) argue that the traditional medical model of disease is inadequate to solve this problem: In its emphasis on biology, personality, or risk behaviors, the traditional medical model underplays the complex origins of spouse abuse. The "political" model of spouse abuse, which emphasizes the use of violence to enforce inequality, finds stronger support than alternative explanations highlighting pathology, risk behaviors, or stress. Yet not only did the CDC funding announcement retain the therapeutic emphasis on risk factors, it also targeted females at risk. This exclusive focus on "female pathology" not only ignores the overwhelming evidence that the basis of this problem derives from male behaviors that are condoned by the existing social belief system, it perpetuates the traditional, patriarchal approach of placing the responsibility for violence against women on the victims of that violence.

Inadequacy of Risk Factors
in Preventing Intimate Violence

A review of what is known about risk factors or "vulnerabilities" for involvement in woman abuse leads to the conclusion that the sensitivity and specificity of any risk profile are inadequate for the purposes of targeting prevention efforts regarding violence against women. Identifying individual risk factors for woman abuse is a difficult task. Very few reliable risk factors have been identified for men who abuse or for women or girls victimized by abuse. The most consistent finding on risk factors for male abusers is the experiencing or witnessing of violence as a child (Stark & Flitcraft, 1991);

however, even for this most consistent risk factor, the majority of men with this background are not violent (Fagan & Browne, 1991). In fact, numerous researchers have concluded in their evaluation of risk factors for men that the single greatest risk factor for a man's being violent is his belief that his violence toward his wife/partner is socially acceptable (Adams, 1989; Dobash & Dobash, 1979).

The search for risk factors associated with women who have been victimized yields similar results. In Hotaling and Sugarman's (1986) review of 42 specific variables from 52 studies that employed case-comparison or experimental designs, only one characteristic is associated with woman abuse: witnessing parental violence as a child or teen. However, even this finding has been questioned. A review of the literature of personality factors indicates that no consistent personality profile has been identified for battered women (Stark & Flitcraft, 1991). Factors of helplessness, low self-esteem, and alcohol consumption are now seen as more likely to be results of being victimized than antecedents of violence.

Other risk factors associated with intimate violence against females include young age, divorce or other problematic marital status, pregnancy, alcohol abuse, and demographic variables, such as unemployment. However, the only consistent risk factor is prior instances of violence (Stark & Flitcraft, 1991). The scarcity of reliable risk factors relevant to prevention efforts confirms that violence against females cuts across all levels of society as opposed to being characteristic of particular economic, family, or social circumstances.

Exclusive reliance on the "microlevel" approach of addressing individual risk factors, primarily on the family level, may be inadequate to prevent intimate violence against women. More all-encompassing "macrolevel" solutions need to be developed and supported (Edleson & Tolman, 1992). The emphasis Stark and Flitcraft (1991) place on the "gender politics" model is supported by the conclusions of other researchers that family violence in general, spousal abuse, and other forms of violence against females are special and distinct types of violent behavior (Dobash & Dobash, 1979; Wardell, Gillespie, & Leffler, 1983). From this perspective, violent men achieve and maintain the level of dominance they consider appropriate through a variety of oppressive strategies, including wife beating, child abuse, marital rape, psychological abuse, punitive economic deprivation, and coerced social isolation (Bowker, Arbitell, & McFerron, 1988).

Implications for Prevention

Although the traditional approaches of the gender-neutral family violence perspective have some value as elements supportive of building healthy families and individuals, such strategies should not constitute the dominant form of intervention. To be effective interventions for particular families in crisis, strategies must be implemented in conjunction with an insistence that the primary problem is abuse and that abusive men need to acknowledge their accountability for their violent behaviors. More important, gender-neutral family violence interventions are ineffective in terms of *preventing* violence because they fail to address the root cause—men's belief that it is acceptable to control and coerce women in order to maintain their authority. Researchers who apply an "ecological" approach note that "gender-absent" or "power-absent" perspectives constitute "microsystem myopia": "Ignoring the historical and cultural power imbalances between men and women in intimate relationships and in society at large strips these interactions of critically important factors that play themselves out in daily life" (Edleson & Tolman, 1992, p. 20).

For example, in terms of the most significant risk factor for intimate violence and family violence, prior witnessing or experiencing of violence, the family violence approach specifies that a particular abuser teaches other family members that violence is an appropriate means of asserting authority and control; from this perspective, the therapist works to intervene in the learning cycle through counseling and therapy. Although the gender-neutral family violence approach may acknowledge the social origins of stress, such as unemployment or poverty, or acknowledge sexism as a variable present in a family dynamic, the emphasis remains on teaching individuals to cope with stress within the context of the family unit rather than on considering such stress in a larger sociopolitical and historical context (Kurz, 1989).

A gender-based approach, on the other hand, is more effective in addressing both intimate violence and other forms of family violence for two reasons. First, it offers interventions (such as reeducation programs for men who batter) into existing violent family situations that address the root of the violent behavior by highlighting the fallacy of the underlying belief system of male superiority that supports this violent behavior. Although such gender-based intervention strategies are useful, this focus on individual men still falls short of preventing original incidents of violence; such programs are implemented after the fact, at the expense of women who have been injured, and tend to reach primarily those men referred by the courts, estimated to be less than 10% of all men who batter (Federal Bureau of Investigation, 1991). Thus, whereas intervention strategies are more important when derived from gender-based analysis, individual interventions alone cannot be the basis for the prevention of men's violence against women. This leads to the second and more important reason a gender-based approach offers effective strategies: It has the potential for preventing the violence in the first place, *before* it manifests in a particular family, because it acknowledges the overall societal systems that teach, perpetuate, and condone the use of such violence by men to maintain their authority.

The gender-based perspective offers additional advantages in that it enables consistency of approaches and strategies. The traditional family violence focus on individual risk factors and therapies, in contrast, often creates an overly narrow focus, fragmentation of approach, and thus lack of consistent and comprehensive preventive strategies. Richard Gelles (1993), a proponent of the family violence approach, comments that the field of family violence has become "balkanized," with experts in each area of family violence (such as spousal abuse, child abuse, and elder abuse) professing independent theories and strategies, and often not even reading one another's research reports. Gelles also states that "a possible exception to this 'balkanization' is the effort of feminists who conceptualize the victimization of women across the age span as the central problem worthy of study" (p. 5).

The gender-based perspective on intimate and family violence thus avoids such fragmentation; the unified approach provided by the gender-based perspective assures consistent and comprehensive prevention strategies. It holds immense value for the discourse on violence prevention. It is a unifying theory that accounts for the wide range and prevalence of violence against females, both in the home and on the streets (from sexual harassment, workplace violence, incest, rape, assault, and homicide), by recognizing how the patriarchal culture systematically discriminates against women and implicitly supports abusive and violent behaviors by men. This perspective offers strategies for change that move beyond the individual and the specific family to encompass broad social changes.

Marginalization of the Gender-Based Perspective

Defining Social Problems

Given the value of the gender-based perspective, why does the full spectrum of male violence against women and other family members, and in society at large, continue to be framed and acted on in the absence of a unified, gender-specific theory? Why is the violence affecting women and girls not recognized as an "epidemic," warranting as full consideration as other social issues, such as the problem of random violence in the United States? Smelser (1988) provides a helpful framework for understanding social problems; the following perspective is drawn largely from his work.

In Smelser's terms, a social problem must first be relevant to some institution that society endows with value. For instance, pregnancy out of wedlock is considered a social problem in large part because it stands in violation of the value placed on the family as the appropriate center of childbearing and child learning. Dropping out of the educational system is viewed as a social problem because of the value placed on learning both in itself and as preparation for entering the workforce.

A second criterion for a behavior to be regarded as a social problem is that the behavior be viewed as deviant in relation to a type of norm or role expectation. Behaviors such as excessive alcohol consumption and teenage pregnancy are not illegal, but they violate social norms relevant to substance abuse, dependency, premarital sex, and childbearing behavior. Societal norms and values undergo constant change, so that behaviors that were once prevalent and considered normal may become unacceptable because they violate new norms and values. For instance, child beating was once widely considered to be normal and appropriate behavior. With new expectations about child rearing and the place of discipline and punishment, and with the rise of the movement for children's rights, even corporal punishment is being challenged as a violation of newly evolved social norms. In many instances, spanking a child is now considered such a serious social problem that there are those who would make it illegal.

There are additional ingredients in the definition of a social problem. The behavior in question must (a) have a significant level of prevalence, (b) involve some economic or social cost (e.g., absenteeism and inefficiency being among the high economic costs of alcoholism and drug dependency), and (c) be viewed as amenable to positive change through application of resources, changes in legislation and social policy, and other methods.

Given the above criteria, the labeling of a social problem becomes primarily a political matter. In order for a social problem to be placed on the public agenda, sufficiently visible and powerful people must persuade those who officially name social problems that the behavior in question meets these criteria. For example, the AIDS epidemic was essentially ignored in its initial years; it was considered to be a small problem isolated among the gay population, a highly marginalized community that was not adequately represented among decision makers. It was only when visible and prominent persons, especially in the entertainment industry, began to experience the impact of the epidemic in their social circles that they took up the cause and advocated for consideration of the epidemic as a serious social problem.

Defining Violence Against Women as a Social Problem

Smelser's (1988) approach offers insight into the definition of violence against women as a social issue and its placement on the public agenda. Consider whether the problem of woman abuse within the context of intimate relationships is perceived as the erosion of a valuable institution. Despite the ongoing efforts of the women's movement, women are still regarded as subordinates, and their contributions are often not valued as highly as those of men. Existing social systems and institutions are still dominated by men and continue to discriminate systematically against women (French, 1992). Current social conditions continue to reinforce male superiority over and exploitation of women and girls. This is seen most readily in the fact that traditionally male occupations still pay more than traditionally female occupations. In the United States, women have only recently achieved earning 70% of men's wages for similar work (French, 1992). As of 1992, women accounted for only 11% of members of the U.S. House of Representatives and 6% of the U.S. Senate (Abzug & Kelber, 1993).

The long history and tradition of violence against women was not even given much attention until activists started the battered women's movement, which established shelters for these women. Abused women then started leaving their homes, taking their children with them. The issue of battered women thus emerged for consideration at the national level, not so much because of the value placed on women and concern for their safety, but primarily because battering was seen as resulting in the breakup of the family, an institution on which much value *is* placed.

The institutions of marriage and family in the Western world (indeed, in most cultures around the world) are predicated on the servitude of wives to husbands. Consider the etymology of the word *family*. It is derived from the Latin word *famulus,* which means domestic slave. *Familia,* or family, referred to the total number of slaves belonging to one man and was used by the Romans to denote the social order of a man ruling over a variety of subordinates, with wife and children collapsed into the category of domestic slaves. The unity of family was thus founded on the refusal to cede to women any independent existence, a legacy that still is present today in the majority of American families (Garske, 1992). Thus, although intimate violence against women has gathered some momentum toward being recognized as a social problem, it is often regarded as such on the basis of the value placed on the institution of the family, which, in its predominant configuration, typically denies value and independence to women and children and places them in positions subordinate to men.

As to the second element in the definition of a social problem, does woman abuse involve a behavior that is deviant in light of an established norm or law? Only recently in the United States has it been considered that a man's beating or raping his wife is a crime. Although the legal mechanisms are in place to deem much of men's violence against women as against the law, the norm still remains that few negative consequences exist to make it unacceptable for men to control and coerce women through violent means, and many types of abuse—verbal, emotional, and economic—are *not* illegal.

In addition, the legal system generally continues to condone implicitly men's acts of violence within intimate relationships. When such cases come to court, the husband is often excused for his violent behavior by "extenuating circumstances," even though the behavior is explicitly illegal. A man arrested for battering his wife can be released on his own recognizance within hours of his arrest. Many men then return to further intimidate the women they have battered and frighten them into dropping the charges. There continue to be few negative consequences for men who are abusive; abusive behavior does not lessen a man's social standing with his friends, family, community, or employer (Marin Abused Women's Services, 1994).

The next criterion for establishing a behavior as a social problem is prevalence. Is violence against women prevalent enough to be regarded as significant? Undeniably so. Some 4 million women are physically battered each year by their partners (including husbands, former husbands, and boyfriends); it is estimated that as many as 30% of all women in the United States have been beaten by their partners at least once. On the average, more than 4,000 women are killed each year by their husbands/boyfriends (Los Angeles County Special Panel on Domestic Violence, 1994). Does the problem result in an economic loss? In the United States, it is estimated that 25% of such workplace problems as absenteeism, lateness, and low productivity are due to domestic violence (Institute for Women's Policy Research, 1995).

The last criterion concerns whether there is a solution to the problem of intimate violence, given appropriate social changes and investment of resources. A positive answer is provided by the achievements of the national battered women's movement and the rape prevention movement, which grew out of the women's movement in the mid-1970s. Today there are more than 1,200 safe homes/shelters for women nationwide, with hotlines and support services for women in almost every community. These two movements have worked together, community by community, state by state, to bring forward an awareness about a major social problem heretofore ignored, denied, or simply passed off with "That's just the way men are." Concrete language and theories to analyze this problem now exist. Laws have been rewritten, and practical solutions are in place to help women and their children live free of violence. These movements have made significant progress over the past 20 years in breaking the hold of men's power over women in the home, in enabling thousands of women to lead violence-free lives, and in actually saving many women's lives.

Most of the elements for defining intimate violence against women as a serious social problem thus pass the litmus test laid out by Smelser (1988). More problematic are questions about the value society places on women, and whether society recognizes men's acts of violence as deviant or transgressive of a social norm.

With women's value being held in high regard, primarily in terms of their ability to maintain the family unit, the approach that family violence theory advances emphasizes women within the context of family, with the preservation of the family serving as the highest ideal. Family violence theory does not emphasize the value of women's basic human right to live free from bodily harm, the same right that is guaranteed to men under the U.S. Constitution (Jones, 1994). The American disregard for women's rights can be seen in the failure of the United States to ratify the United Nations Convention on the Elimination of All Forms of Discrimination Against Women, which has been ratified by more than 100 other nations and which outlines women's rights and requires nations to enact legal sanctions to support these rights (Edleson & Tolman, 1992).

This framework for defining social problems identifies the only reason that the problem of male violence against women has not acquired the full attention it deserves on the public agenda: The U.S. sociocultural system is severely lacking in a social norm that values women as individuals rather than in terms of their relationships to others. Successful efforts to eliminate violence against women must be driven by an agenda that promotes the basic human right of women and girls as individuals (separate from their roles as family members) to live free of harassment, intimidation, and violence. Until this basic right is established and widely supported, the problem of men's violence toward women will continue. The replacement of current social practices and beliefs that deny this basic right with those that elevate women's value and status will have radical and far-reaching effects.

Prevention Strategies Based on Gender-Specific Analysis

The gender-based approach to intimate violence provides a theory to explain the experience of females' being victimized by all types of male violence, and, indeed, illuminates male violence in general. The gender-based perspective is thus the most valuable strategy for prevention of all forms of male violence. This sociopolitical perspective provides a broad-level analysis that sheds light on the intimate interrelationship between women's freedom from violence and their freedom from political, economic, and social exploitation. Because violence is a tool used by men to maintain their authority over women (Adams, 1989; Dobash & Dobash, 1979; Gondolf, 1985; Sinclair, 1988), eradicating violence against females will require changes at the most fundamental levels of society. These changes must eliminate the policies and practices perpetuated by the male-dominated culture that sexualize women as objects, demean their value, restrict their participation in decision making, dehumanize them with labels, control their rights over their own bodies, and marginalize and demean their presence. At the same time, the eradication of all forms of male violence against women is a necessary precursor to the prevention of all forms of violence in general. Examination of the gender-derived bases of violence against women will lead to a greater understanding of all violence and its prevention.

Prevention of Violence
Against Females: Vision, Values

Prevention, as a psychosocial term, is understood to encompass efforts to alter learning, environmental factors, and problematic behaviors before they become serious problems. Though useful, this concept is limiting because it defines change solely on the basis of the absence of a problem, such as a "smoke-free" environment or "nonviolent" relationships. Some practitioners in fields of social transformation have instead chosen strategies and language within the framework of "promotion" in order to provide more positive and meaningful descriptions of what must be created in order for significant change to occur, rather than focusing on defining issues primarily in the negative terms of what must be eliminated (Pransky, 1991).

Just as Martin Luther King, Jr. noted that " 'peace is not the absence of conflict, but the presence of justice' " (quoted in True, 1991, p. 43), so too must the values and characteristics of what must be present or promoted be identified if we are to end violence against women. Given that the problem reflects the deeply rooted sociocultural belief that men are entitled to have authority over women and that our society is replete with individual, interpersonal, and institutional manifestations of this belief, effective change will require not only the elimination of this belief system, but its replacement with a coherent alternative that offers positive benefits to all. A "new reality" must be promoted, one that supports the right of women and girls to safety, equality, and justice.

Programs that serve battered and raped women, along with programs that serve victims of other forms of family violence, are needed to address the external manifestations of these problems by providing intervention services. However, such programs will have limited impact as long as the conditions that give rise to the problem remain unchanged (Pransky, 1991). Thus, those concerned with preventing domestic violence and other forms of family violence must, in addition to providing the necessary short-term, stopgap measures, progress beyond these strategies to create long-term transformation of society. Individuals and organizations using gender-based approaches to effect such transformation need to be supported financially and otherwise in these vital efforts. The transformation of deeply ingrained beliefs and attitudes requires the commitment and participation of the entire community. The advocates who have led this effort for the past 20 years are rich with experience and vision to promote an agenda of prevention to the broader community.

Although the task of transforming society at this level is enormous, it is essential if we are to effect long-lasting progress in the prevention of violence within families and against women and girls: "Only by changing the social and cultural institutions that have given rise to the problem can a lasting solution be achieved" (Goodman, Koss, Fitzgerald, Russo, & Keita, 1993, p. 1054).

Recent studies in the emerging field of prevention in the realms of substance abuse and HIV/AIDS indicate that community-based prevention efforts yield promising results and offer hope that the primary prevention of complex problems can be brought about when an entire community endorses the necessary societal changes and works actively to implement these changes at all levels (Bracht & Gleason, 1990).

Social Transformation:
A Communitywide Approach

Even after 20 years of impressive efforts on the part of the women's antiviolence movement, the movement still lacks the critical mass required to replace current problem-causing images, values, and practices with problem-solving ones in a sufficient number of individuals. How might such critical mass be achieved? What is known about other efforts that have successfully created change by galvanizing entire communities?

A valuable source of information and methodology on this topic is social movement theory (SMT), which provides a strategic framework and analytic tools for organizing and evaluating social movements. A social movement is defined as a collective action in which the populace is alerted, educated, and mobilized over years and decades to challenge the whole society to redress social problems and restore critical social values (Moyer, 1987). SMT acknowledges that such movements occur in complex, open systems in which there are no instant, single solutions; problems are not "solved"— rather, the system itself is transformed. SMT's emphasis on the principles of participatory democracy ensures active community involvement and formulation of the widest possible spectrum of alternative solutions. Priority is given to community residents rather than to professionals in terms of decision making and development of strategies. SMT grounds social movements in strongly felt and widely held human and cultural values and traditions of the general population, such as freedom, democracy, and justice (Burns, 1990; Moyer, 1987).

SMT's analytic tools can be applied productively to the movement to end violence against women, family violence perpetrated by men, and violence in general, especially in terms of envisioning an alternative, problem-solving reality that promotes safety, equality, and justice. It may be somewhat inaccurate to discuss "restoring" to women rights that many believe they have never possessed, but in this case the approach of the civil rights movement provides an appropriate parallel. Slaves were never granted civil rights, but the civil rights movement worked to have these rights extended to African Americans. Indeed, some theorists claim that women did possess these rights in ancient times; Eisler (1987) posits an ancient Greek culture characterized by a "joyful and equal" partnership between men and women at all levels of society. Although many may dispute such claims, this work is still valuable in helping us to envision a new, positive reality.

Examples of previous successful efforts to create fundamental change in the dominant social and political beliefs and socially acceptable patterns of behavior can be found in various social movements, such as the peace, civil rights, and women's suffrage movements; these movements all arose from the grassroots level and achieved fundamental change through reliance on community-based development of strategies.

The grassroots movement to end drunk driving conducted by Mothers Against Drunk Driving (MADD) offers an inspiring model for successful community-based transformation of norms and behaviors. Although it must be acknowledged that MADD addresses norms and behaviors that do not have the immense scope and historical support of those associated with men's violence, MADD's grassroots tactics provide excellent models. As a result of efforts stimulated by MADD, drunk driving is now recognized as a serious threat to our communities, is strongly discouraged by community residents, is responded to with strictly enforced sentences, and has declined dramatically. In 1982, alcohol-related traffic fatalities in the United States represented 57.2% of all traffic fatalities; in 1993 the proportion declined to 43.5%. It is important to emphasize that this success was brought about not by professionals, but by grassroots activists:

> The actions taken by police departments and courts all over the country to ferret out and to imprison drunk drivers did not come from Masters in Public Health. This effort was triggered by groups of angry, hurt and disgusted mothers whose children had been killed by drunk drivers. These grief-stricken women rose up and shouted, "no more, no more, no more!" Their moral outrage galvanized the nation. (Prothrow-Stith, 1991, p. 143)

Considerations for Future Directions

Transforming communities so that women and girls experience safety, equality, and justice requires a daring approach that can best be thought of as parallel to the challenge the civil rights movement faced when confronted with eradicating racism in the United States. In the words of Martin Luther King, Jr., " 'Just as Socrates felt that it was necessary to create a tension in the mind, so that the individual could rise from the bondage of myths and half-truths, so must we create the kind of tension in society that will help men rise from the dark depths of prejudice and racism' " (quoted in True, 1991, p. 32).

In terms of the emerging movement to transform sociocultural norms and behaviors, in order to prevent intimate violence and other forms of family violence perpetrated by men, this "creative tension" is derived from competing values and rights: for women, the acquisition of equal value and participation in decision making, freedom from harm and injury, and the right to safety, equality, and justice; and for men, their historically and socially supported right to dominate and control women, family members, and other perceived subordinates.

It would be naive to suggest that such tensions do not exist and will not be exacerbated as the movement for women's right to safety, equality, and justice and for violence prevention continues and expands. It will continue to be extremely difficult to implement or even place on the public agenda strategies and policies that identify and challenge male domination. A crucial element in the dynamic of any system is the drive to preserve its own existence. As a manifestation of that reality, gender-based analyses and strategies are consistently shelved, ignored, neutralized, unfunded, or otherwise diverted from being effective. The male-dominated culture has resisted framing this issue in a way that truthfully acknowledges women's experience of violence and men's accountability for that violence. Indeed, the degree of male defensiveness aroused by this movement functions as a measure of the extent of the problem.

The challenge lies in promoting *creative* tension—tension that interrupts problematic attitudes and behaviors unequivocally while offering men and the male-dominated system the opportunity to participate in the benefits of a society based on equal partnerships. Men in general are not the problem, but rather abusive male attitudes, behaviors, and the male-dominated system. The new reality will benefit both men and women and will ease the stresses to which men are prone as they strive for predominance in a competitive world.

Given the changes required by such a vision of violence prevention, great challenges will also be faced by those working in the fields of family violence and domestic violence. It is tempting to opt for less demanding and more easily managed solutions—for what is outlined here represents a fundamental shift in beliefs that demands moving beyond a tidy role as a professional. Advocating for "prevention" means advocating for social transformation and being willing to undergo personal changes and transformation in order to bring about the "new reality"—a safe and just world for women and girls.

The Transforming Communities Project:
A Working Model

In 1992, Marin Abused Women's Services, in Marin County, California, launched a new organization called Transforming Communities: Creating Safety and Justice for Women and Girls. Transforming Communities derives its principles from a gender-based approach to violence against women. It provides a learning environment for the advancement of new thinking, practices, and strategies aimed at transforming existing social belief systems and practices so that violence, abuse, and intimidation of women and girls will cease to exist. Currently under way are four projects, all in varying stages of development, implementation, and testing, that have begun to incorporate the following basic operating principles into practice.

1. Strategies must reflect the values of safety, equality, and justice for women and girls. They must promote women's personal safety as a matter of public safety and as a basis for men's relationships to women.

2. Community intervention and organizing strategies must be designed and implemented by the residents of each community. In order to be effective, strategies must reflect the needs, values, and cultural and ethnic composition of each community.

3. Strategies are aimed at reaching an ever-expanding number of diverse individuals to build a broad-based social movement that will challenge existing personal and social understandings and beliefs about relationships, the spectrum of violence and abusive behaviors, and women's and girls' individual human rights.

4. Strategies have been designed that (a) seek to create formal and informal sanctions that hold men accountable for the full spectrum of their abuse and violence, (b) build men's awareness of and accountability for stopping their own beliefs and attitudes that support these behaviors, and (c) encourage men to become advocates to other men to do the same.

5. Women and men interested in the community organizing work of the project shall receive training so that all participants learn to relate to and interact with each other based on the values of safety, equality, and respect.

6. Problematic institutional practices such as criminal justice responses are directly addressed and, as needed, confronted and challenged by community members rather than by project staff.

7. Changes in attitudes, beliefs, and practices with regard to men's violence toward women will be measured through a research and evaluation component in order to validate the effectiveness of the project's community-organizing methods, so that communities around the country can be confident in adopting similar strategies.

8. New thinking and learning shall be incorporated into strategies along the way from the actual experience of conducting the work and from other disciplines working to advance social transformation.

In summary, Transforming Communities holds a vision that the epidemic of men's violence in general and specifically against women and girls can function as a catalyst for broad-based community and political action, which, by acknowledging and addressing the root cause of men's violence, works to create a socially just society. To that end, success and advancement toward this change shall be celebrated every step along the way. It is hoped that other communities around the country will be encouraged by the eventual proven success of Transforming Communities to implement similar strategies in order to support an ever-expanding national movement to eradicate violence against women and girls.

References

Abzug, B., & Kelber, M. (1993). *Women's government: New ways to political power.* New York: Women's USA Fund.

Adams, D. (1989). *Family violence: Emerging issues of a national crisis.* Washington, DC: American Psychiatric Press.

Bowker, L. H., Arbitell, M., & McFerron, J. R. (1988). On the relationship between wife beating and child abuse. In K. Yllö & M. Bograd (Eds.), *Feminist perspectives on wife abuse* (pp. 158-174). Newbury Park, CA: Sage.

Bracht, N., & Gleason, J. (1990). Strategies and structures for citizen partnerships. In N. Bracht (Ed.), *Health promotion at the community level* (pp. 109-124). Newbury Park, CA: Sage.

Buchwald, E., Fletcher, P., & Roth, M. (1993). *Transforming a rape culture.* Minneapolis: Milkweed Editions.

Burns, S. (1990). *Social movements of the 1960s: Searching for democracy.* Boston: Twayne.

California Office of Criminal Justice Planning. (1994). *Overview of crime in the state of California* [Report]. Sacramento, CA: Author.

Conte, J. R. (1993). Sexual abuse of children. In R. L. Hampton, T. P. Gullotta, G. R. Adams, E. H. Potter III, & R. P. Weissberg (Eds.), *Family violence: Prevention and treatment* (pp. 56-85). Newbury Park, CA: Sage.

Dobash, R. E., & Dobash, R. P. (1979). *Violence against wives: A case against the patriarchy.* New York: Free Press.

Dobash, R. E., & Dobash, R. P. (1992). *Women, violence and social change.* London: Routledge.

Edleson, J., & Tolman, R. (1992). *Intervention for men who batter: An ecological approach.* Newbury Park, CA: Sage.

Eisler, D. (1987). *The chalice and the blade.* New York: Harper & Row.

Fagan, J., & Browne, A. (1991). *Violence between spouses and intimates: Physical aggression between women and men in intimate relationships.* Washington, DC: National Research Council.

Federal Bureau of Investigation. (1991). *Uniform crime reports.* Washington, DC: Government Printing Office.

French, M. (1985). *Beyond power: On women, men and morals.* New York: Summit.

French, M. (1992). *The war against women.* New York: Summit.

Garske, D. (1992, November 22). Illusions of family values [Opinion editorial]. *Marin Independent Journal,* p. B8.

Gelles, R. (1993). *Family violence: Prevention and solutions.* Newbury Park, CA: Sage.

Gondolf, E. (1985). *Men who batter: An integrated approach for stopping wife abuse.* Holmes Beach, FL: Learning Publications.

Goodman, L. A., Koss, M. P., Fitzgerald, L. F., Russo, N. F., & Keita, G. P. (1993, October). Male violence against women: Current research and future directions. *American Psychologist, 48.*

Hotaling, G. T., & Sugarman, D. B. (1986). An analysis of risk markers in husband to wife violence: The current state of knowledge. *Violence and Victims, 1,* 101-124.

Institute for Women's Policy Research. (1995). *Report on the impact of domestic violence.* Washington, DC: Author.

Jones, A. (1994). *Next time she'll be dead: Battering and how to stop it.* Boston: Beacon.

Kurz, D. (1989). Social science perspectives on wife abuse: Current debates and future directions. *Gender & Society, 3,* 489-505.

Los Angeles County Special Panel on Domestic Violence. (1994). *Domestic violence: The war on the home front.* Los Angeles: Los Angeles County Board of Supervisors.

Marin Abused Women's Services. (1994). *Man to Man Study: Findings from 400 men on their knowledge, attitudes and behaviors regarding woman abuse.* San Rafael, CA: Author.

Minnesota Women's Fund. (1993). *Everyday fear: A systemic analysis of violence against women.* Minneapolis: Author.

Moyer, B. (1987). *The movement action plan: A strategic framework describing the eight stages of successful social movements.* San Francisco: Social Movement Empowerment Project.

Pransky, J. (1991). *Prevention: The critical need.* Springfield, MO: Burrell Foundation.

Prothrow-Stith, D. (1991). *Deadly consequences: How violence is destroying our teenage population and a plan to begin solving the problem.* New York: Harper-Collins.

Relationship Abuse Prevention Project. (1987). *Findings from teen abuse survey.* San Rafael, CA: Marin Abused Women's Services.

Sinclair, H. (1988). *Manalive training manual for violent men.* San Rafael, CA: Manalive, Inc.

Sinclair, H. (1995). *I am not a violent man.* New York: Ballantine.

Smelser, N. J. (1988). *An introduction to social problems.* Unpublished manuscript.

Stark, E., & Flitcraft, A. H. (1991). Spouse abuse. In M. L. Rosenberg & M. A. Fenley (Eds.), *Violence in America: A public health approach.* New York: Oxford University Press.

True, M. (1991). *Ordinary people: Family life and global values.* New York: Orbis.

U.S. Department of Justice. (1994). *Violence against women: National crime victimization survey report.* Washington, DC: Government Printing Office.

Wardell, L., Gillespie, D. L., & Leffler, A. (1983). Science and violence against wives. In D. Finkelhor, R. J. Gelles, G. T. Hotaling, & M. A. Straus (Eds.), *The dark side of families: Current family violence research* (pp. 69-84). Beverly Hills, CA: Sage.

Author Index

Subject Index

About the Editors

Robert L. Hampton, Ph.D., is Associate Provost for Academic Affairs and Dean for Undergraduate Studies and Professor of Family Studies and Sociology at the University of Maryland, College Park. He is also a Research Associate in the Family Development Program, Children's Hospital Center, and a Research Associate in Medicine (general pediatrics) at Harvard Medical School. He has published extensively in the field of family violence and is editor of *Violence in the Black Family: Correlates and Consequences* (1987) and *Black Family Violence: Current Research and Theory* (1991) and coeditor of *Family Violence: Prevention and Treatment* (1993). His research interests include interspousal violence, family abuse, male violence, community violence, stress and social support, and institutional responses to violence.

Pamela Jenkins, Ph.D., is Associate Professor of Sociology and Director of Grants and Development for the Women's Center at the University of New Orleans. She has combined an active research agenda with social action in her community. Her research interests include a long-term study of incarcerated battered women, class issues in shelter life, and the links between domestic and community violence. She is coeditor of the recent book *Witnessing for Sociology: Sociologists on the Court,* which examines the use of sociologists as courtroom expert witnesses. In New Orleans, she is working on building coalitions among academics, activists, and service providers who define child and family safety from a community-based framework.

Thomas P. Gullotta is CEO of one of the nation's oldest children's service agencies, the Child and Family Agency of Southeastern

Connecticut. A nationally recognized authority in the fields of primary prevention and adolescence, he holds an academic appointment at Eastern Connecticut State University in the Psychology and Education Departments. He is the founding editor of the *Journal of Primary Prevention,* serves as general series editor for the book series **Advances in Adolescent Development,** and is the senior book series editor for **Issues in Children's and Families' Lives.** He currently serves on the editorial boards of the *Journal of Early Adolescence* and *Adolescence.*

About the Contributors

Lynn Andrews, M.S., is the Coordinator of Violence Prevention Programs at the Child and Family Agency of Southeastern Connecticut. She has worked extensively with child care providers, school personnel, community providers, and parents on violence prevention and child abuse prevention and has worked directly with children and families in a variety of education and social service settings in New York City, Connecticut, and West Africa. She is also trained as a community mediator and is a member of the editorial board of the *Primary Prevention Newsletter.*

Kathleen R. Beland, M.Ed., is the author of *Second Step: A Violence-Prevention Curriculum* (grades K-8) and the writer/executive producer of 10 award-winning videos on child abuse and youth violence.

Martin Bloom, Ph.D., currently teaches at the University of Connecticut School of Social Work. He has written several books, including *Primary Prevention: The Possible Science* (1981); *Configurations of Human Behavior: Life Span Development in Social Environments* (1984); *Introduction to the Drama of Social Work* (1990); *Evaluating Practice: Guidelines for the Accountable Professional,* with Joel Fischer and John Orme (1995); and the forthcoming *Primary Prevention Practices.* He is currently studying his first grandson's progress toward resilience in a loving environment.

Mary Braddock, M.D., M.P.H., is the Medical Director of Community Initiatives at Children's Health Care-St. Paul, Minnesota, where she also practices general pediatrics. She is a Research Associate at the Connecticut Childhood Injury Prevention Center,

307

where she was formerly Director of Research and Education. Her research interests include the prevention of unintentional and intentional childhood injuries, improving the health care status of medically underserved children, and policy and program development for community health and preventive medicine.

Steven J. Danish, Ph.D., is the Director of the Life Skills Center and Professor of Psychology and Preventative Medicine at Virginia Commonwealth University. He previously served as Chair of the Department of Psychology and has held academic positions at Penn State University and Southern Illinois University. He is a licensed psychologist and a diplomate in counseling psychology of the American Board of Professional Psychology as well as a registered sport psychologist for the Sports Medicine Division of the U.S. Olympic Committee. He has written more than 80 articles and eight books on the subjects of counseling, community, and life-span developmental psychology; health and nutrition; substance abuse prevention; and sport psychology.

Thomas R. Donohue, Ph.D., is a Professor of Mass Communications and Coordinator of Television Projects at the Life Skills Center at Virginia Commonwealth University. He previously served there as the Director of the Mass Communications Program and has held academic positions at the University of New Orleans, University of Hartford, University of Kentucky, and Boston University. He has consulted widely on media issues for various companies, including the Kellogg Corporation, the American Broadcasting Corporation, Knight-Ridder Newspapers, the Taft Broadcasting Company, Communication Research Corporation, and the Media Institute. He is also the author of a number of articles and chapters on children's television issues. Currently, he is the executive producer of *Kids Like You and Me,* a Saturday-morning children's television program on the Richmond, Virginia, NBC-affiliate station.

Stephen E. Gardner, D.S.W., is the Associate Director for Program Development and Special Projects, Division of Demonstrations for High-Risk Populations/Center for Substance Abuse Prevention (CSAP), in Rockville, Maryland. He was previously the Chief of the High Risk Youth Branch. CSAP has recently begun a prevention initiative targeting violence related to alcohol and other drugs.

Donna Garske, M.P.A., has been a part of the international move-ment to end violence against women for the past 16 years. Cur-rently, she is Executive Director of Marin Abused Women's Services (MAWS) in San Rafael, California, Cochair of the California Alli-ance Against Domestic Violence, and Project Director of Transform-ing Communities: Creating Safety and Justice for Women and Girls (a prevention project of MAWS). She also works with the Network of East-West Women to create dialogue and linkages with women in Eastern and Central Europe and the former Soviet Union about violence against women. She was selected as 1994-1995 national scholar by the Gimbel Foundation and the *Journal of Primary Prevention* for her work on the prevention of woman abuse.

Garry Lapidus, PA-C, M.P.H., is the Associate Director of the Connecticut Childhood Injury Prevention Center. He has worked for 15 years as a physician's assistant and is Assistant Professor of Pediatrics and Public Health at Hartford Hospital and the Univer-sity of Connecticut School of Medicine. He is Director of the Hartford Violence Prevention Project and conducts research and teaching in both unintentional childhood injury and violence pre-vention. He has expertise in injury data sources and surveillance systems and is Past Chair of the Injury Control and Emergency Health Services Section of the American Public Health Association.

Linda Lausell, M.S.W., is the Director of the School Mediation and Violence Prevention Services Division at Victim Services in New York City, where she has developed and expanded the agency's school-based programs. She has also developed and implemented peer mediation and violence prevention programs in 45 New York City schools. She has developed training materials and curricula in conflict resolution, peer mediation, and victim assistance. Prior to her work at Victim Services, she was Director of the Children's Aid Society's Parent-Child Mediation Program. She also has experience in counseling youth and their families.

Aleta L. Meyer, Ph.D., specializes in human development interven-tion research. She is currently Assistant Professor of Psychology at Virginia Commonwealth University, where she conducts evaluation research on a peer-led life-skills program, Going for the Goal, and is coinvestigator for Responding in Peaceful and Positive Ways, a violence prevention program funded by the Centers for Disease Control and Prevention. Her current interests include collaborating with local communities to create and evaluate contemporary rites-of-passage programs for adolescents.

Hank Resnik, M.A., is a writer and editor who has written extensively about youth, education, and community-based substance abuse and violence prevention strategies. He is a senior writer for the CDM Group in Chevy Chase, Maryland, and is the editor of *Partnership Perspectives,* the bulletin of the Center for Substance Abuse Prevention Community Partnership Demonstration Grant Program.

Jeffrey Trawick-Smith, Ed.D., is Professor of Education at Eastern Connecticut University and Director of Project ACCESS, a federally funded violence prevention initiative. He is the author of five books on early childhood education and child development. His research has focused on young children's social competence and early play behavior and language development. He has worked with children and families as a teacher and administrator in urban early intervention programs in Louisville, Kentucky, and Minneapolis, Minnesota.

Billie P. Weiss, M.P.H., is the Executive Director and one of the cofounders of the Violence Prevention Coalition of Greater Los Angeles. She is an epidemiologist and Director of the Injury and Violence Prevention Program of the Los Angeles County Department of Health Services. In addition to studying violence as a public health issue, she is currently working on the epidemiology of gang-related homicides and assaults, pedestrian injuries among preschool children, iron poisoning, and residential pool drownings. She is a regional member of the American Academy of Pediatrics Poison Prevention and Injury Control Committee and a member of the American Public Health Association, the Los Angeles County Inter-Agency Gang Task Force, the Los Angeles County Child Death Review Committee, and the National HELP Network, which addresses gun violence from a public health perspective.

Betty R. Yung, Ph.D., is Clinical Associate Professor at the School of Professional Psychology, Wright State University. Since 1989, she has served as Program Research and Evaluation Coordinator for

Positive Adolescent Choices Training, a violence prevention initiative she helped develop for middle school-age African American youth. She is the lead author of a clinical guide to establishing and operating adolescent violence prevention training groups. In 1994, she won a Gimbel Child and Family Scholars Award for violence prevention. In 1994, she and her coauthor, Dr. Rodney Hammond, received the Best Journal Article on Adolescent Social Policy Award from the Society for Research on Adolescence for their *American Psychologist* article on psychology's role in the public health response to assaultive violence among young African American men.